THE ENGLISH
CHURCH & THE
PAPACY IN THE
MIDDLE AGES

THE ENGLISH CHURCH & THE PAPACY IN THE MIDDLE AGES

C. H. LAWRENCE

SUTTON PUBLISHING

First published in 1965 by Burns & Oates Ltd

This revised edition published in 1999 by Sutton Publishing Limited
Phoenix Mill · Thrupp · Stroud · Gloucestershire GL5 2BU

A catalogue record for this book is available from the British Library

ISBN 0 7509 1947 7

*Cover illustration: Coronation of Pope Boniface IX (1389–1404), from Froissart's
Chronicle (British Library; photograph Bridgeman Art Library)*

ALAN SUTTON™ and SUTTON™ are the
trade marks of Sutton Publishing Limited

Printed and bound in Great Britain by
Biddles Limited, Guildford, Surrey.

CONTENTS

INTRODUCTION

The six essays in this book provide a study of the relationship between England and the papacy from the conversion of the heathen English until the eve of the Reformation. The papacy is a doctrine embodied in a unique institution, the oldest in fact of all Western institutions, with an unbroken existence from the age of imperial Rome to the present day. Its history occupies a central place in our understanding of the medieval world. The long process by which a spiritual authority, which traced its origins to a divine commission, was translated into organs of government and gradually welded the churches of the West into a united and articulated body under a common system of law, forms the ever-changing background to these studies of the links that bound the English Church to the Apostolic See.

After the lapse of Roman imperial administration in the West, the papacy, located in the ancient capital, remained the repository of the imperial tradition. But the claims of the popes to spiritual authority over all members of the Church, including secular rulers, rested upon a deeper basis than the imperial status of Rome and one that was unquestioned in the middle ages. This was the tradition that the Apostolic See had been founded by St Peter, to whom Christ had entrusted the keys of the kingdom of heaven with the power to bind and loose, and had commanded him, with reiterated emphasis after the resurrection, to 'feed my sheep'. The bishop of Rome was the successor of Peter and the heir to his pastoral office. The historian's task is one of explanation. This doctrinal premiss, which informed the actions of successive popes, inspired the whole process of institutional development which in time gave the medieval Church a centralized monarchic structure, but the question of its ultimate validity lies outside the scope of this book.

England had a unique role in the early stages of this process because the church of the English was a colony directly planted from Rome. Augustine's mission founded a church which, so far as the politics and demography of the Anglo-Saxon kingdoms allowed, was organized on the Roman model proposed by Pope Gregory himself, and guided by his repeated instructions. Ties between the infant English Church and the papacy remained strong in the century that followed. The popes continued to confer the pallium – the woollen stole symbolising the delegation of authority to a metropolitan – on Augustine's successors at Canterbury. Veneration for the see of Peter and his shrine drew many English pilgrims to Rome, among them kings of Wessex, two of whom abdicated and elected to live in Rome at 'the threshold of the apostles'.

This Roman orientation of the early English Church had far-reaching consequences for the organization and ethos of western christendom. In the East, the primatial claims of the popes had to contend with the caesaropapism of the Byzantine emperor; whereas in the West the way lay open for the realization of the Petrine mission to the Germanic peoples. It is arguable that when Pope Gregory dispatched a mission to convert the barbarian high-king of the southern English, he was, perhaps unconsciously, calling a new world into existence to redress the spiritual balance of the old. In the eighth century, English veneration for the successor of St Peter in the old Rome was disseminated among the Germanic peoples settled in Germany and Gaul by St Boniface and other missionaries from English monasteries. They transmitted their notions of ecclesiastical order to their foundations on the continent. In the course of time, they instructed the Carolingian dynasty and the Frankish Church in the authoritative status of Roman customs and liturgy and in the centrality of the Apostolic See in the ecclesiastical cosmos.

In the last age of the Anglo-Saxon monarchy, when often unworthy popes were immersed in the dynastic politics of Rome and papal influence in the churches of northern Europe was at low tide, regular intercourse between England and the papacy was maintained by archbishops visiting Rome to seek ratification of their appointment and to receive the pallium. It was in this period that veneration for the mother-church was expressed by the annual alms of Rome-scot or Peter's Pence, collected from the people by royal command and dispatched to Rome for the support of St Peter's basilica and the Schola Saxonica – the English colony in the Leonine City.

A new era in Anglo-papal relations began with the Gregorian Reform movement of the eleventh century, which initiated a great expansion of papal government. The reform movement was a reaction against the widespread secularisation of ecclesiastical office. Its object was to renew the Church by restoring what the reformers believed to be the proper hierarchical order of christian society. A cardinal item of this agenda was the exaltation of the Apostolic See and the assertion of its right and duty, implicit in the Petrine commission, to oversee and direct the life of the universal Church. Reverberations of all this were brought to England during the reign of Edward the Confessor by English bishops attending the councils of Pope Leo IX. But it was the Norman Conquest, followed by an influx of prelates and monks from the continent, that exposed the English Church to the reforming spirit of the Gregorian age and the mounting assertion of papal authority in the affairs of local churches.

The reformers found a vital agency for disseminating Gregorian ideals and implementing the reform programme in the new literature of canon law. Here again England made a significant contribution to the growth of papal sovereignty through collections of papal decretals compiled by English canonists. These, like Gratian's classical Concordance of ancient law, which appeared at Bologna about 1140, pointed to the legal supremacy of the pope as ultimate judge and law-maker. In due course, Gratian's text was supplemented by official collections containing the decretals of subsequent popes, and these were promulgated by the expedient of sending them to the Bologna schools for copying and scholastic commentary. Through the lectures of the law-doctors and the students who flocked to hear them from all parts of Europe the new law was transfused into the mental bloodstream of the whole western Church. Its reception in England was assured by the large number of English students who frequented the Bologna law-schools and returned home to staff the courts and chanceries of English bishops.

From the twelfth century onwards The English Church, like the other churches of western christendom, experienced the unfolding process of papal sovereignty. This meant a constant growth in the volume of appeals to Rome by individuals, monasteries and collegiate bodies, a stream of travellers leaving England for the papal Curia – royal ambassadors and clerks, attorneys, prelates, penitents and pilgrims – and more frequent visits by legates *a latere*, usually cardinals, invested with the full panoply of papal powers. In the thirteenth century, the expansion of the central power was manifested by a growing number of papal provisions to English benefices and by papal taxation of benefices to finance the crusades. Bishops were summoned to a series of ecumenical councils, culminating in the Fourth Lateran Council summoned by Innocent III in 1215, which set out the Gregorian agenda for the eradication of abuses, the moral reform of the clergy, improvement of the pastoral ministry, and the liberation of the Church from lay control.

Most of the English bishops who attended these assemblies made genuine efforts to apply the conciliar programme in their own dioceses, but at home they belonged to a different sort of world. They were part of a long-established political and social structure in which the activities of church and state were inextricably intertwined; in which bishops and abbots were not only spiritual pastors, but also royal councillors and administrators, landlords and agents of local government; and in which laymen were not only spiritual sheep, but also benefactors of monasteries and patrons of churches, with important rights over them which the courts would uphold. In this world, the reforming ideals of theologians, and the sharp distinctions of the canonists, only slowly penetrated the stubborn realities of power and patronage.

Collisions between the claims of the Gregorian canonists and the advancing powers of the Norman and Angevin monarchy there were bound to be. Yet dramatic conflicts like that between Henry II and Becket over clerical immunities and the competence of ecclesiastical courts, or that between King John and Pope Innocent III over the election to the archbishopric of Canterbury, were only occasional collapses of the tacit compromises that governed normal relationships between church and state. There were a number of tussles between Henry III and cathedral chapters who resisted the king's nomination to bishoprics, but memories of the Great Interdict that Innocent III imposed upon England made John's successors more cautious in opposing the claims of a candidate who had won papal support. In the fourteenth century, the assertion of the papal 'plenitude of power' was pressed a stage further when, largely for financial reasons, the popes at Avignon reserved certain categories of bishoprics to be filled by papal provision. The English monarchy and the papacy now settled down to a working arrangement by which the pope usually provided to bishoprics those whom the king nominated, without regard to the electoral claims of the chapters concerned. This ever-changing relationship between spiritual authority and secular power is a major theme of this book.

With the exception of a fresh chapter on the Anglo-Saxon Church and Rome written by Dr Ortenberg, these essays are reprinted as they first appeared without change. Since they were first published thirty-four years ago, a number of important studies of Anglo-papal relations have appeared in print. Our knowledge of the documents has been enlarged, there have been striking advances in the history of medieval canon law, and various phases of the story have been elucidated by the work of Christopher Cheney, Leonard Boyle, Charles and Anne Duggan, Jane Sayers, Margaret Harvey and others. Yet it remains that no other book has attempted to provide a conspectus of the subject over the whole of the middle ages. A selection of the new work on the subject that has appeared in the interim is listed in the bibliographies at the end of each chapter. These selective bibliographies are confined to 'secondary sources' and are designed to provide guidance for further study. Perhaps a final word is called for to reconcile the title of the book with the subject of its first chapter written by Kathleen Hughes, whose early death was such a grievous loss to British Celtic studies. The Celtic Church, which evangelized the north of Britain, contributed an important ingredient to the culture of the Anglo-Saxon Church and to that of continental Europe, and for this reason it was felt that our survey would not be complete without it.

C.H. LAWRENCE

THE CELTIC CHURCH AND THE PAPACY

Kathleen Hughes

1

THE CELTIC CHURCH AND THE PAPACY[1]

To a fourth-century Briton of the lowland zone, Rome was the centre of a great empire. All around him stood the evidence of Roman power. The army protected the civilian population, and consumed the local produce. A network of roads linked the centres of population in the civil zone and ran out into the highlands; the Romano-British towns with their solid stone buildings, baths and markets formed a sharp contrast to the conglomerations of small huts which made up the hill cities of the barbarians; Romano-British art, with its judicious naturalism, demonstrated the rational, the obvious and humane, usually avoiding the ingenuity and fantasy of Celtic craftsmen. In economy and administration Britain was part of the empire, so that goods were imported to Britain from overseas, imperial tribute was collected, and the Briton, from childhood onwards, was familiar with the emperor's head on the circulating coins. The simplest person could not but be aware of the material evidences of Rome.

The educated Briton was also conscious of his debt to Rome in language and philosophy. Latin was the language of government and polite society, though the Latin spoken by the Romano-British gentry would have sounded a little old-fashioned and pedantic to the ears of a Gallo-Roman. Early in the fifth century a debate (presumably held in Latin) on the freedom of men's will could draw a crowd of supporters, while Pelagius' ideas show the

[1] Professor Francis Shaw (*Studies*, no. 206, 1963, p. 182) has recently objected that the terms 'the Irish Church', 'the Celtic Church' distort ecclesiastical history. They are, however, convenient abbreviations, which I shall use to mean 'the Catholic Church in Ireland', 'the Catholic Church in Celtic-speaking areas'.

I should like to thank Père Paul Grosjean, S. J., Bollandiste, for his kindness in reading this chapter, criticizing it in detail, and saving me from a number of errors. Professor Whitelock has also kindly read and discussed it with me.

stamp of classical philosophy in their emphasis on the importance of human reason and the responsibility of the rational man. Pelagius, though a Briton, spent most of his adult life on the continent, his ideas compelled so much attention in his own age that he was attacked by no less a polemist than Jerome and opposed by no less a philosopher than Augustine, and the heresy he launched was of such fundamental interest that it has recurred in one form or another throughout the history of Christian thought. His career demonstrates how a Briton of the late fourth century could move into the centre of intellectual life in Europe.

Christianity came to Britain along with other Roman exports, material and spiritual, and in the persecutions of the third and early fourth centuries the Church gained its native martyrs. In the fourth and fifth centuries the British Church was organized like the Church elsewhere in the empire, governed by bishops whose seats were in towns and who attended Church councils at Arles (314), Sardica (347) and Rimini (359), where three of them had their travelling expenses paid by the imperial treasury. The Christian inscriptions of fifth-century Britain demonstrate a close connection with the Gaulish Church. The most popular of the early formulae (*Hic iacit* [*sic*] with the name of the person commemorated in the nominative case) had a restricted vogue in Gaul, confined to the first half of the fifth century and to the Lyon-Vienne and Rhineland districts, and must have been introduced into Britain in the fifth century. British churchmen travelled to the continent: one, Faustus, became a monk at Lérins and later bishop of Riez; another, Riocatus, brought books back home from Gaul. One pilgrim, who seems to have been a Briton, was dissuaded from travelling to the East by a religious lady in Sicily, to whom he committed his daughter. The educated Briton felt himself more at home in Mediterranean lands than among the barbarian Picts and Scots. His frontiers were the imperial frontiers, and Rome's special significance for him was as the heart of the empire to which he proudly belonged.

During all this period, British Christians must have been aware of the pope as bishop of Rome, a city which was both imperial capital and burial place of SS. Peter and Paul, but our earliest evidence for any specific contact between the papacy and the Celtic west comes from the pontificate of Celestine I. Celestine, deeply concerned by the spread of Pelagianism, sent Germanus to Britain in 429 to combat the heresy.[2] The deacon Palladius was the pope's adviser, and it was almost certainly this same Palladius whom Celestine sent to Ireland in 431, as first bishop to 'the Irish believing in Christ'. It is quite likely that Celestine sent, with the first bishop, those relics of Peter and Paul, Stephen and Lawrence which were treasured by the church of Armagh two or three hundred years later. Early in the seventh century the Irishman Columbanus believed that the popes had first delivered the faith to Ireland, so it would appear that a papal-sponsored ministry was not forgotten. Nevertheless, it was Patrick the Briton whom the Irish recognized as their apostle, and although a paragraph probably written towards the end of the seventh century claims that Pope Celestine, together with the angel Victor, sent him, it is probably confusing the Palladian and Patrician missions, for Patrick's own writings make no such claim to papal support. It seems, indeed, that the conversion of the Celtic areas which lay outside the civil zone of Roman Britain was due mainly to British initiative. Dubricius, the *papa* of the Welsh saints, worked in Archenfeld, the Romanized area on the Welsh border. Ninian, who founded a church at Whithorn and later converted the southern Picts, was a British bishop, and although Bede tells us that he was 'regularly instructed' at Rome, there is no suggestion that the pope in any way inspired his mission. The first conversions among the Irish may have arisen from casual contacts with Britain or Gaul, and the pope appointed Ireland's first bishop; nevertheless the main work of evangelization was performed by a Briton, conducting an unconventional mission which, in the fifth century, failed to win universal support outside Ireland. Iona was founded among the Scots in 563, and its Irish founder Columcille became the apostle to the Northern Picts. Thus it would seem that the foundation and expansion of

[2] This is according to the contemporary account of Prosper of Aquitaine, *Chronicon*, s.a. 429. Migne, *P.L.* li, 594–5, Mommsen, *Chronica Minora* I (1892) 473. Constantius, writing his Life of Germanus about sixty years later, says that a Gaulish synod appointed Germanus and Lupus after the Britons had sent a request for help. *MGH. Script. Rer. Mer.*, vii (1920), p. 259.

Christianity in the Celtic areas was to a considerable extent, though not entirely, independent of Roman initiative.

During the fifth century, the position of Britain underwent a profound change. Early in the century the Roman legions were withdrawn and the Britons were forced to take up their defence against both Celtic raiders from the north and west and Teutonic settlers from the east. Against the Picts and Scots they were, on the whole, successful, but by about 500 the Anglo-Saxons were occupying the eastern half of the island. This was still the position when Gildas wrote towards the middle of the sixth century.

Gildas represented a new movement of ascetic monasticism, and was not sympathetic to the established Church. He describes a Church rich, influential and worldly. Men bought their way into the priesthood, purchasing office from the native princes and encouraging their sons to do the same. Priests took an active part in secular life, enjoyed public games and listening to secular tales, and were exceedingly well versed in the false windings of worldly affairs. Contacts with the continental Church were maintained via the western sea-routes, in spite of the hostile Saxon settlements in the eastern half of the island. We have evidence that the British Church kept up its communications with southern Gaul from an inscription in Caernarvonshire which reads *in tempore Iustini consulis*, thus dating the memorial to 540 in a phrase used only in the Lyon district. New formulae were introduced from the continent during the sixth century: the older form was sometimes modified to *Hic in tumulo iacit* [*sic*] in the manner of late fifth and early sixth century Gaulish inscriptions, and occasionally *memoria* was used with the name in the genitive case as in sixth-century North African and Italian styles. The original majuscule lettering was modified by uncial and half-uncial scripts probably introduced from southern Gaul or Italy, though these in time gained special Celtic peculiarities. Thus comparatively recent work on the British inscriptions has shown conclusively that the British Church was not completely cut off from her fellow Christians on the continent by the Saxon invasions, as used to be supposed.

The writings of Gildas the Briton and Columbanus the Irishman gives us some idea of the attitude of Celtic churchmen to the papacy in the period before the Easter controversy arose in Celtic lands, but before examining their works it is necessary to consider the position of the papacy within the Church. From very early times the popes had been regarded with veneration as bishops of the only great apostolic see in the West, their advice had been sought and given in decretals. They held a primacy of honour, and other churches might submit their cases to Rome for papal jurisdiction. Yet though the popes were recognized as successors of Peter, the commission to bind and to loose had been granted not only to Peter, but to all the apostles. The bishops as a body were successors of the apostles, with responsibility for the Church, and each church enjoyed a high degree of local autonomy, though a council of bishops might overrule any individual decision. Cyprian, quoted later in the Easter controversy, stressed the unity of the Church, a unity which began in the commission of power to Peter, but continued after the resurrection, by extending authority equally to all the apostles, though according to one version of his text, primacy among the apostles was granted to Peter. Augustine saw St. Peter as representing the Church; the powers granted to Peter were inherited by the Church. It was Pope Leo I (440–61) who, summing up the work of his immediate predecessors, gave clear definition to the judicial conception of the papal office, by establishing the legal connection between St. Peter and the reigning pope. Papal theory, as it developed in the later fourth and fifth centuries, viewed the pope as the *indignus haeres beati Petri*, the heir who, in Roman law, legally continued the deceased, taking over his rights and duties. The Roman Church was the source of all other churches, the pope had *gubernacula* and *potestas* over the whole Church, and while other bishops had authority within their own sees, the pope held a plenitude of power. There is here a considerable development in the theory of papal authority.

Although the theory of papal authority within the Church had now been defined, its practice remained insecure and uncertain. The spirit of autonomy in the provincial churches was strong, and Leo himself was opposed in Gaul by St. Hilary of Arles when he attempted to intervene in a case already tried by a Gaulish council. Leo was given the support of an imperial rescript which asserted his authority over the Gaulish bishops and required the provincial governor, if necessary, to force their attendance at the papal court when they were summoned, but soon the emperors were unable to afford the popes much help. The popes were not always well-informed, their machinery of government was quite inadequate to exercise their claims, and their political power tenuous, so that even a pope as able and upright as Gregory the Great was forced to flatter brutal and vicious rulers in his attempts to gain his ends. It is, indeed, difficult to see how the theory of papal power enunciated by the popes from Damasus to Leo could have been fully carried out in practice under the changed conditions of the seventh century. Gregory's achievement was astonishing, his vision splendid, his courage great.

The attitude of both Gildas and Columbanus towards the papacy is in line with Patristic thought. Gildas, writing in the mid sixth century, has nothing specific to say about papal authority, but his oblique references are of considerable interest. He regards Peter as *princeps apostolorum*, but he uses the phrase *sedis Petri apostoli* to mean the office of any *sacerdos*. He comments on the phrase of the Petrine commission in the following terms:

> . . . As the Lord asked whom the disciples thought him to be, Peter answered, 'Thou art the Christ, the son of the living God.' And the Lord for such a confession said: 'Blessed art thou, Simon bar Jonah, for flesh and blood hath not revealed it unto thee, but my Father which is in heaven.' Thus Peter, taught by the Father, rightly confesses Christ; but you (i.e. the priests of Britain), instructed by your father the devil, iniquitously deny the Saviour by evil deeds. To the true priest it is said: 'Thou art Peter, and upon this rock will I build my church.' You, however, are likened 'unto a foolish man who built his house upon sand.' . . . To Peter and his successors the Lord says: 'And unto thee will I give the keys of the kingdom of heaven'; but to you: 'I know you not, depart from me, ye workers of iniquity . . . ' To every holy *sacerdos* it is also promised: 'And whatsoever thou shalt loose on earth, shall be loosed in heaven; and whatsoever thou shalt bind on earth, shall be bound also in heaven.' But how do you loose anything so that it shall be loosed in

heaven also, when because of crimes, you are severed from heaven and fettered by bands of monstrous sins. . . .

Gildas is very much aware of the divine powers granted to all the true successors of the apostles. The whole episcopal order exercises spiritual authority in the Church and inherits the power which Christ first granted to Peter. Gildas lays particular emphasis on the importance of a pure life in those who hold episcopal office, and fiercely attacks the sin of simony. It is likely that anyone educated in the Gildasian tradition would set a very high value on purity of life, and that, in any dispute, he might be expected to appeal to the spiritual quality of the protagonists rather than to papal judgement.

The dispute which, in fact, arose within the seventh-century Celtic Church concerned the reckoning of the date of Easter. The Catholic Church in the West, though united in doctrine, varied considerably in its liturgical practices, and one of the most disturbing of variations concerned the date of Easter. The early Church had found it difficult to agree; the Council of Arles (314), where British bishops were present, required the pope to inform the churches each year of the date of Easter, while the Council of Nicaea (325) repeated the principle that the churches should follow a uniform practice. But the Nicene Council had laid down no rules for fixing a proper date, so the problem was by no means solved. Rome normally followed the reckoning of Alexandrine computists, but the popes never gave their official approval to any one Easter cycle, and although the Quartodecimans, who kept Easter on the Jewish Passover, had been condemned at the Council of Nicaea, other deviations from current Roman usage were not regarded as heretical. It was difficult to secure uniformity: in 577 the Victorian calculations accepted by Rome gave 18 April as the date of Easter, the Dionysian reckoning accepted by Alexandria gave 25 April, while the Spanish Church observed Easter on 21 March. In 590 Gregory of Tours complained that he was celebrating a Latin Easter, while many around him were celebrating the Greek festival. The Gallican bishops in 541 adopted the Victorian cycle, which they were observing in the lifetime of Columbanus, while Gregory the Great, though he imposed no one cycle, seems to have been following the Dionysian calculations. The Dionysian tables were accepted in Spain before 627, though a canon of the Fourth Council of Toledo shows varieties of practice there in 633. Thus it is clear that controversies over the date of Easter were not a peculiarity of the Celtic Church.

Nevertheless, although during the period 591 (the probable date of Columbanus' arrival in Gaul) and 664, the Western Churches, excepting the Celtic areas, were in the main using two different sets of Easter tables (the Victorian and Dionysian), the calculations based on them happened to result in a high degree of similarity during that period, whereas the Irish calculations, following yet another, and older, cycle, showed blatant discrepancies with the Easter date practised elsewhere. Between 591 and 612 (when Columbanus left Gaul) there seem to have been at least seven occasions when the Irish and Gaulish Easters differed. The claim made in the seventh century by the Romanizing party that the Celtic Church, a mere pimple on the outermost extremity of the earth, held out against the combined usages of Western christendom was rather tendentious, but not completely false.

When the Easter controversy spread to Britain, at the turn of the sixth and seventh centuries, it was pursued with a bitterness which may have been partly due to political circumstances. For it was their Anglo-Saxon enemies who brought the British Church into the Easter dispute, enemies whom the Britons still hoped to expel rather than convert. The Pope's representative was Augustine, to whom Pope Gregory had granted authority over the British bishops, ordering him to 'correct the obstinate'. The Britons, who had been Christians for centuries, could not have looked with pleasure on the prospect of control by the leader of the recently formed English Church. During the half century since Gildas had written, the British Church had been stormed by the ascetics, monasticism was now flourishing, and the Church was conscious not only of material but of spiritual power.

Augustine, acting in accordance with papal instructions, called a conference of the bishops and doctors of one of the British kingdoms on the border. The Britons made the initial concessions by accepting Augustine's invitation and travelling into enemy-

occupied territory for the meeting. Augustine seems to have opened the proceedings with a speech urging unity of observance (by
which he meant that the Britons should abandon certain customs
which conflicted with those practised by the Roman Church) and
assistance from the Britons in the conversion of the English. A
long discussion followed, centring on the observance of Easter.
At last, when no conclusion could be reached, Augustine suggested that the matter should be decided by a contest in miracle
working. The learned British bishops were most reluctant to
agree: did they doubt the logic of such a decision, were they suspicious of Augustine's good faith, or did they merely fear their
own inadequacy? Suspicions could hardly have been allayed when
a blind Englishman was brought in, upon whom their ministry
had no avail, but who responded to Augustine's treatment.
Throughout this initial interview the Britons acted towards
Augustine with courtesy.[3] They themselves had no authority over
the other bishops and *sapientes* of their Church, and suggested that
a fuller conference should be held when they had had time to
refer the matter back to their own people.

The second conference was attended by seven British bishops
and many *viri doctissimi*, mostly drawn from the monastery of
Bangor. They had consulted a wise and holy anchorite, and on his
advice had agreed to let the decision rest on Augustine's personal
sanctity, which they intended to judge by that specifically Christian virtue, his degree of humility. At the first interview Augustine
had submitted the Britons to a test which they had failed: at the
second the Britons submitted Augustine to a test, subtler but no
less decisive. Both contests leave a slightly artificial and contrived
impression on the reader.

> Those who were to go to the aforesaid council [says Bede]
> came first to a certain holy and discreet man, who led the life of
> an anchorite among them, to consult with him whether they
> ought to desert their own traditions at the preaching of Augus-

---

[3] It must be remembered that Bede was writing a century and a quarter after
these events, when the Christian position over Easter had become much better
defined. Round about 600 the position was much more fluid than in 731. See
above, p. 9. According to Bede, the Britons admitted that Augustine's teaching
was true and right, an admission in direct opposition to all their actions.

tine. He replied: 'If he is a man of God, follow him.' They said: 'And how can we prove that?' And he said: 'The Lord says: "Take my yoke upon you and learn of Me, for I am meek and humble of heart." If, therefore, that Augustine is meek and humble of heart, it is to be believed that he himself bears Christ's yoke, and offers it for you to bear; but if he is stern and proud, it is evident that he is not of God, nor are we to regard his words.' They said again: 'And how can we tell even this?' 'Contrive', he said, 'that he may first arrive with his company at the place of the synod, and if on your approach he rises to meet you, hear him submissively, knowing that he is a servant of Christ; but if he despises you, and will not rise up in your presence, when you are more in number, let him also be despised by you.'

Augustine failed to rise in greeting, the Britons angrily accused him of pride and refused to recognize him as their archbishop, 'arguing that if he would not rise to greet them in the first instance, he would have little regard for them once they had submitted to his authority'. Augustine resorted to warnings of disaster, and Bede saw the fulfilment of Augustine's prophecy of their downfall in the British defeat at Chester a decade or more later, when 1,200 non-combatant monks were cut down by the Saxons. Bede's account makes it clear that the synod composed of bishops and *viri doctissimi* held authority in the British Church, an authority more decisive than that of a foreign bishop sent by the pope, whose advice he was attempting to follow.

Throughout the seventh century the Britons were fighting a losing battle against the Saxons, with undiminished antagonism. Aldhelm writes in 705 to King Geraint of Dumnonia that the priests of Dyfed (the kingdom in the south-west of Wales) will not worship in the same church or sit at the same table with Saxons. In the century when Irish and Northumbrian traditions fused to form a splendid manuscript art, the Welsh scriptoria, such as they were, existed behind an iron curtain, isolated from Anglo-Saxon influence.[4] Nor is there any record of contact between the

---

[4] With the possible exception of the Book of St. Chad, *if* this was written in Wales (which is very doubtful).

Welsh Church and Rome throughout this century of British defeat. But though British evidence for the seventh century fails, Irish evidence is abundant, and relations between the Celtic Church and the papacy enter upon a new phase.

Gregory I was a pope deeply and unusually concerned about the whole of christendom. The mission of Augustine had informed him of the Britons, the pilgrimage of Columbanus forced the Irish on his attention. Columbanus, Master of the Schools at Bangor, arrived on the continent probably in 591 with a little band of monks, and was soon on very uneasy terms with the Frankish bishops. The Franks concentrated their opposition on the Irishman's method of keeping Easter, but before they could launch their attack, Columbanus addressed himself to the pope, Gregory the Great. He knew quite well that the pope was aware of the difficulties presented by the Victorian cycle, and that Gregory, whose learning and zeal he admired, could not approve the simonaical practices of some of the Gaulish clergy. He hoped for a decision against his opponents, and writes as one *savant* to another, expressing his arguments with freedom, confident in the learning of his fellow-countrymen.

> Why then, with all your learning, when indeed the streams of your holy wisdom are, as of old, shed abroad over the earth with great brightness, do you favour a dark Easter? I am surprised, I must confess, that this error of Gaul has not long since been scraped away by you, as if it were a warty growth. . . . For you must know that Victorius has not been accepted by our teachers, by the former scholars of Ireland, by the mathematicians skilled in reckoning chronology, but has earned ridicule and pity rather than authority.

He goes on to deride those who claim that the Irish hold the Quartodeciman heresy. 'What, I ask, is this so frivolous and so uneducated judgement, which is based on no proofs from holy scripture?' He points out to Pope Gregory the discrepancies between the authorities, and begs him not to put the Irish into the intolerable situation of having to decide between Pope Gregory and St. Jerome: 'For I admit to you simply, that anyone impugning the authority of St. Jerome will be a heretic or reprobate in the eyes of the western churches, whoever that man may be.' He concludes by asking the pope to advise him and to pardon his plain-speaking, but even after this he cannot forbear to add a post-script: 'And should you wish (as we have heard from holy Candidus your officer) to make the reply that what has been confirmed by long passage of time cannot be changed: clearly the error is of long standing, but truth has stood longer and refutes it.'

The content of this letter is unexceptionable. Columbanus is asking the pope for an opinion, as he had every encouragement to do. Even the implied threat that the Irish will turn from him should he give a heretical opinion is in accordance with the accepted principle that a heretic cannot hold papal office. Nevertheless the tone is extraordinarily independent, and although Columbanus says he is asking for advice, he seems in fact to be demanding a judgement against his adversaries. We can only guess how he would have responded to a decision against himself, for he seems to have received no reply. Perhaps Gregory, caught between Columbanus and the Merovingian bishops, thought it better to maintain a discreet silence.[5]

By the time Columbanus addressed his second letter to the Holy See (during a vacancy) his own position had worsened. The Frankish bishops had summoned him to a council which he had refused to attend, preferring to seek for papal support. He enclosed his previous correspondence with a covering letter, the tone of which is considerably less assured than that of his first epistle. This time he is not so much hoping to convert the pope to his own views as asking for toleration. The Irish settled in Gaul dwell in seclusion, he says, harming no one: can they not be allowed to practise their own customs? He begs the pope to 'grant to us pilgrims in our travail the godly consolation of your judgement, thus confirming, if it is not contrary to the faith, the tradi-

---

[5] See Grosjean, *Analecta Bollandiana*, lxiv (1946), 214. The early ninth century *Vita S. Sadalbergae*, c.2 (ed. B. Krusch, *MGH. Script. Rer. Merov.*, V. 52) says that Gregory *melliflua remisit scripta*. His authority is not good, for he is inaccurate in another statement concerning Columbanus and Gregory. Above all, there is no record of any reply from Gregory to Columbanus in the Papal Register.

tion of our predecessors'. There is here a much clearer recognition of papal authority than in the previous letter, he accords to the pope a judgement on a matter of faith which supersedes his own, and even gives a hint, before completely absent, that Irish scholars might possibly be wrong.

Columbanus' third and last surviving letter to the papal see was addressed to Pope Boniface IV in 613, who had been suspected of schismatical leanings by some of Columbanus' associates for his part in the Three Chapters controversy. He is begging the pope to clear himself from all imputation of heresy, and in so doing he defines more specifically than ever before his attitude to papal power. The glory of Rome rests no longer upon imperial might, but on 'the dear relics' of Peter and Paul. Rome is now 'head (*caput*) of all the churches of the world, saving the special privilege of the place of the Lord's resurrection'. Because of this, the pope has a pre-eminence of dignity: 'your honour is great in proportion to the dignity of your see'. But papal honour is attached to papal office, and passes away from an unworthy recipient. 'For power will be in your hands just so long as your principles remain sound; for he is the appointed key-bearer of the kingdom of heaven, who opens by true knowledge to the worthy and shuts to the unworthy; otherwise, if he does the opposite, he shall be able neither to open or shut.' There is here nothing contrary to orthodox contemporary principles.

Moreover, in this letter, Columbanus clearly recognizes the pope as the proper leader of the Church:

I, like a trembler, while I am no brave soldier, since I see that our enemies' army has surrounded us, try to awaken you as the chief of our leaders with cries that I admit to be importunate; for it is you that are concerned with the danger of the Lord's whole army in those regions, sleeping rather than fighting in the field, and partly (which gives even more cause for tears) surrendering rather than opposing the foe. You are awaited by the whole, you have the power of ordering all things, of declaring war, arousing the generals, bidding arms to be taken up, forming the battle-array, sounding the trumpets on every side, and finally of entering the conflict with your own person

in the van. . . . In grief and fear I look to you only, who are the
sole hope among the chiefs in your power that flows from the
honour of St. Peter the Apostle. . . .

This seems to be a recognition, in vague and rhetorical language,
of the papal plenitude of power.

Yet even the successor of Peter, endowed with such authority,
may not pervert the faith; if he does so, the whole Church must
rise up to correct him:

> Therefore, since those things (i.e. the necessity for sound
> doctrine in a pope) are true and accepted without gainsaying
> by all who think truly, though it is known to all and there is
> none ignorant of how Our Saviour bestowed the keys of the
> kingdom of Heaven upon St. Peter, and you perhaps on this
> account claim for yourself before all things some proud meas-
> ure of greater authority and power in things divine; *you ought*
> *to know that your power will be the less in the Lord's eyes, if you*
> *even think this in your heart,* since the unity of the faith has pro-
> duced in the whole world a unity of power and privilege, in
> such wise that by all men everywhere freedom should be given
> to the truth, and the approach of error should be denied by all
> alike, since it was his right confession that privileged even the
> holy bearer of the keys, the common teacher of us all. . . .

On matters of doctrine, the Pope must be guided by the consensus
of opinion within the Church. He is, as it were, the commander-
in-chief, but he cannot change its law.

Gildas and Columbanus thus reveal a Church in line with
patristic opinion. Gildas stresses the divine authority of the whole
episcopate, as Cyprian and Augustine had done; Columbanus
recognizes, in doctrinal matters, a power vested in the whole
Church which is superior to that of any individual pope. Celtic
churchmen of the sixth and early seventh century recognized the
popes as leaders of the Church and successors of Peter, yet they
did not give up their powers of independent judgement. The
British clergy refused to accept Augustine of Canterbury, appointed by Gregory the Great, and Columbanus did not hesitate
to argue and rebuke the popes. Gildas' comment on the *Tu es*
Petrus passage seems hardly consistent with the Leonine view that

the authority of the bishops is mediated through St. Peter and his heirs, while Columbanus' confidence in the rightness of his own views rides rather uncomfortably with the claim that the pope was the divinely appointed mouthpiece. Though the position of Gildas and Columbanus is not unorthodox, their views and expressions could hardly have been entirely satisfactory to papal opinion.

In the dispute on the date of Easter which continued later in the century between the Anglo-Saxons and Celts, the Roman party clung to the thesis that the pope was the heir of Peter, who kept the keys of heaven and whose word could not be disputed. The Celts agreed that the church was founded on Peter the key-bearer, yet they refused to adopt the Easter advocated by the party of the *Romani*. How can this action be explained?

According to Bede's account, Wilfrid, speaking for bishop Agilberht of the Roman party, argued that the customs followed at Rome were derived from St. Peter; that they were accepted not only in Rome but throughout Italy and Gaul, in Africa, Asia, Egypt, Greece and indeed everywhere except among the Scots, Picts and Britons; they had been reaffirmed by the Council of Nicaea; and Catholics were obliged to follow them. 'But if you and your fellows', he says to Colman, the Celtic leader, 'having heard the decrees of the apostolic see, nay of the universal Church, confirmed as they are by the sacred scriptures, if you scorn to follow them, *without any doubt, you sin*.' This is the crux of the matter. Wilfrid is treating the date of Easter as though it were a matter of belief, on which no divergence is permissible. Forty years later, Aldhelm, writing to the British king Geraint, re-iterates the same point of view with even greater clarity and emphasis:

Si ergo Petro claves caelestis regni a Christo conlatae sunt, (de quo poeta ait: *Claviger aetherius, portam qui pandit in aethra,*) quis, ecclesiae eius statuta principalia spernens et doctrinae mandata contemnens, per caelestis paradisi portam gratulabundus ingreditur?

Uniformity is essential: failure to conform imperils the soul.

We have no rejoinder to Aldhelm's Letter, and no report of the Celtic arguments at Whitby by a historian who agreed with their views. But, taking what we know of the actions of the Celtic leaders, together with the letters of Columbanus, it is legitimate to assume that the Celtic party regarded the date of Easter as a matter of ritual, not a matter of belief. Everyone knew that ritual might vary, without danger of sin. There must be unity of belief, but there need be no uniformity in ritual practices. 'Let Gaul, I beg, contain us side by side, whom the kingdom of heaven shall contain,' writes Columbanus to the Frankish clergy, who were attacking his methods of keeping Easter. Fintan Munnu, the Celtic spokesman at the Synod of Mag Ailbe, which was held about 630 in southern Ireland to discuss the Easter question, pleaded for the toleration of diverse practices: 'Therefore let each of us do what he believes, and as seems to him right.' The Celtic spokesmen, accustomed to diversity in their religious practices, recognized no obligation in conscience to conform to the Easter advocated by the *Romani*.

For this view they had considerable justification. Although Pope Honorius had written to the Irish asking them to conform to the current practice, he does not appear to have treated the issue as a matter of faith. Pope John, who wrote in stronger terms, of 'heresy', appears to have been misinformed about the Irish, whom he mistakenly believed to be Quartodecimans. The Celts were diverging from Roman *ritual*, not deliberately withholding obedience to an order of the pope on a matter of belief.

Columbanus, Fintan Munnu and Colman were all adherents to the conservative Celtic view on the Easter question: Cummian's Paschal Letter addressed to Segene of Iona and Beccan the Hermit, about 632 or 633, gives the arguments of an Irishman whose sympathies were with the *Romani*. He describes how a group of romanizing abbots, mainly from north-west Munster, had met at Mag-Léna near Durrow to discuss the Easter question, had agreed to seek further information from Rome, and to celebrate Easter in future with the rest of the Church. One abbot, to Cummian's indignation, went back on this decision, pleading the traditions of the elders.

Then it seemed to our elders (according to the commandment that if a difference has arisen over a case, and judgement has varied between what is leprosy and what is not, that they should go to the place which the Lord has chosen), that if there should be more important cases, these must be referred to the chief of cities, according to the synodical decree. We sent those whom we knew to be wise and humble, as sons to a mother.

From this it is clear that the *Romani* in Ireland, and probably the rest of the Irish Church, recognized a synodical decree which advised referring difficult cases to Rome, but that one abbot at least preferred the 'traditions of the elders' to papal judgement.

This is the first time that Irish sources mention the 'synodical decree' which advised reference to Rome, and there is considerable controversy as to its origin. Some historians claim that it is to be identified with a canon which reads:

Patricius: if any questions arise in this island, let them be referred to the apostolic see.

But this canon appears in an early eighth century collection,[6] compiled by Irish scholars of the Roman party. Other canons in the collection lay down the principle that cases must be referred to a higher court when agreement cannot be reached, encourage trial by Irish synod, and warn against referring disputed cases to the Britons, 'who are contrary to everybody, and cut themselves off from Roman custom and the unity of the Church'. The compilers, who cite both native and foreign sources, may be quoting a genuine early Irish source in the canon which orders reference to Rome. But the attribution to Patrick cannot in itself command much confidence, since other passages in the same collection which are attributed to Patrick are known to be from non-Patrician authorities.

It is, however, clear that in the 630's the *Romani* were familiar with the decree and that by about 700 Patrick was believed to be the author of some such ruling. Cummian of the Roman party had

[6] *Collectio Canonum Hibernensis*, ed. H. Wasserschleben, Leipzig 1885, p. 61. Professor Ryan assumes, inaccurately (*Mediaeval Studies*, pp. 5–6), that this canon is contained in the Circular Letter attributed to Patrick, Auxilius and Iserninus.

claimed him as *noster papa*, and by the time the Book of the Angel was compiled, probably in the seventh or perhaps the early eighth century, Auxilius, Patrick, Secundinus and Benignus were said to have laid down the following ruling:

> If any difficult cause shall arise beyond the competence of all the judges of the tribes of the Irish, it is duly to be referred to the see of the archbishop of the Irish, that is Patrick, and to the examination of that prelate (*antistes*). But if, in the examination of that prelate with his *sapientes*, such a case as we have mentioned cannot be easily decided, we have decreed that it shall be referred to the apostolic see, that is, to the chair of Peter, having authority over the city of Rome.

This, the 'Armagh canon', seems to be a more elaborate version of the ruling attributed to Patrick alone in the *Collectio Canonum Hibernensis*. It is perfectly in accordance with the spirit of the early eighth century *Collectio*, while the reference to Patrick as *archiepiscopus* accords very ill with fifth century conditions.

This Irish legislation in favour of Roman jurisdiction is found in no sources earlier than the seventh century, the period of the Easter controversy. Was it drawn up by the contemporary Romanizing party, or does it go back, as it claims, to the beginning of the Irish Church? The pre-seventh century Celtic Church, like the Church elsewhere in the West, must have known that important matters causing local controversy could and should be referred to Rome. It is possible that this principle was stated in some early Irish synod, though our scanty evidence tells of no fifth or sixth century Irish case which was referred to Rome. It is certain that such a practice would be, and was, canvassed by the Roman party as soon as the Easter controversy became acute. It seems to me likely that seventh century *Romani* gave precise legal form to a general principle which had long been recognized.

How much difference, then, did the Easter controversy make in the relationship between the Celtic Church and Rome? Celtic churchmen from the beginning recognized the primacy of Rome, but nevertheless there is a real difference between an abstract and an applied principle: Columbanus had consulted the pope in his difficulties with the Gaulish bishops, but the independence of his tone is in sharp contrast to the reverence of Cummian's. Throughout the sixth century the popes seem to have been ignorant of what was going on in the Celtic West: the debate over Easter brought them again into contact.

Nevertheless, although contacts between the Irish and the papacy were resumed in the seventh century, although between about 630 and 768 all the *Scotti* and the Britons made changes in their liturgical practices, and although Irish canon law now clearly recognized Rome as a supreme court, the organization of the Celtic Church was little affected until the eleventh century. Once the Easter controversy was settled, cases were not transferred from Ireland, Scotland or Wales to Rome, though the problems created by Celtic churchmen on the Continent were familiar to the popes. The monastic system was already too strong for organization of the Continental type to be imposed; none of the Celtic areas had a metropolitan see like Canterbury, as far as we know no Celtic bishop went to fetch a pallium from the pope, no tribute for the papacy was collected, and the popes sent no legatine commissions to the Celtic Church.[7]

Celtic Christians of the eighth, ninth and tenth centuries travelled to Rome, not to lay their cases before the papal curia, but to visit the shrines of the apostles and martyrs. To a Celtic Christian the body of a saint, entombed at the place where he had died, signified not only the place of his death, but also the 'place of his resurrection'. The saint's grave was a link with heaven. Monastic story-tellers knew of a service of angels between heaven

---

[7] The two legates sent by Pope Hadrian in 786 to the English Church proceeded together as far as Mercia. Then, 'considering that that corner of the world extends far and wide', one went on into Northumbria, while the other stayed 'to visit the King of the Mercians and the parts of Britain (*Britanniae partes*)'. Haddan and Stubbs (*Councils*, III, 461) suggest that these 'parts of Britain' lay in north-west Wales, where, eighteen years before, Elfodd of Gwynedd had introduced the Roman Easter (768). No certainty is possible, but it seems to me likely that the *Britanniae partes* were the border districts, where Offa was fighting (battles are recorded in 760, 778 and 784) and seeking to define his frontier. The legates' report is translated by D. Whitelock, *English Historical Documents*, I, London 1955, 770–4. No British bishops appear to have attended the synod held in Mercia, for none signed its decrees, though the English bishop of Mayo (in Ireland) attended the Northumbrian synod, and signed.

and the saint's tomb, and the poets of Derry described their en-
closure as 'angel-haunted', 'full of white angels from one end to
the other'. The cemeteries and tombs of the Celtic saints at home
were sought out for the spiritual protection they could give, and
Rome, with its crowd of great saints, including Peter the key-
bearer, must bring the gates of heaven almost within sight. So
learned clerics travelled to Rome, like the three who arrived in
Cornwall and went to King Alfred's court in 891, of whom one,
at least, was 'a man blossoming in the arts, learned in literature, an
eminent teacher of the Irish'. The three set out for Rome, 'as
magistri Christi are often accustomed to do', intending to go on
from Rome to Jerusalem. Sometimes such Irish scholars were men
of wealth, accompanied by dependants and servants, like that
Irish bishop Marcus who remained at St. Gall on his way home,
keeping his books and valuables, but dividing his horses, mules
and 'many coins' among his angry servants, who had to make
their way home as best they could without him. Poor pilgrims set
out *ad limima*, like the old priest, footsore and ill, who begged
help from the bishop of Liège. Princes occasionally journeyed
there, as did Cyngen, King of Powys, who died in Rome in
854/6, or Dwnwallon, the North-British prince of Strathclyde,
who visited it in 975. Busy ecclesiastical administrators sometimes
retired from office and set out for Rome, intending to seek the
place of their own resurrection near the tombs of the apostles.
Most of them journeyed in devotion and gained the peace which
they sought, though some seem to have been disillusioned, like
that ninth-century Irishman who found:

> To go to Rome
> Is much of trouble, little of profit:
> The King whom you seek here,
> Unless you bring him with you, you will not find.

The Celtic Christian's idea of Rome as the burial place of the
saints was so powerful a conception that the word *róm* in the Irish
language gained a secondary meaning as a burying ground. One
poet *c.* 800, writing a martyrology on the festivals of the saints,
comments that the tiny settlements once occupied by twos and

threes are now the burial places of multitudes. A later life of Coemgen describes Glendalough as one of the 'four best Romes of burial in Ireland'. Bardsey Island, off the north-west coast of Wales, the burial ground of 'twenty thousand holy confessors and martyrs', was proverbially known in the twelfth century as *Roma Britannie*. This idiomatic use of the word *róm* clearly shows Rome's primary significance in the Celtic imagination. The living pope was respected, but it was his great predecessor Peter, with the other saints and martyrs, who drew Celtic pilgrims to Rome. The power of the dead saints was a far more potent force than that of the living pope.

During the eleventh century direct contacts were re-established between Ireland and the papacy. Professor Aubrey Gwynn, S. J., who has examined the history of the period in a series of admirable articles, shows that pilgrimage to Rome not only maintained its hold on the imagination of the clergy, but gained an unprecedented popularity among the laity. Between 1026 and 1064 Irish or Hiberno-Norse princes set out for Rome on six known occasions. Twice they went with other native princes (1029, 1064), one went with his wife (1051), one died there and was buried in the monastery of St. Stephen. Towards the end of the century there was a small community of Irish in Rome, established in a church called S. Trinitas in the contemporary sources, which may be identified as S. Trinitas Scottorum on the Palatine Hill. Here Irish pilgrims most probably stayed. Some aimed farther east, for the Holy Land, like that Domnall Déisech who died in 1060, having 'journeyed all that Christ journeyed on earth'. We do not know the country of origin of the five Jews from oversea who came in 1079 with gifts to Tordelbach, king of Munster, but the following year one of the sub-kings of Munster, Úa Cinn Faelad of the Déisi, set out for Jerusalem. It was probably some crusader who brought back the camel which the king of Scotland gave to the Irish king Muircertach in 1105.

Professor Gwynn sees in the spate of Roman pilgrimage following 1027 the influence of King Cnut, who on his visit to Rome in that year negotiated better conditions for travellers. Sitric, king of Dublin, went to Rome in 1028, accompanied by the king of

Bregia and many others. Professor Gwynn argues that this Norse-Irish pilgrimage brought the papacy into closer touch with Irish affairs, and that plans for a diocese of Dublin were probably discussed then. It is certain that, half a century later, Gregory VII was interesting himself in Irish affairs. In a letter addressed to 'Tordelbach, noble king of Ireland, and to the archbishops, bishops, abbots, nobles and all Christians dwelling in Ireland', Gregory expresses the papal plenitude of power, and urges the Irish to refer cases to his judgement:

> [Christ's] authority has founded holy church on a solid rock, and he has entrusted his rights to blessed Peter. . . . He has also placed His church over all kingdoms of this world, and has subjected to her rule principalities and powers. . . . Wherefore the whole world owes obedience and reverence to blessed Peter and to his Vicars. . . . Be mindful ever devoutly to revere and obey the holy Roman church. We exhort you, as our most dear children, to practise justice. . . . But if any matters have arisen among you that seem to need our help, be prompt and ready to inform us of them, and, with God's help, you shall obtain what you have justly asked.[8]

From this time on, if not considerably earlier, the reformed papacy was extending its influence over Irish affairs. It is possible that Mael Muire Ua Dúnáin was acting as a specially appointed papal legate in the Synod of Cashel, 1101, where he is described as 'chief legate, chief bishop, and chief senior of the island of Ireland, with authority from the pope himself'. Certainly Gilbert, bishop of Limerick 1107-40, was papal legate, and presided as such over the synod of Rath Breasail in 1111, when Ireland was divided into territorial dioceses according to the Roman pattern. Malachy, visiting Rome in person, was appointed his successor as papal legate by Innocent II, and although the pope refused the saint's plea for two pallia, on the grounds that they must be requested by a national council, he treated Malachy with honour and made close

---

[8] Ussher, *Works*, iv, p. 498. Professor Gwynn defends the authenticity of this letter, *IER*, lviii (1941), 98–100. No year is given in the dating clause of the letter, but on the other evidence Professor Gwynn suggests 1076, 1078 and 1080 as possible dates.

enquiries 'concerning the affairs of their country, the morals of the people, the state of the churches and the great things that God had wrought by him in the land'. It was left for Cardinal Paparo, papal legate at the Synod of Kells, to bring from Rome in 1152 four pallia for the metropolitans of Armagh, Cashel, Dublin and Tuam. Thus, in Ireland, papal influence in ecclesiastical jurisdiction seems to have preceded the establishment of territorial dioceses.

It is impossible to consider the influence of Rome on eleventh century Ireland in isolation from the influence of England, for the two progressed together. The Church of Dublin, a Viking settlement, could not claim to be founded by any early Irish saint. It was, moreover, an urban settlement, in close touch by sea with Scandinavian colonies elsewhere in Ireland and across the Irish sea. English coins were circulating fairly freely in Dublin throughout the tenth century, and when, at the close of the century, the Hiberno-Norse kings started to strike their own coins, they followed English models. It is thus not surprising to find that the first bishops of the Hiberno-Norse kingdoms were closely connected with England, a country which had absorbed large numbers of Scandinavian settlers and which, between 1013 and 1035, with one brief interruption, was ruled by Scandinavian kings.

The early bishops of the kingdom of Dublin were Irishmen who had in most cases been trained in English Benedictine houses. We do not know the origins of Dunan, the first bishop, but his successor, Patrick (bishop from 1074 to 1084) spent some time at Worcester. Patrick sent his successor, Donatus (bishop from 1084 to 1095), to be trained at Christ Church, Canterbury, and there he must surely have come into contact with Lanfranc. Donatus' successor Samuel (bishop 1095–1122) was trained at St. Albans. Malchus, the first bishop of the Norse colony in Waterford, elected in 1096, was 'a monk of Walkelin, the bishop of Winchester', while Gilbert of Limerick (bishop 1107–40), though probably not consecrated by the English primate, was a friend of St. Anselm of Canterbury. All these except the first bishop of Dublin[9] and probably Gilbert took oaths of obedience to Canter-

---

[9] It is likely that Dunan was consecrated by the archbishop to Canterbury, though without any formal profession of obedience. See Gwynn, *IER*, lvii,

bury, and when the Synod of Rath Breasail (1111) divided Ireland into diocesan sees under two metropolitans (Armagh and Cashel), Dublin was significantly omitted. Anselm addressed a letter to his 'revered fellow bishops, the senior Domnaldus (bishop of Munster), Donatus (bishop of Dublin) and others in the island of Ireland who are eminent by their pontifical dignity' in which he urged the Irish Church to submit its difficulties to him.

> If anything that touches our holy religion, such as the consecration of bishops or the transaction of ecclesiastical business or other similar matters, should arise among you which you are unable to settle according to canon law, we advise you in charity to bring it to our notice, so that you may receive from us counsel and consolation, rather than fall under God's judgement as transgressors of his commandments.

The English archbishops were aiming to extend their influence from the Norse colonies over all Ireland, and there is evidence that they met with some success. The bishops of Dublin were Irishmen, in touch with their colleagues in Irish sees. Their kingdom was under the overlordship of Tordelbach and his son Muircertach, kings of Munster, who claimed the high kingship of Ireland. Donnall Ua hEnna (died 1098), the leading bishop in Munster, and other unnamed bishops, had sent letters of enquiry and requests for advice to Lanfranc. The archbishop dealt with the theological problem which had been raised, but to their questions on secular literature he replied that it was 'not seemly for a bishop to pay much attention to these studies'. Contacts with England probably did as much to forward the reformers' programme as contacts with Rome. Nevertheless, when Ireland re-affirmed diocesan organization at the Synod of Kells in 1152, her Church was placed under four native archbishops, and was made independent of Canterbury.

Direct contacts between the British Church and the papacy seem to have been re-established only after Roman diocesan

(1941), 107–12. Lanfranc, writing to the king of Dublin after the consecration of Patrick, says: 'We have sent him [Patrick] back after consecration to his own see, with the testimony of our letters, *more antecessorum nostrorum*'. Ussher, *Works*, iv, 490.

organization had been accepted. Urban took the first oath of obedience to Canterbury as *Clamorgatensis ecclesiae antistes*,[10] and in the next few decades the other Welsh bishops followed with similar professions, Bernard of St. David's in 1115, David of Bangor in 1120, Gilbert of St. Asaph's in 1143.[11] From this time on the jurisdictional powers of the papacy were exercised in Welsh affairs, for bishops of Llandaff and St. David's brought their appeals to Rome. The historians of both Llandaff and St. David's sought in the popes the origin of the British Church, elaborating Bede's account of Lucius' appeal to Pope Eleutherius.[12] Hagiographers now sometimes sent their patrons to Rome, and one scribe copied into the Book of Llandaff an account of the walls of Rome, her principal churches and cardinals. Urban built a new church at Llandaff, dedicating it to St. Peter, and all over Wales churches were re-named under Norman influence, so that Peter and others of the Roman calendar replaced the saints of the British Church.

Thus the changes in the Celtic attitude to the papacy implied so long before in the acceptance of the Roman Easter were consummated in the twelfth century. The Church now gained her hierarchy of courts and officials, and appeals to Rome became a part of the normal machinery of government. But even while the Church became Roman in organization it remained to a large extent native in imagery. The Irish phrase *comarba Petair* might be translated 'abbot of Rome', yet it is a literal translation of the phrase

[10] The Book of Llandaff would have us believe that bishops of Llandaff had been consecrated at Canterbury from the time of Dunstan onwards, and that a see organized on Roman lines existed at least from the time of Herewald. See E. D. Jones, *National Library of Wales Jrnl.*, iv (1946), 123–57, for a discussion of the value of this evidence.

[11] In Cornwall the process of incorporation had taken place earlier. Kenstec had made a profession of obedience to Ceolnoth (archbishop of Canterbury 838–870), but Celtic customs must have died hard, for well over a century later King Aethelred granted the see of Cornwall to Ealdred (994) with the order that he should 'govern and rule his diocese like the other bishops who are in my realm' (Haddan and Stubbs, I, 685). In Scotland Queen Margaret (grand-daughter of Edmund Ironside and wife of Malcolm III, died 1093) corresponded with Lanfranc; she and her sons brought the Scottish Church into line with Roman practices.

[12] This story was probably due to a misunderstanding of the *Liber Pontificalis*. See A. H. Thompson, *Bede His Life Times and Writings*, p. 135, n. 2, for references. For the various versions of this legend see Brooke, *Studies in the Early British Church*, pp. 240–2, p. 207.

used first by the fourth-century popes, *heres Petri,* one who inherits in his own person all the rights and privileges of his predecessors. A twelfth-century Welsh pilgrim sums up for us the
Celtic recognition of the Petrine powers, even while he prays, as
none but a Welshman could, for burial in his native 'Rome', the
isle of Bardsey.

> May I, the poet Meilyr, pilgrim to Peter,
> gatekeeper who judges the sum of virtues,
> when the time comes for us to arise
> who are in the grave, have thy support.
> May I be at home awaiting the call
> in a fold with the moving sea near it,
> a hermitage of perpetual honour,
> with a bosom of brine about its graves.

SELECT BIBLIOGRAPHY

Kathleen Hughes, *The Church in Early Irish Society* (1966)

Charles Thomas, *Christianity in Roman Britain to AD 500* (1981)

J.C. McNaught, *The Celtic Church and the See of Peter* (1927)

Nora Chadwick, *The Age of the Saints in the Early Celtic Church* (1963)

L. Gougaud, *Christianity in Celtic Lands, transl. M. Joynt* (1932)

M. Lapidge, ed. *Columbanus: Studies on the Latin Writings* (1997)

P. Grosjean, 'Recherches sur les débuts de la controverse pascale chez les
  Celtes': *Analecta Bollandiana* 64 (1946), pp. 200–244

D. Binchy, 'Patrick and his Biographers': *Studia Hibernica* 2 (1962),
  pp. 7–173

L. Bieler, *The Works of St Patrick* (1953)

Wendy Davies, 'The myth of the Celtic Church' in *The Early Church in
  Wales and the West,* ed. Nancy Edwards & A. Lane (1992), pp. 12–21

Próinséas Ni Chatháin & M. Richter eds. *Irland und Europa/Ireland and
  Europe: Die Kirche im Frühmittelalter/The Early Church* (Stuttgart 1984)

Dáibhi Ó Cróinin, *Early Medieval Ireland 400–1200* (1995)

Aubrey Gwynn, *The Irish Church in the Eleventh and Twelfth Centuries,* ed.
  Gerard O'Brien (Dublin 1992)

THE ANGLO-SAXON CHURCH AND THE PAPACY

Veronica Ortenberg

2

THE ANGLO-SAXON CHURCH AND THE PAPACY

To say that the Anglo-Saxons were the blue-eyed boys of the early medieval popes is more than just another pun on the Whitby monk's account of Gregory the Great's encounter with the English boys in a Roman market. 'The faithful narrate that before [Gregory's] pontificate, certain of our nation, beautiful in form and fair-haired, came to Rome. When he heard of their coming, he was at once eager to see them; and receiving them . . . and, God prompting him inwardly, he asked of what race they were. And when they replied: 'Those from whom we are sprung are called Angles', he said: 'Angels of God'. Then he said: 'What is the name of the king of that people? And they said: 'Aelle'; he said: 'Alleluia, for the praise of God ought to be there'. He also inquired the name of the tribe from which they specially came, and they said: 'The Deire'. And he said: 'Fleeing together from the wrath [de ira] of God to the faith".[1] This encounter, according to Gregory's first, English, biographer, fired Gregory with missionary zeal for the newly settled inhabitants of the old Roman province of Britannia. While the incident may have its roots in legend, it sheds an unmistakable light on the way in which the still relatively recently converted Anglo-Saxons of the eighth century perceived their debt and their attachment to Rome and the papacy. This is a characteristic phenomenon of the Anglo-Saxon period: at no time in their history would the English, for whom,

---

1. *The Earliest Life of Gregory the Great By an Anonymous Monk of Whitby*, ed. and tr. B. Colgrave (Lawrence, 1968), p. 90–1.

after the sixteenth century, 'popishness' would become a terrible taint, enjoy such a close relationship, emotional as well as institutional, with the Roman popes.

The Whitby monk's account of Gregory's meeting with the Deiran boys in Rome is not the first claimed link with the papacy. Bede, relying in his account on his copy of the *Liber Pontificalis*, makes another pope, Eleutherius, well before the 590s, take an interest in the conversion of the Romano-Britons to Christianity by responding to a letter from the British 'king' Lucius, who requested from him instruction in the christian faith. Once again, what matters far more than the legendary story is the importance attached in Anglo-Saxon England to the antiquity of this connection.

Both British churchmen and Irish monks greatly venerated St Peter, Prince of the Apostles, and his successor the pope. In addition to the regard for the apostle himself, the British were clearly aware of their conversion from Rome in 'apostolic' times, while the Irish were keen to emphasize both Palladius and of course their apostle Patrick's link with the papacy. The first had been a papal envoy to the Irish Christians in the 430s, while Patrick, a Romano-Briton educated in Gaul, was said to have visited Rome and been confirmed by the pope. However, none had a relationship as close as that of the Anglo-Saxons with the successors of St Peter. This particular attachment was due to a combination of two factors. On the one hand was the general awareness of the power of St Peter, head of the 'apostolic college' but mainly 'gatekeeper of heaven', as so many English texts call him. No one put it more clearly than king Oswiu at the synod of Whitby in 664: he asked all participants: 'Tell me which is greater in the kingdom of heaven, Columba or the Apostle Peter?' The whole synod answered . . . 'The Lord settled this when he declared: "Thou art Peter and upon this rock . . . [Matt. xvi. 18–19]"'. The king wisely replied: "He is the porter and keeps the keys. With him I will have no differences nor will I agree with those who have such, nor in any single particular will I gainsay his decisions so long as I live"'.[2]

Bede's account is even more powerful when he makes Oswiu state: "since he is the doorkeeper I will not contradict him . . . otherwise when I come to the gates of the kingdom of heaven, there may be no one to open them because the one who . . . holds the keys has turned his back on me".[3]

In addition to this, the Anglo-Saxons had another reason for their emotional involvement with Rome: their conversion by, and hence veneration for, Pope Gregory I, the 'Apostle of the English'. This finds an echo in Bede's account of Gregory's life but, earlier still, in the tradition enshrined in the first-ever written Life of Gregory, by a monk from the abbey of Whitby, composed around 700. Not only the origin, but also the date are significant. By 700, Gregory was still not a very popular figure with those who staffed the Roman curia, just as he had not been popular in such circles during his lifetime, possibly because of his unusual monastic background, and his strained relations with the Emperor and the Byzantine patriarchate. While it was the people of Rome who had brought him to power, the clergy of the papal curia were wary of his monastic lifestyle and bias, as well as of his involvement in the day-to-day running of the city and his increasing interest in creating closer links with the Lombard conquerors of Italy. After his death, they were reluctant to commemorate him, as the entry in the *Liber Pontificalis* shows, let alone to sanctify his memory. Not until the English, especially Bede, whose *Ecclesiastical History* began to circulate soon after his death, made him into a national saint, did the Roman curia itself come to acknowledge the advantages of promoting his holy status.

Recent work has placed Gregory's missionary attempts into a more general perspective, and has shown how essential was his turning away from Constantinople towards the West. This overall change in papal policies, begun under Gregory through, for

---

2. *The Life of Bishop Wilfrid by Eddius Stephanus*, ed. and tr. B. Colgrave (Cambridge, 1927 repr. 1985), p. 22–3.

3. Bede, *Ecclesiastical History of the English People*, ed. and tr. B. Colgrave and R.A.B. Mynors (Oxford, 1969), p. 306–7.

example, the attention paid to the conversion of western
barbarian kings either from Arianism to catholic Christianity, as in
the case of the Visigothic and Lombard kings, or from paganism
to catholicism in the case of the English, was part of an overall
policy of looking towards the West, towards the Latin world with
its new masters, rather than waiting resentfully and often uselessly
for help and attention from the Eastern Emperor. This policy,
launched largely by Gregory and later implemented by seventh-
century popes, was to change the face of European history.
Gregory's efforts in that direction are clearly shown in his
correspondence: his congratulatory letter to the Visigothic king
Reccared on his conversion from Arianism, supporting letters to
the catholic Queen Theodelinda encouraging her to convert her
Arian Lombard husband, great attention paid to the Frankish
bishops, kings and especially the all-powerful Queen Brunhild.
For a long time, Gregory's missionary efforts towards Britain were
perceived as unique, notably because this is how Anglo-Saxon
writers like Bede thought of them, and of England's privileged
place in the great pope's plan. Although it is increasingly clear that
this was not entirely so, nevertheless these efforts were still
particularly noteworthy and did hold a special place in Gregory's
heart, since the Anglo-Saxons represented the last major challenge
of conversion from paganism to Christianity in what had been
part of the Roman Empire but which had reverted to paganism
in the fifth century.

Gregory's involvement began with the despatch of a group of
missionaries. Legend has it that he wanted to lead the mission
himself but found that the Roman people were not prepared to
let him go away; he thus had to send his representative, a monk of
his own monastic foundation in his family home on the Coelian
Hill, Augustine. While it might have appeared somewhat unusual
in sixth century Italy that monks should be involved in
missionary work, Gregory knew that Benedict of Nursia himself,
and before him Martin of Tours, had occasionally been engaged
in such endeavours around their monastic foundations. Moreover,
it seems likely that Gregory could have heard, from both his

contacts and their reputation, about the Irish monk Columbanus and his followers, settled in Francia since *c.* 590. It is likely that he would have come to recognize the value of missionary monasticism in the Irish tradition. This seed was implanted into the newly-converted Anglo-Saxon Church both directly by Irish missionaries working in the kingdom of Northumbria in the seventh century, but also by Augustine and his monks, themselves directed by a pope by then probably familiar with the Columbian tradition. It would later lead to what would be regarded as typical Anglo-Saxon missionary activity of the kind carried out by the monks Willibrord and Boniface in Germany in the next century.

Gregory sent Augustine to an area which he knew only as an administrative province of the Roman empire, possibly from imperial administrative documents, but much more likely from the list of signatories at fourth century Church councils, available in Rome. He would have seen in the first instance the list of three British bishops present at the council of Arles in 314, the first two described specifically as bishops of the cities of York and London in the province of Britain. Thus Augustine was briefed to establish two metropolitan sees in what had been the two major Roman centres, London and York, and to organize twelve dependent episcopal sees for each. This naturally proved impracticable on the ground, since Gregory knew nothing of the shape and nature of Anglo-Saxon settlements, except for what he might have assumed to be a not unfriendly king in Kent; for King Aethelberht had earlier married a Frankish catholic princess, and had allowed her to keep her faith and her chaplain in her new home. This was the king to whom Augustine was sent. Augustine travelled through Gaul, with letters from Gregory to a large number of bishops on his way, and one to Aethelberht's Queen, Bertha, whose protection the pope requested for the missionary party. The travels were not entirely smooth and Augustine, on the verge of leaving his familiar Mediterranean landscape in Southern Gaul, got cold feet; only by a mixture of cajoling and threatening did Gregory's epistolary encouragement finally lead the party to pursue its route and reach the isle of Thanet in 597, a year after first setting off.

Augustine finally settled in Canterbury with Aethelberht's permission and started preaching there. The king was gradually convinced of the interest that the new religion might have for him, both individually, for his political and military success, and perhaps in diplomatic terms for good relations with his close neighbours and trade partners in Francia. He became a christian before his death in *c.* 616. Augustine, however, was hardly an experienced missionary and he needed advice on, and answers to, a variety of problems. For that purpose, he naturally appealed to Gregory and sent him some queries, to which the pope replied in a group of letters, subsequently put together by Bede in what he termed a 'Libellus Responsionum'. These letters and their advice set out the norm for conversion policies, not only in England, but more generally in the West, in particular for subsequent Anglo-Saxon missions to Germany, Frisia and Scandinavia. They advocated the christianization rather than destruction of pagan cult places and practices, the toleration of some traditional social customs, especially those relating to marriage, the creation of a hierarchy of clergy closely linked to the Roman Church and modelled on it, a style of preaching based on debate and argument as well as miracles, and the use of queens for the purpose of converting their royal husbands. While this last strategy had already been deployed with some success by Gregory in the case of Bertha, some years later Pope Boniface V was to pursue the policy with Aethelberht's daughter, Aethelburh, to whom he wrote when she left Canterbury to be married to the pagan king of Deira, Edwin.

Augustine crossed over to Gaul to be consecrated bishop, and he subsequently received from Rome the *pallium*, which was to become gradually in the West the insignia of office of archbishop. He placed his new see at Canterbury. While the mission settled and performed its task successfully in Kent and the south (two new episcopal sees were to be established in Rochester and London, occupied by two of the Roman team, Justus and Mellitus, the latter having joined Augustine's first band of monks in 601 from Rome), another small group of missionaries left Kent between 619 and 625, to go further north, to York in Deira, under the leadership of Paulinus. Paulinus was to succeed in converting King Edwin about 628, but other parts of England would only accept the new religion more slowly or not at all. The kingdom of East Anglia, after at first appearing to adopt Christianity, possibly as a result of its subservient status to the king of Kent, soon experienced a strong pagan reaction, when its king, Redwald, became in turn powerful enough to be more autonomous and exercise overlordship over the Saxon settlers south of the Humber. Mercia showed a blank refusal to take Christianity on board for over fifty years.

It has been argued that Christianity may have been widely perceived by a king such as Redwald, and indeed at first by Aethelberht himself, as a ploy to bring the Anglo-Saxon kingdoms within the orbit of Frankish power in Gaul. As such, it was to be accepted if it was seen to be associated with Rome, in a way that it would not if it was thought to promote Frankish interests. Thus was explained the time taken by Aethelberht himself before embarking on it, and it may have been regarded in the same way by Redwald, politically sensitive about Kentish overlordship. An alternative but more speculative interpretation suggests that a first attempt by Aethelred to interest Frankish bishops in converting Kent had failed, and that only then did he actively seek Gregory's help. Similar political reasons, this time of opposition to another rival royal line, may also explain Edwin's slow decision to convert, only to be later convinced by the superior advantages of the new religion after his victory over his enemies. After Edwin's death in battle in 633, however, power passed on to the royal family of the northernmost kingdom of Bernicia. It would in turn become christian but through the influence of another agency, that of its Irish-reared king Oswald, rather than that of the by then dispirited Roman missionaries who, with the exception of James the Deacon, had fled Northumbria a little earlier.

A great deal of ink has flowed on this issue, and it has been customary for a long time to contrast the Roman tradition and that which some still like to call the 'Celtic Church' in England. Historians used to emphasize an Irish-style Church whose basic unit was, not the episcopal 'civitas' in a country without towns, but the great monastic 'paruchia', founded by a venerated saintly figure, which developed into a pastoral unit around the abbot and the monks, and where the bishop was a rather shadowy figure, sometimes subordinated to the abbot. This style of organization, particularly noticeable at Iona and through the 'paruchia' of its founder, St Columba, was often also ascribed to the Northumbrian Church, imported by the Iona monks invited to work in Northumbria by Oswald. This pattern has been seriously challenged by recent research, which considers it inaccurate not only with regard to the Northumbrian, but even to the Irish church itself. The prevalent monastic organization was indeed more appropriate in a rural and tribal society, but this does not undermine the role of the bishops, whose existence and participation was anything but minor – simply they, too, were essentially bishops of a tribe, rather than of a 'civitas' in a Mediterranean sense.

Thus it is now quite widely accepted that on the ground and in practice, there was no actual rivalry between the two traditions, which differed in style rather than in fundamentals. The Irish monks illustrated both a more charismatic and more rural lifestyle and approach and maintained what had by then become contested traditions for calculating the date of Easter and the shape of the ecclesiastical tonsure, but they were not themselves theoretically hostile to Canterbury, the Roman missionaries or the pope's authority. The two traditions were not properly speaking opposed to each other, even though the representatives of the by then current 'Roman' view were rather irritated by what they saw as the outmoded Irish view on Easter; mainly they functioned in parallel. Thus, while Northumbria was still clearly dominated by Irish christianity, the attachment to both the veneration for St Peter and more specifically for Gregory the Great remained paramount, even in such a stronghold of Irish-style monasticism as Abbess Hild's monastery at Streonescalh, more famously known by its later name of Whitby. But the practical aspects of the Roman tradition finally prevailed, being acknowledged by the king of Northumbria and Oswald's brother, Oswiu, as more universal, and thus ensured the institutional success of the current Roman views.

The story as it is told uses the anecdote of Oswiu and his court celebrating Easter on the Sunday that his Queen and her court were still keeping as Palm Sunday – according to Bede, everyone was uncomfortable about this fact, which brought home the oddity of the situation. It is not unlikely that, as the most powerful king on the island at this stage, Oswiu might have realized, as others had before him, the advantage of religious unity throughout his lands, and that he used this opportunity to decide on enforcing one or the other styles. Not surprisingly, the more tautly organized, hierarchical and international Roman Church won. This victory was related, probably conflating a longer debate, by both Bede and Eddius Stephanus, Bishop Wilfrid's biographer, as the dramatic confrontation in front of Oswiu between the representative of the Roman party, Wilfrid, and that of the Irish party, Bishop Colman, at the 'synod' of Whitby in 664. The triumph was that of Peter over Columba, the head of the apostles and gatekeeper of heaven, in Oswiu's words, over the founder and patron of Irish–Northumbrian monasticism, Columba, abbot of Iona. By then, St Peter was already venerated as the greatest saint throughout the island: Oswiu's words reflect his popularity, which was to give rise to the practice and extraordinary popularity of the Roman pilgrimage in England.

The pilgrimage was one of the three main aspects of the Rome-centred and papally-aware ecclesiastical style very strongly promoted by Wilfrid. The other two were his gaining of papal privileges for exemption from local secular and episcopal interference for his monastic foundations in England, and his two appeals to the popes against the king of Northumbria and once against the new Archbishop of Canterbury, Theodore, ironically enough sent there by the pope himself. Until Theodore's arrival in England in 669, the links of the English Church with Rome and the papacy had been essentially of a personal and emotional nature; with Theodore, a major reorganization of the Anglo-Saxon Church was to take place, which was to mould it into the Roman model in a practical and institutional manner as well.

Until Theodore's predecessor, Wigheard, most archbishops of Canterbury had been appointed from Rome, and all with the exception of Deusdedit had been 'Romans'. Wigheard, an Englishman, was appointed by kings Oswiu and Egbert to succeed Deusdedit as archbishop in 667; he went to Rome to collect his *pallium*, but died there of the plague. Pope Vitalian appointed a Greek-speaking abbot from Tarsus in Cilicia, then living in Rome, and sent him to Canterbury together with a helper, the Neapolitan abbot Hadrian, an African by birth. Theodore was by no means a shadowy figure; he was well known as the foremost scholar of his time together with Maximos the Confessor, and they were both at the forefront of the opposition to the monothelite heterodoxy supported by the Eastern emperors and the Byzantine patriarch, which the papacy was fighting. To lose a man of such prestige and support, not to mention proficiency in Greek, in a city which was increasingly losing such knowledge, was no easy decision to make for the popes, and Pope Agatho's letter to the emperor in Constantinople in 680 makes this loss clear. By the second half of the seventh century, the importance of the young English Church to the papacy was already such that it was prepared to lose one of its best men for its benefit. We will see later why this was so.

When Theodore arrived in England, he found a Church loosely based on Augustine's model, divided into episcopal provinces but in a way far removed from the purely Roman tradition. The founding of dioceses had followed the progress of the conversion, and had generally stopped at the level of the kingdom or people (Gewisse, Middle Angles, East Saxons, Lindsey, Northumbrians and so on) in the 'barbarian' tradition, with a bishop servicing a whole people and sometimes an enormous diocese, such as that of Northumbria for Wilfrid.

Several sees were without a bishop and Theodore's first job was to appoint and consecrate new ones to fill the gaps. He then resolved to divide the larger dioceses and create smaller, more manageable ones: thus the Mercian diocese was divided between the sees of Worcester for the Hwicce and Hereford for the Magonsaete; London was assigned to the East Saxons, and the East Anglian diocese was divided between the two sees of Dunwich and Elmham. Whenever possible, he favoured the settling of episcopal sees in towns. He reinforced the hierarchy of dependence of bishops, archbishop and pope and he established the need for papal approval for major changes in the ecclesiastical hierarchy and geography. Several such changes were later made in this way, in particular in the well-documented case of the contested and short-lived metropolitan see of Lichfield and, in the eleventh century, when the poor and remote see of Crediton was transferred to the prosperous city of Exeter in 1050.

Theodore also introduced the idea of regular annual meetings of Church councils, and himself called several, including the two very important ones at Hertford in 672 and 'Hatfield' in 679. Through them, he promoted a much greater awareness of canon law. Both his councils were reforming ones and, like the other great councils of the next century, especially 'Clovesho' in 747 and the legatine councils of 786–7, greatly concerned with pastoral issues. But they were innovative in another sense too, since they brought to England the Roman formal style of Church councils, with their written proceedings and resolutions, and their reminder of previous conciliar canons, which constituted a major source of canon law. Significantly, at the council of Hertford, Theodore also legislated against 'wandering' bishops and recommended that bishops should reside in one place where their see was fixed, surely a feature of his constitutional Mediterranean style reorganization going against the grain of the 'barbarian' style of episcopal behaviour.

One of the dioceses reorganized by Theodore was that of Northumbria, which he divided into three smaller ones, and from which he evicted its reluctant bishop Wilfrid, to the latter's great displeasure. As a result, Wilfrid appealed to Rome against Theodore and King Ecgfrith, who supported the Archbishop, and later appealed a second time against Theodore's successor Berhtwald and the then king Aldfrith, in 679 and 704. Appeals to Rome of this sort were not unknown in principle, and we have a few prior examples from Gaul and from Ireland. But none had the decisive impact that Wilfrid's was to have in setting the trend for such appeals, and possibly none for a long time exercised papal ingenuity to such an extent: it was a matter of not disappointing a rare 'customer' when he addressed the papacy with his problem, without countermanding the papal envoy himself, Theodore, or antagonizing the English Church. The first time, Pope Agatho compromized by accepting the principle of the division but suggesting that Wilfrid should be reinstated and the division carried out with his approval. The second time, Pope John VI simply requested Archbishop Berhtwald to summon a council to solve the problem.

In fact, it seems likely that Wilfrid's views of the episcopal function had been fashioned by his stays in Gaul and by the status and behaviour of the great aristocratic bishops of the Gallo-Roman tradition, with their enormous power and wealth, like Aunemundus of Lyons, with whom he had spent three years; hence his puzzled reaction to Thedore's reorganization, which was more in accordance with the traditional and genuinely Mediterranean and Italian style of diocese and episcopal government. Two points about these appeals are worthy of comment. The first is the attention paid by the papacy to this internal problem of the English Church, at its request; a large part of the Roman synod's business was taken up by this issue, at a time when the papacy was otherwise deeply engaged in the antimonothelite fight and the preparation of the great council of Constantinople in 680, consecrated to this debate. The second concerns the Anglo-Saxon reaction to the appeals. No king or archbishop denied Wilfrid's right to appeal or indeed the principle of an overruling papal judgement pronounced in Rome; when they refused to take on board such a ruling, it was on the grounds that Wilfrid had been in breach of canon law by not obeying an English council when it had deposed him, or that he had bribed his way in Rome. The principle itself was not denied and the precedent set.

While he pulled the English Church into the orbit of Roman and Western style of ecclesiastical government, and even into the major theological debate about monothelitism (at 'Hatfield', the Anglo-Saxon Church had been required to produce a statement confirming its orthodoxy by subscribing to the decrees of the Roman synod, brought over by John, the precentor of St Peter's), Theodore was also bringing to it that which had made him famous in the first place: his scholarship. The school he and Hadrian set up at Canterbury rapidly became the best known educational centre in Britain, supplanting the Irish-founded monasteries and schools. As well as grammar and the Scriptures, metre, computation and music, it also taught Greek language and philosophy, Roman and canon law, medicine and astronomy. Some of these subjects were by then largely ignored elsewhere in the West. While Theodore brought his knowledge to England, he was not the only one to do so. Wilfrid and especially his contemporary, the founder and abbot of Wearmouth-Jarrow in Northumbria, Benedict Biscop, were also interested in learning. Biscop contributed to the creation of a library at Wearmouth which was almost on a par with Canterbury. Its holdings were made up of books brought back by him from his travels in Gaul and especially Rome, where he went on pilgrimage six times. Both he and Wilfrid had also collected on these travels artefacts, especially icons, and relics, as well as acquiring papal charters of exemption for their monastic foundations. They thus launched the great English tradition of the Roman pilgrimage, which would remain one of the most distinctive features of the Anglo-Saxon Church until the end of the eleventh century.

Biscop and Wilfrid were the first two pilgrims to Rome. Their collections of books, relics and artefacts, added to those which Augustine had brought with him, were the nucleus of monastic libraries, decorative schemes and architectural innovations such as the use of the round *confessio*-style crypt on the model of that in St Peter's basilica, in churches such as Brixworth. Other pilgrims followed in their wake. Kings set the example: the first to go was Caedwalla of Wessex who, after being baptized in Rome, died there and was buried in the Vatican basilica, where his tomb became one of the highlights of the visit to Rome for later pilgrims. Ine of Wessex, together with his wife Aethelburh, followed, and he was reputed to have founded the Schola Saxonum, a sort of 'English Quarter' with its houses, hospice, church and cemetery, which was to function successfully throughout the Anglo-Saxon period; Ine too died in Rome in 726. Next went Coenred of Mercia and Offa of East Anglia in 709, a fact so worthy of notice that it too, like Caedwalla's visit, was to be recorded in the *Liber Pontificalis*; and Burhred of Mercia, who also died there and was buried in the Schola Saxonum. Archbishops of Canterbury, such as Cuthbert *c.* 740 and Bregwin in 761 followed, as did other ecclesiastics: bishops, Daniel of Winchester in 721, Egbert of York in 733 and 735 and Cuthwin of East Anglia *c.* 750; Abbot Hwaetberht and some of his monks from Wearmouth *c.* 700, Aldhelm *c.* 701, Ceolfrid and some monks from Jarrow in 716, Willibald and Winnibald, together in 721 and 730 and the first on his own in 739. About 725, a priest from London, Nothelm, was asked to search the papal archives for information on the conversion of the English; he managed to acquire most of Gregory the Great's letters relevant to England and, having brought back copies, he gave them to Abbot Albinus at Canterbury. Thanks to Albinus who was a correspondent of Bede, the letters were then sent to him to be included in his work. Other figures are also known to have visited Rome: abbot Forthred in 757, Alcuin twice in 767 and 780, another priest, Odberht, in 795 and an abbot Wada in 797. Laymen also went there, such as the two thegns Cildas and Ceolbert in 798, and even women: some Northumbrian nuns *c.* 713, Wethburh *c.* 716, who 'retired' to lead a quiet life near the shrine of St Peter, two friends of Eangyth and Bugge *c.* 722 and the latter herself in 738, when she met Boniface there and toured the shrines of the martyrs in his company. In Bede's words, 'nobles and common, layfolk and clergy, men and women' went to Rome during the first two centuries after the Conversion.

From the very first, the Anglo-Saxon Church had adopted Roman liturgical customs, introduced by St Augustine and reinforced by the addition of the 'correct', that is Roman, practices, by men such as Wilfrid and Benedict Biscop, who brought from Rome liturgical books, a teacher of the papal style of chanting, the archchanter John, liturgical objects for the veneration of the people and relics. Interestingly, John was the archchanter at St Peter's, not at the official papal residence and cathedral of the Lateran, far more important to Romans; for English pilgrims, again, what mattered was, more than anything, to follow the liturgy of St Peter's church, even when that was different from the pope's own cathedral church. The books used, sacramentaries and pontificals, were closely modelled on the 'Roman' so-called 'Gregorian' Sacramentary then attributed to Gregory the Great, and on the *ordines* used by the popes themselves, going as far as to preserve the entries of the processional churches in Rome, and the names of purely Roman feasts such as those of Sta Maria ad Martyres (dedication of the Pantheon) and S. Giovanni ante portam latinam. Roman liturgical innovations such as those which occurred under Pope Sergius: feast of the Cross, singing of the Agnus Dei at Mass and celebration of the four feasts of the Virgin, reached English centres within less than twenty years of their introduction or enforcement by the papacy.

Wilfrid and Benedict Biscop had brought large collections of relics from Rome. The importance to the papacy of English pilgrims in the seventh century is again displayed when Wilfrid's biographer Stephanus implies quite clearly that his patron was the first pilgrim to have obtained (officially, at any rate) actual bodily relics of the Roman martyrs to take home with him, at a time when the papacy was still clinging to the principle of only allowing relics by association to leave Rome: pieces of cloth, dust or wax from the tombs of the saints. Later, other relics were sent to English kings by the popes: those of SS Pancras, Laurence, Gregory and John and Paul were sent to King Oswiu of

Northumbria by Pope Vitalian in the seventh century, and some of the Holy Cross to King Alfred by Pope Marinus. Archbishop Plegmund brought back some relics of St Blaise from Rome in 909, later given to Canterbury, and Abbot Aelfstan also brought some back from his pilgrimage, which he gave to St Augustine's in 1022. The importance of these relics is easily perceived from the importance of liturgical celebrations for the respective saints in the English churches where they were kept: for example, even such relatively minor Roman saints as the martyrs Pancras and John and Paul were celebrated with somewhat more elaborate texts than those of numerous English saints. Naturally, this applied on a much larger scale to the main saints associated in England with Rome and the papacy: St Peter, St Gregory and St Benedict.

First and foremost came St Peter. Through its association with St Peter, Rome, always regarded as the Apostle's city, had become the major goal of numerous Anglo-Saxon pilgrims who desired to die near the tomb of the Apostle, 'ad limina Sancti Petri', thereby securing almost certain access to heaven. The devotion for the 'owner' of the city, St Peter, ensured the continuous success of the pilgrimage, prompting many pilgrims to visit and venerate the relics of the Apostle in all the places associated with him in Rome; but the pilgrims also paid their respects to the pope, who was perceived as the embodiment of St Peter on earth. Veneration for St Peter was thus originally initiated and later fuelled by England's privileged links with Rome, the original source of the conversion of England, and remained throughout the period the expression of an emotional link with the Prince of the Apostles, rather than a mere political gesture. It indeed found its expression through the pilgrimage to Rome, but also through the great number of dedications of churches in England itself, twenty-one to St Peter on his own and six to SS Peter and Paul in the early Anglo-Saxon period alone, not counting smaller chapels, altars and so on. Offa of Mercia alone acquired monastic houses placed under the patronage of Peter, such as Bath and Bredon, or dedicated new foundations to him, like the nunnery in Winchester. It is also Offa who is credited with having been at the origin of 'Peter's Pence', an annual tax levied throughout the later Anglo-Saxon period and sent to Rome (the only such occurrence in the West), when he made a large gift of money to St Peter's for the poor and for the maintenance of candles, and proposed to renew it every year in future. Subsequent legislation, notably the law-codes of Edgar and Aethelred at the turn of the tenth and eleventh centuries, show this tax, variably called Peter's Pence, 'Rome money' or Romscot, to be still very much a permanent impost throughout the country.

St Peter's cult was widespread in Western Europe at the time, even outside Rome. Numerous Frankish churches were dedicated to him and the German Emperors, whose imperial ideology was closely linked to their involvement with Rome, upheld it. Great imperial abbeys, such as Reichenau, were dedicated to SS Peter and Paul, as was the most prestigious abbey in the West from the tenth century onwards, Cluny, favoured by both popes and emperors. But, however significant this cult may have been in Western Europe outside Rome, nowhere does it appear to have been as strong as it was in England, where no local saint ever superseded it during the Anglo-Saxon period. The English cult was underlaid by a considerable official, ecclesiastical and royal devotion to St Peter, fostered by the Conversion, supported by the close links of the English Church with Rome, and made manifest in the liturgy, dedications and patronage of kings. While this 'official' cult of St Peter was considerable in England, even more overwhelming was the personal veneration for him, a characteristically English feature. The prayers addressed to St Peter express a devotion due to his role in the process of intercession, remission of sins and salvation, as well as to his official status as Prince of the Apostles. It was St Peter, and not local or minor saints, on whom English saints focused their veneration; for example, he appears to St Dunstan in a vision, exhorting him. This very personal and emotional link bears witness to a stronger individual cult than anywhere in the West outside Rome itself.

Second to Peter, Gregory the Great himself was one of the most popular saints, as was St Benedict, the founder of

Benedictine monasticism. From the first years after the Conversion, the Anglo-Saxon Church viewed St Gregory as the initiator of the mission to England, and he rapidly became one of the most highly regarded saints in the English Church. Although Benedictine monasticism as such did not become the predominant form of monastic life in the West before the reforms of Benedict of Aniane at the beginning of the ninth century, and before the tenth-century reform in England, great veneration for St Bendict himself was already common by the eighth century in England. It was in fact in England that the first still extant copy of the Rule of St Benedict was produced. This cult was rooted in the admiration shown towards the saint by Gregory the Great in his *Dialogues*. For English pilgrims, Rome was not only the city of St Peter, but also that of Gregory. Devotion to the great pope did not stop at the writing of his Life, but remained constant through the study of his theological, pastoral and homiletical writings, as well as through the influence of his spirituality, hagiographical techniques and pastoral outlook. These derived from Gregory's homilies, commentaries on the Gospels, *Dialogues, Pastoral Care* and correspondence with St Augustine of Canterbury. In every other respect, English hagiography also remained faithful to Roman models and saints, as models of martyrdom, charity (St Laurence) or virginity (St Agnes). Most significant in Aelfric's collections of Lives are those of St Peter, St Gregory, St Benedict and the main Roman martyrs mentioned above.

During the tenth and eleventh centuries, these close links with the city of St Peter were maintained and reinforced. Englishmen of all ranks and status from the kings down continued to go to Rome. In 853, King Aelthelwulf of Wessex sent his son Alfred on pilgrimage to Rome, and in 855, he went there himself, taking Alfred with him. In 1027, it was King Cnut, a convert to Christianity when already of mature age, who followed the English tradition and went on pilgrimage. When in Rome, he used the opportunity to do some business as well, meeting the pope, asking him to allow the archbishops coming for the *pallium* to obtain it without having to pay extortionate sums for it in gifts! The archbishops Plegmund in 909, Aelfsige in 958–9 (who died on his way in the Alps), Dunstan in 960, Sigeric in 990, Aelfric in 997, Aethelnoth in 1020, Robert of Jumièges in 1051 and the archbishops of York Cynesige and Ealdred in 1033 and 1061 went to Rome to collect the *pallium* or on business. The only archbishop of Canterbury who did not collect his *pallium* in Rome and is expressly said not to have done so was Stigand, appointed by King Edward in 1052, whom the 'correctly' elected Pope Leo IX had refused to consecrate as bishop of London in 1051, and who was sent the *pallium* in 1058 by the anti-pope Benedict X. In this refusal of a pope to approve the choice of a royal candidate are made apparent the first attempts of the papacy to obtain control over episcopal elections. The papacy's arguments in this case were that Stigand had been appointed by the king despite the fact that the incumbent of the see, Robert, was still alive at the time, even though exiled. Stigand's irregular position was further weakened by William I's refusal to be crowned by him. The knot was untied only in 1070, on the initiative and to the satisfaction of the papal reforming party by the two papal legates sent to England to depose Stigand.

Other ecclesiastics, of lower rank, went on pilgrimage to Rome too, during the tenth and eleventh centuries, such as Bishop Herman of Ramsbury and Abbot Aelfwine of Ramsey, who attended the council of 1050, together with Ealdred; and Abbot Aelfstan of St Augustine's, who spent some time in Rome in 1022. Among the laity, both the higher ranks, such as the earls Harold and Tostig with his wife, and the lower, like the simple thegn mentioned in the Life of St Swithun by Lantfred, and Aelfric Modercope. Immediately after the conquest, a couple called Ulf and Maselin left a will disposing of their property before undertaking the pilgrimage. A nobleman who had entered an illicit marriage condemned by Dunstan went to Rome to ask the pope for a letter addressed to Dunstan, which would support his claim. The statutes of an Exeter guild of the first half of the tenth century mention the pilgrimage to Rome of its members as a fairly common occurrence. Despite Boniface's warning as to the fate of women and nuns going to Rome on pilgrimage and ending up in Italian cities as prostitutes, women continued to go to Rome; we know of one Sifflaed, who made a will before leaving, and another one is mentioned by Symeon of Durham among the visitors to the shrine of St Cuthbert at Durham.

Traffic did not flow in one direction only, however. The first bishops had been sent to England from Rome. Once the Anglo-Saxon Church stood on its own feet, emissaries sent by the popes visited it. The first, after Theodore, were the two legates bishops George of Ostia and Theophylact of Todi, two very important figures in the papal entourage, George as a diplomat and envoy to Charlemagne's court and Theophylact the papal librarian and foremost scholar. It is quite possible that it was King Offa of Mercia himself who had suggested that a legatine visit should take place. Only a little time before, he had put into motion his plans to raise Lichfield to metropolitan status and to have his son crowned king the following year. In practical terms, while a king might take the initiative for the erection of a new archbishopric, it was nevertheless universally recognized that only the pope could sanction such an innovation. But Offa's motives may not have been only practical. He may well have felt that an Anglo-Saxon king who had reached the climax of his power needed the prestige of papal approval and underwriting of his actions, in order fully to function as more than a warlord, as a king worthy of exercizing the *imperium*, (an as yet not common concept in the West, but one already used by Boniface and Alcuin), the moral as well as political authority over the island. Alcuin, who held Offa in great regard, would not have been ignorant of such views by the time he left England for Charlemagne's court, where he would then be the main thinker behind both the Carolingian reforming policies and the revival of the imperial title in 800.

The legates toured the country and presided over the legatine council of 786 in the south, after carrying out a thorough mission of observation. George had gone to Northumbria while Theophylact visited the south. Both parties comprised papal and Frankish clergy, as well as the most distinguished living Anglo-

Saxon who accompanied the legates from Francia, Alcuin. In Northumbria, George presided over a synod at York; Alcuin is thought by some historians to have played an important part in discussing and drafting the acts of this synod with Bishop George, particularly in matters relating to royal ideology. It is hardly possible to ascertain whether he, or George himself, was responsible for the strong Gelasian slant in political theory, then current in Rome, emphasizing the subordination of secular to spiritual power. George then brought the acts of this council of the Northumbrian province back south to the main council of the following year, presided over by Offa of Mercia and the Archbishop of Canterbury, Jaenberht. There, a great deal of reforming activity took place, most of it well-known from the report sent by the legates to the pope.

Attempts have been made to demonstrate that the similarities between the legatine decrees of 786 and the second half of the great Carolingian reforming text known as the *Admonitio Generalis* of 789 cannot be entirely coincidental, thus implying a considerable part played by Alcuin in the drafting of the *Admonitio* too, and of Carolingian reforming policies, as a result of his Roman contacts of only a few years earlier. Again, such similarities may be ascribed to Alcuin, but they may also have been the more direct result of George's own views, in both cases. Whichever way one considers it, the impact of Roman political as well as pastoral ideas was crucial during those years in England as well as, only a few years later, in Francia. One is strongly tempted to relate the Roman slant of the Frankish reforms to Bishop George's efforts in Francia; but one needs also to remember Alcuin's presence, his familiarity with George's ideas implemented in the reforming legatine councils, and his characteristically English enthusiasm and support for a similar Roman-led reform.

Another major council, that of 747, was also convened at the pope's request, indeed on his order, and Zacharias' letter to that effect is appended to the acts of the council. In 808, we hear of another example of a papal emissary sent to England, an

Englishman this time, a deacon who, as a papal legate and together with Archbishop Eanbald and Charlemagne himself, was responsible for the restoration to the throne of Northumbria of the deposed king Eardulf. In 824, a papal legate, Nothelm, was present at the council held at 'Clovesho' that year, and witnessed the settlement of a dispute in favour of the church of Worcester. We then encounter a gap of over two centuries before the next legatine visits, which did not occur until 1061 and 1070. The reasons for this absence of visits may be due to the later Anglo-Saxon kings' major preoccupation, fighting the Vikings; no legation could take place without the king's consent and, frequently, on his invitation, and their lack of interest is understandable. Equally, the gap may be due to the more frequent journeys made by the archbishops to Rome to collect their *pallia*, which they invariably did after the mid-tenth century. One can nevertheless speculate as to whether the renewed legatine missions in the second half of the century may not have been at least suggested by the popes themselves, in their new mood of assertiveness and their attempts to intervene more closely in the affairs of national Churches. The first time, in 1061, the legates came back from Rome with the Archbishop of York Ealdred to solve the problem of his irregular position as a holder of the two dioceses of York and Worcester, and only consecrated him archbishop of York when he resigned the see of Worcester to Wulfstan. Then, as later in 1070 with the visit of the cardinals John and Peter and Bishop Ermenfrid of Sion, to resolve the question of Archbishop Stigand's position, the action of the Roman reforming party can be seen at work, attempting to enforce the principles laid down by the popes of the second half of the eleventh century from Leo IX to Gregory VII, in the matter of appointments to episcopal sees and stricter ecclesiastical discipline.

A less strenuous but no less potent form of communication between the English and the papacy throughout the period was through the constant exchange of letters. The popes continued the custom begun by Gregory of sending letters to English kings and ecclesiastics. After Boniface V's correspondence with Aethelburh and her husband Edwin, as well as with Augustine's successor at Canterbury, Justus, letters were constantly sent back and forth between the popes and Englishmen. Pope Honorius wrote to both King Edwin and Archbishop Honorius on sending the *pallium* to Canterbury and York. A letter, now lost, was sent by the two kings Oswiu of Northumbria and Egbert of Kent on the election of Wigheard to the see of Canterbury, and Pope Vitalian replied to Oswiu in 667 to inform him of the archbishop-elect's death in Rome. The same Vitalian then proceeded to appoint Theodore in Rome and tried to smooth his way both in practical terms, by recommending him to John, Bishop of Arles, and other Frankish prelates, and probably also by stating the supremacy of Canterbury in England. About 701, a letter from Pope Sergius to Ceolfrid, Abbot of Jarrow, discusses the possible trip to Rome of one of the monks. John VI wrote twice probably in 704, once jointly to Aethelred of Mercia and Ealdfrith of Northumbria concerning Wilfrid's appeal to Rome, and once generally to the archbishop and clergy of England for the same purpose. In 716, the abbot of Wearmouth wrote in turn to recommend Ceolfrid, then on his way to Rome, to Pope Gregory II. Rather less agreeably, Pope Paul II in 757–8 sent a letter to Eadberht of Northumbria and Archbishop Egbert of York to request the restoration of monasteries taken by the king from Abbot Forthred.

A matter which once again engaged the attention of the English Church was that of the rights of Canterbury. After Offa of Mercia's attempt to raise Lichfield to metropolitan status by dividing the see of Canterbury and obtaining from Pope Hadrian the *pallium* for the bishop of Lichfield in 788, King Coenwulf of Mercia wrote to Leo III in 798, explaining the English bishops' unease at this action, which went so clearly against Augustine's and especially Gregory's plan. The Archbishop of Canterbury Aethelheard went to Rome to discuss the matter; the pope replied to the king and to Aethelheard in 802, to inform them of his decision to anul the metropolitan status of the new see. Thus, finally, the archbishopric of Lichfield was abolished by Aethelheard at the council of 'Clovesho' in 803, on the order of Pope Leo III.

Leo continued his intense involvement with English affairs, even indirectly, since he deals with such affairs several times in his correspondence with Charlemagne. For example, Leo wrote to the emperor about the relations of the kings of Northumbria and Mercia with their respective archbishops, and his involvement in the restoration of Eardwulf has already been mentioned. Leo was not the first to discuss English matters in a letter to Charlemagne; Hadrian a few years earlier had also written to the Frankish emperor a most extraordinary letter, in which he appeared to believe that some plan was afoot by Offa of Mercia to depose him. Some of the papal correspondence had also been in the form of privileges of exemption for Anglo-Saxon monasteries, from the first such privilege granted by Pope Adeodatus to St Augustine's, Canterbury in 673, to those of Agatho to Wearmouth in 679 (later extended to Jarrow) and of Constantine to Bermondsey and Woking sometime between 708 and 715.

Such letters continued from the ninth century onwards. Pastoral issues, privileges, changes of sees, rights of various sees, relations between Canterbury and York are mentioned. The papal correspondence with England was frequent and wide-ranging, covering both political and disciplinary problems relating to the life of the Church in general. Some letters came from the popes for the purpose of granting privileges or confirming episcopal elections; one from John XII accompanied the grant of the *pallium* to Dunstan in 960 and two from Nicholas II to Giso of Wells and Wulfwig of Dorchester confirmed the privileges of their sees. Others allowed various administrative changes: the ejection of secular canons from the Old Minster at Winchester and their replacement with monks by Bishop Aethelwold in 963 and the removal of sees to new centres, as in the case of Leofric's from Crediton to Exeter in 1050. Others deal with various matters of ecclesiastical discipline or pastoral care: John VIII wrote to the English archbishops, bishops and clergy *c.* 873–5 on such matters, and wrote again to Archbishop Aethelred referring to some problem between him and the king, while in 891–6, Pope Formosus sent a rather fierce letter accusing the English bishops of not putting enough efforts into preaching christianity to the 'pagans', doubtless meaning the Viking settlers. Such letters went in the other direction too, since in 1020 the English bishops in turn wrote to the pope complaining about the problems they were facing because of the obligation to go to Rome to collect the *pallium*, not least of which was having to spend large sums of money to bribe their way into the papal curia. As often in previous times, letters were also sent and received by the kings themselves. From the late ninth century onwards, we have a letter of John VIII to Burghred of Mercia of 873–4 on marriage practices, and other letters to and from that pope to King Alfred. John XIV attempted to make peace between King Aethelred and the Duke of Normandy, Richard I, and Victor II sent letters to Edward the Confessor, granting privileges to the abbeys of Chertsey and Ely, some time between 1055 and 1057. A pope John even wrote directly to a layman, the Earldorman Aelfric, condemning his attempts to seize some lands belonging to the abbey of Glastonbury.

My analysis so far has insisted heavily on the importance of the links with the papacy for the Anglo-Saxons. They developed throughout the period in four successive phases. The first was, of course, the conversion from Rome, under the aegis of Gregory the Great, by Augustine and his mission in the south, and Paulinus in Northumbria. The second was the radical restructuring, in administrative as well as scholarly terms, carried out by Theodore. The third was the renewal under King Alfred and his successors, which gave new impetus to the Roman connection after the Viking disruptions, an impetus which was to last until the Norman Conquest. These are more or less definite chronological phases. The fourth phase is not, but underpins and supports the others. It is, quite simply, Bede's work, especially his *Ecclesiastical History*.

It was largely due to Bede's understanding and propounding of the Roman connections of the English and his description of Theodore's age as the Golden Age of the Anglo-Saxon Church, that these views came to be perceived as the only right way of doing things. Particularly significant in this respect is, of course, King Alfred in the second half of the ninth century. He translated, or had translated, several books which he considered absolutely essential to ensure the revival of civilization after the Viking devastation. Among these books, on a level with the most important, Gregory's *Pastoral Care*, was Bede's *Ecclesiastical History*. These two texts were distributed to various centres throughout England on the king's order, a fact to which the large number of extant manuscripts of both these Old English translations bears witness. Alfred spent a great deal of time pondering over Bede's views of the world, kingship, the English and the Church. Bede's account of the establishment and triumph of the Christian Church among the English from Augustine's arrival to his own day was paramount in the king's perception of his people's fate and his own mission. Bede idealized the happy years of the second half of the seventh century under Theodore, Cuthbert and Wilfrid; he also provided the English with a strong sense of their own identity and common Christian past. On both counts, Alfred could recognize his ideals: to recreate this golden age, and to unite the English by giving them comfort in times of difficulties with the Vikings and by making them unite against the common, pagan, enemy. More importantly even, Bede's fundamental premise was that from the king's support of the Church came, not only the salvation of the Christian people, but also the material prosperity of the kingdom, peace and victory in war. The Church had to be restored and reformed; but it was the Church described by Bede that Alfred was attempting to revive. This ideological framework became so overwhelming that when a non-English king like Cnut in the first half of the eleventh century wanted to mould himself into a 'good' king in the English tradition, the best he could do was to follow Bedan models, even down to undertaking the Roman pilgrimage. Cnut's archbishop, Wulfstan, would have taken care to point the way to the king.

Wulfstan's case would be only one among many. Bede's prestige in England, which began shortly after his death, was such that he became the key formative influence on English ecclesiastics – from the mid-eighth century onwards, his work would have been 'bedtime reading' for people like Boniface and Alcuin. When the Anglo-Saxon missionaries left England for the Continent, they knew about Augustine and his mission, Wilfrid and Theodore, and they became, as one would say in modern terms, conditioned to see them as the models for setting up or reforming any Church. Willibrord and Boniface immediately went to Rome to see the pope and to gain papal approval for their missions to Frisia and Germany. They were constantly exchanging letters with the popes in the following years, especially Boniface, and they even took new names, with Roman and papal connotations: Willibrord became Clement and Winfrith, Boniface. In terms of missionary techniques in Germany, what strikes one forcibly in Boniface's correspondence with the pope or with his mentor, Bishop Daniel of Winchester, is his use of Gregorian policies as defined in the 'Libellus Responsionum': assimilation, christianization rather than destruction, debate and so on.

In terms of Church reforms, when asked by Carloman and Pepin III to reform the Frankish Church, Boniface attempted to implement no more and no less than Theodore's policies: the hierarchy of bishops and archbishops under Roman control, regular meetings of Church councils, and the ultimate authority of papal jurisdiction. If he did not altogether succeed, it was because of Pepin III's reluctance to allow such a degree of Roman control over his Church. Charlemagne and Louis the Pious would take on board more of Boniface's ideas in some respects, while still tailoring them to their own requirements. Concomitantly, Alcuin would be behind the impetus for the adoption of the Roman liturgy with Charlemagne's acquisition of a copy of the Roman sacramentary, supplemented in Francia, and known as the Hadrianum, and of Roman collections of canon law, in response to the emperor's request to the pope to be sent a copy of the compilation known as the Dionysio-Hadriana. Alcuin further requested, from English libraries this time, both secular texts for teaching purposes, and ecclesiastical ones – many such books being themselves originally Roman or copies of Roman manuscripts.

The role played by Anglo-Saxon monks in the Carolingian world in terms of a *rapprochement* with Rome cannot be too strongly emphasized. Ascertaining whether they inspired the Carolingian alliance with the papacy around the middle of the eighth century or whether Pepin III had thought of it all by himself so as to create the legitimacy he needed after usurping the Frankish throne, and then used the Anglo-Saxons because their views favoured his, is rather like working out the egg and the chicken problem. What is not in doubt is that they supported one another, the Carolingians for political safety, the Anglo-Saxons because this is how they had been taught to think, especially by Bede. While the Frankish world was becoming increasingly closer to Rome, its impact on England from the end of the ninth century onwards was also growing. Under the joint influence of Bede's views, on the one hand, and their Carolingian neighbours on the other, Alfred, then Aethelstan and his successors would once again bring foward the Roman connections, in what might be termed an almost self-fulfilling process.

The English were not to break this emotional link until the reformed papacy of the late eleventh century, associated with the Norman conquest, would lead them to do so. At this stage, the papacy came to be seen as making too many demands and being too interventionist on its own initiative in the internal affairs of the English Church, and thus came to clash with William I in a battle of wills – William, who, unlike his Anglo-Saxon predecessors, had not been brought up with the same affection and respect for the papacy. Even when problems occurred, as they not infrequently did, between the English and the popes, over the archbishops' resentment at being obliged to collect the *pallium* in Rome, and the accusations of corruption at the papal court, no radical questioning of papal authority would have been likely before 1050.

In the years immediately following the Norman Conquest, during Lanfranc's archiepiscopate, links between England and

Rome were still close, and few legates in England had as much power and influence as Ermenfrid of Sion, who contributed to ecclesiastical legislation at William's council of 1070, reflecting the preoccupations of Roman reformers. One of these, the issue of clerical marriage, was specifically dealt with. On the whole, however, it must be noted that papal directions were no longer the ultimate law in England, once William I became powerful enough, though his conquest of England had been legitimized by the popes in the first place. Thus, although William accepted to pay all the arrears of Peter's Pence when Pope Alexander II asked him to do so, he remained firmly opposed to the placing of his kingdom under the feudal authority of the popes, and continued to refuse to bow to Gregory VII's demands in the matter of episcopal elections, to the point of attempting to forbid his clergy to go to Rome on any pretext after 1080. Both Lanfranc and William remained closely involved in papal politics, however, and their support was sought by both Clement III and Urban II in their rival claims to the papacy, after Gregory VII's death. Sometimes, the popes tried to intervene in English affairs, for example, in a matrimonial case in the diocese of Chichester or in a claim to land made by St Mary's at Wilton; in the first case, it was Lanfranc who eventually solved the case. Interestingly, the appeal in the second case emanated from a member of the Anglo-Saxon aristocracy: this rather supports the view that it was the Anglo-Saxon tradition, with its emotional link with St Peter and Rome, which was much more strongly attached to Rome, than the Norman one, despite the efforts of a reformed papacy.

So far, I have analysed essentially the Anglo-Saxon need, affection and veneration for the papacy throughout the period. However, such feelings were anything but one-sided. We saw earlier how closely the popes were interested and involved in the life of the English Church, how they protected it and even made considerable sacrifices for it, such as sending over Theodore and accepting to part with important relics, for its sake. Even leaving aside the emotional connection, what did the papacy have to gain from thus nurturing this link?

The first and most obvious benefit to the popes was the development of the cult of St Peter. Its importance in England has already been discussed. But the point has also been made that others in the West were interested in the cult too, the Lombards and the Franks in particular. What made the Anglo-Saxon devotion special was that, for the English, Peter was not simply a *major* saint: he was irrevocably associated with Rome, his city, and with his successor on earth, the living pope. While others, notably the Franks, tried to appropriate St Peter, to 'bring him to Gaul', the Anglo-Saxons never attempted to separate the three, to them forever linked, entities of Peter, Rome and the popes. Hence, of course, their willingness to obey the popes and acknowledge their primacy and authority in the West.

In addition, it so happened that the seventh century, the very century which saw the conversion of England, was a particularly decisive, but also very difficult, time for the papacy. Challenged on the one hand by the Eastern emperors' high-handed religious policies of monothelitism, and on the other by Lombard military pressure and Arian affiliation in Italy, the popes' confidence in their own status was being eroded. But, precisely at that time, they were also faced with a newly converted people who actually forced those same popes to exercise authority over the English, at *their* request, to legislate and provide for them, in short, to *act* as the foremost ecclesiastical authority in the West. Furthermore, the popes geared themselves during the second half of the seventh century towards winning the monothelite debate. To do so successfully, their main weapon was to demonstrate to Constantinople the perfect unanimity in its staunch orthodoxy of the whole Latin western Church, especially in the post-Roman kingdoms where the Church saw itself as the natural heir of the Roman world and its values. The English Church was one such, and its orthodoxy was vouched for at a major national Church council at 'Hatfield', and by Wildrid's engagement in Rome.

Another valuable asset to the papacy was the English devotion to Gregory the Great. It is not unlikely that, without the Anglo-Saxon veneration for *their* Apostle, without the production of a first hagiographical text devoted to Gregory, not so much at Whitby as in Bede's *Ecclesiastical History*, the cult of Gregory in the West would have been slower to take off. This English-born cult was only then seriously taken up and used by the popes, who promoted it from the eighth century onwards. Furthermore, these popes, especially the significantly self-styled Gregory III, clearly understood the lessons to be drawn from Gregory's western involvement. They, too, finally gave up on being part of the Byzantine world and its problems and turned more definitely towards the western churches. One might even say that the papacy was forced to take this line by these peoples, Franks, Lombards and Anglo-Saxons, whose main concern was with issues relating to conversion and ecclesiastical organization rather than with debates on the nature of Christ, peoples for whom St Peter and his earthly representative, the pope, were the supreme authority one turned to when in doubt or difficulty.

The Anglo-Saxons, whose links with the papacy began at the very time when it was under severe political pressure in the seventh century, were an essential element in propping it up when it most needed support, and providing it with the example to others, East and West, of a Church fully accepting papal authority, indeed requesting it to exercise this authority. In the second half of the eighth century, with the new alliance between the popes and the Carolingian kings, partly under the inspiration and certainly with the support of such Anglo-Saxon missionaries and reformers as Boniface, papal influence grew in moral terms at least. One could perhaps claim that the maintenance of the authority of Rome in Europe was due to the English devotion to the Roman Church and pope, its veneration for St Peter and Gregory the Great, and its respect for Bede's writings, which the Anglo-Saxon missionaries spread to the Continent. Through the later contacts of the English, both with Rome directly and with the Carolingians, the association with Rome and the papacy continued throughout the later Anglo-Saxon period. The eleventh-century reform movement of the papacy, and its insistence on the authority delegated by Christ to St Peter, may

have contributed to reinforcing English views since at least some of
the reforming ideas must have been known in England through the
journeys of ecclesiastics to Rome and to the all-important council
of Reims in 1049, where Pope Leo IX initiated the papal reform
movement. Ultimately, however, there is little evidence of these
changes having had any direct effect in England before the twelfth
century, so pervasive was the association with the papacy in its
traditional form; an association stronger, if anything, with the
unreformed papacy, one that many Englishmen may have preferred
to the late-eleventh century papacy which had, after all, supported
William's Conquest of England.

SELECT BIBLIOGRAPHY

J. Richards, *The Popes and the Papacy in the Early Middle Ages 476–752* (1979)
J. Campbell, E. John and P. Wormald, *The Anglo-Saxons* (2nd ed., 1991)
F. Stenton, *Anglo-Saxon England* (3rd ed., 1971)
H. Mayr-Harting, *The Coming of Christianity to Anglo-Saxon England* (3rd ed., 1991)
F. Barlow, *The English Church 1000–1066* (2nd ed., 1979)
W.J. Moore, *The Saxon Pilgrims to Rome and the Schola Saxonum* (1937)
W. Levison, *England and the Continent in the Eighth Century* (1946)
R. Markus, 'Gregory the Great's Europe' and 'Gregory the Great and a papal missionary strategy', in his *From Augustine to Gregory the Great* (1983), p. 21–36 and 29–38.
R. Markus, *Gregory the Great and his World* (1997)
T. Zwölfer, *Sankt Peter, Apostelfürst und Himmelspförter: Seine Verehrung bei den Angelsachsen und Franken* (1929)
M. Lapidge, 'The career of Theodore' in *Archbishop Theodore: Commemorative Studies on his Life and Influence*, ed. M. Lapidge (1995), p. 1–29.
C. Cubitt, *Anglo-Saxon Church Councils c. 650–850* (1995) ch. 6
V. Ortenberg, '*Angli aut angeli*: les Anglo-Saxons ont-ils "sauvé" la papauté au VIIe siècle?', *Revue Mabillon* n.s. 6 (t.67) (1995)
I. Wood, 'The mission of Augustine of Canterbury to the English', *Speculum* 69 (1994), pp. 1–17

I should like to thank Prof. H. Lawrence and Prof. H. Mayr-Harting for their most useful comments on this paper.

FROM THE CONQUEST TO
THE DEATH OF JOHN

Charles Duggan

3

FROM THE CONQUEST TO THE
DEATH OF JOHN

THE period from the Norman Conquest to the death of John marks a decisive turning point in the history of Anglo-papal relations. In no previous age were the affairs of the English Church so closely interwoven with those of the Western Church as a whole; and in no other phase did English ecclesiastics exert a more pervasive influence on the ideological and canonical developments which buttressed the rise of papal supremacy over the entire Church. For England, the period opened with the arrival of the Norman conquerors bearing a papal banner, yet resolute in their determination to resist the implications which that impressive symbol contained. It ended with the Angevin John conceding defeat after a protracted and bitter struggle with Innocent III, taking the Crusader's vow and yielding his kingdom to the pope in feudal subjection. Within these limits, three archbishops of Canterbury—Anselm, Becket and Langton—suffered long periods of exile in circumstances reflecting the clash of royal and papal interests, while Becket further endured the ultimate penalty of martyrdom in his own cathedral. The only English pope in the history of the Church, Adrian IV, reigned in the central years of the period. Beginning with Robert Pullen, English ecclesiastics were found for the first time in the college of cardinals in the mid-twelfth century; Englishmen, from King Edward the Confessor to St. Thomas of Canterbury, were inscribed in the catalogue of the saints with formal papal approval. Papal legates *a latere* appeared in England on many occasions with temporary jurisdiction to deal with particular situations; and English prelates were also appointed as papal legates with less specific commissions. With the advance of the twelfth century, papal judges delegate were named in ever-increasing numbers to deal with problems of law and to settle disputes by virtue of the pope's universal jurisdiction: a development which also reflected the swelling stream of appeals from England to the Roman Curia. Englishmen, many of them no longer known to us, shared in the intensive and creative growth of canon law, sometimes with lasting results for the Western Church as a whole. These channels of interrelation were of mutual concern and advantage: the English Church contributed to the increase of papal influence, just as it bore itself the imprint of the rising papal power.

It follows that no history of the English Church in the period is intelligible except in both its insular and its continental frameworks. This rather obvious judgement might appear at first superfluous, were it not that many existing commentaries are weakened by too great a preoccupation with local conditions and a failure to recognize the common pattern in the growth of the Church both in England and elsewhere in Europe simultaneously. Thus, the reforms of the English Church in the later-eleventh century and the introduction of the Investiture Dispute into England are matters which are naturally and validly linked with the policies of the first three Norman kings; but crucial and epoch-making changes for the whole of the Western Church coincided in time with the Norman Conquest of England; and, in one form or another, the issues they posed would certainly have been raised in England, independently of the change of the English dynasty. Had this conceivably not been so, the English Church would have proved a striking exception to the general pattern of the Western Church at the time. Nevertheless, the precise evolution of events was conditioned by the policies assumed by secular and ecclesiastical leaders in England in the light of the existing circumstances. Again, it is a commonplace judgement to consider the reign of Stephen as an intermission of weakness in English secular government, coming between the strong rules of Henry I and his grandson Henry II; according to this theory, in a period of unprecedented opportunity, the English Church advanced to a position of great strength and many-sided privilege: a position which Henry II felt naturally constrained to challenge. But Stephen's reign ran parallel in time with a phase of remarkable development in papal central-ization and jurisdiction, especially through the agency of canon law, throughout the Church. This was the age which witnessed a vital point of departure in the history of ecclesiastical law: the 'Great Divide' between *ius antiquum* and *ius novum*, marked by the completion of Gratian's *Decretum* at Bologna, *c.* 1140–1. Clearly, both the local and the general factors played their part.

The Becket dispute is among the most familiar stories in English history; and conventionally the clash of personalities which it in-volved has formed the principal focus of interest in numerous evaluations of the contest. Alternatively, a diligent scrutiny of the life and practices of the English Church, its traditions and customs, and of the policies of the English kings affecting these, has provided an important yet entirely insular foundation for other assessments. Yet Becket expressed and championed the ascendant ideology of the popes and canon lawyers of the mid-twelfth century; and the conflict of secular and ecclesiastical interests and jurisdictions, which revolved in England round his personality, was also re-flected in many other parts of the contemporary Church: in Sicily and Hungary, to mention but two examples, and in the reawaken-ing of the papal-imperial struggle between Alexander III and Frederick Barbarossa. The English dispute was complex and has given rise to many contrasting interpretations, but it can never be understood divorced from its European context. Lastly, to cite one final instance, the affairs of the English Church in the reign of John involved repeated papal intervention so directly that their briefest outlines will serve to illustrate this general theme: Langton was appointed archbishop of Canterbury and consecrated by Innocent III against the wish of the king; the English kingdom was sub-jected to interdict for resistance to the papal action; the king him-self was excommunicated at first and threatened later with deposi-tion; papal authority and local secular problems, expressed in the baronial opposition to John, were intermingled in the struggle for the Charter and its subsequent condemnation by the pope; and the period ended, as mentioned above, with John's surrender and his submitting the kingdom to papal feudal overlordship. Nevertheless, throughout this well-known story, the basic tenets and principles on which the papacy acted were independent of the particular problems of the English kingdom, and can be accurately judged only against the wider background of Innocent's conception of the papal office and the place of the English Church within the *totum corpus* of Western Christianity.

The fortunes of the papacy itself form, therefore, the necessary backcloth to our story: within the limits of this long period of one and a half centuries, the plenitude of papal power advanced from confident, though frequently resisted, definition to a very high point of practical realization. At the outset, Gregory VII crystallized the essential principles of many centuries of doctrinal and ideological growth touching the themes of sacerdotal superiority in Christian Society and of papal supremacy over the Universal Church. But, despite his immense achievements and the lasting influence of his transcendent personality, his policies were often contradicted and frustrated in his own lifetime; and, despite the decisive and formative phase which his pontificate is retrospectively seen to mark in the evolution of the Church's history, Gregory died in fact in exile, with much of his work in temporary ruins. The principles for which he fought were not fully realized in practice for many decades. Mainly through the influence of theological and canonical exposition on the theoretical plane, and on the practical level through the ever-increasing efficiency of the administrative and judicial machinery of the Curia, the popes of the twelfth century rose to a peak of prestige and authority, until with Innocent III a Christian ethos was attained in which the *plenitudo potestatis* was, in Haller's striking phrase, not merely an exorbitant pretension of the pope, but the belief of the century. Through the long path by which this summit of power was reached, the fluctuations of papal successes and failures conditioned relations between the popes individually and the Churches and rulers in the separate countries. Axiomatically, a strong ruler, as was William I or Henry II in England, resisted ecclesiastical pretensions with greater success than would otherwise have been the case; and, conversely, the problems confronting a given pope, such as Alexander

III in his dangerous contest with Frederick I, induced a temporary or diplomatic abatement of the widest papal claims and an opportunity which secular rulers elsewhere could be expected to exploit. Nevertheless, despite all such vicissitudes of papal fortune, the total story is one of gradual and inexorable papal advance throughout the period, within which the power of the papacy over the Church as a whole, as over the Church in England in particular, increased beyond all previous recognition, whatever qualification of this judgement may seem appropriate in any narrower context.

Some aspects of papal history from the mid-eleventh century affected the life of the English Church so intimately that their nature and evolution must be briefly mentioned. In the first place, the twin and interlocking movements of Church reform and the Investiture Contest permeated by degrees into every province of the Western Church. In its narrowest and technical meaning, the Investiture Contest was the product of a papal reaction against long centuries of secular control of the Church at all its levels, exercised chiefly through a decisive voice in the selection of ecclesiastical officials. The Germanic traditions of a proprietary church system, or *Eigenkirchenwesen*, and of regional churches subject to the control of their local rulers, or *Landeskirchentum*, resulted in such officials becoming increasingly subject to secular rulers and magnates and at the same time involved in secular business; and, as a corollary of this, bishops became important property holders and influential ministers in royal and feudal administration: a development reflected most directly in their dual possession of spiritual office and material benefice. Both Church and State drew benefit in some respects from this co-operation; and secular rulers came naturally to expect some measure of control over the activities of the Church in their dominions and over the appointment of the more important ecclesiastical officials. But a new situation resulted from the spiritual and juridical reform movements of the eleventh century, which upset the existing and traditional delicate balance. The papacy had fallen on evil days by that time, and the nomination of the popes themselves had passed into the control of the Italian and Roman factions. This regrettable situation was amended by an intervention of the German ruler Henry III, who at the synod of Sutri in 1046 secured the deposition of rival claimants for the papal title, and in the person of Clement II inaugurated a line of popes of far superior character and suitability for their office. This secular action was viewed in retrospect by reforming ecclesiastics as an unlawful usurpation.

Nevertheless, the papacy, being itself reformed from without, went forward now to take the initiative in a broad and deeply-penetrating reform of almost every aspect of its life and that of the whole Church; the work of Leo IX, Nicholas II and Gregory VII in particular, taken up and further developed by Urban II, was of outstanding importance. With the reforming movement now pushed forward on a very wide front, the investiture question revolved within it round a single but highly significant problem: to the clerical reformers it seemed an intolerable abuse that bishops and other ecclesiastics should be invested with the symbols of their rank, dependent essentially on its spiritual functions, by secular persons, while, for the historical reasons already mentioned above, secular rulers felt unable to distinguish so sharply the spiritual and material competence of the holders of these important positions. For itself, the papacy cast off the constraints of external secular pressure in the matter of papal elections, and by a decree of Nicholas II in the Lenten Synod of 1059 placed for the future their effective control in the hands of the cardinal bishops. Then Gregory VII, from 1075, and Urban II laid down rules prohibiting the practice of lay investiture at all levels in the Church; and these injunctions were repeated from time to time by their successors. The most dramatic dispute resulting from these measures took place between two series of popes and emperors, spanning the period from 1076 until 1122, and ending in the Concordat of Worms in the latter year. During that long period, the issue was contested in England also, within the space of a very few years, in the reigns of Rufus and Henry I, while Anselm was archbishop of Canterbury; and an agreement was reached between Anselm and Henry I in 1107, comparable in terms with the more famous agreement at Worms referred to above.

But however important the Investiture Contest appears in

political history, it was in fact merely symptomatic of far deeper problems in the interplay of secular and ecclesiastical forces in the period. It was, in Tellenbach's familiar judgement, not simply a dispute over investitures, but 'a struggle for right order in the world': a struggle for all that was summed up in the Gregorian concept of *iustitia*, or righteousness and true order in Christian Society.[1] The intervention of the emperor Henry III could not have produced such far-reaching results, paradoxically so injurious in their consequences to the imperial power itself, had not already-existing currents of reform in the Church provided a promising foundation. These currents were mainly of a spiritual and juristic nature. The revivified spirituality of the Church, which was basic to any authentic religious reformation, is recognized most clearly in the history of the religious orders in the period: above all, though not exclusively, in the earliest phases in the expansion and influence of the Cluniac movement from the early-tenth century, and later attaining an all-pervasive penetration of the life of the Church through the rise of the Cistercian movement in the twelfth. This new religious zeal, with its characteristic emphasis on the monastic virtues and disciplines, conditioned the general state of the Church as well as, in a more particular way, the minds of such leading reformers as Peter Damian and Gregory VII himself. It played a vital role in effecting a wider movement of reform, and was in the event itself still further stimulated by it.

But in producing an efficient instrument of reform and a means of expressing its manifold aspects in concrete terms, the growth of canon law was even more important. Jedin has recently argued that the historical transition marked out by the ending of the old canon law, and the emergence of the new, is more significant in fact than the conventional classification of historical epochs; and, from a different viewpoint, Knowles has suggested that canon law was soon to eclipse, if only for a time, theology itself as an influential discipline in the Church. The canonical tradition had never in fact died out since the early centuries; but, in a more proximate con-

---

[1] For a stimulating, if controversial, account of the Investiture Contest, see G. Tellenbach, *Church, State and Christian Society at the Time of the Investiture Contest*, trans. R. P. Bennett, Oxford (1948).

text, the canonical background of Gregorian Reform and its impact on twelfth-century developments can be retraced in its
origins to the publication of the pseudo-Isidorian collection in the
mid-ninth century, a fountain-head of canonical transmission from
that time, through the proliferation of collections in the hands of
the eleventh-century reformers, and culminating in the *Decretum*
of Gratian in the mid-twelfth century.[2] From that time, at least
until the pontificate of John XXII at Avignon, every significant
pope was also an experienced canon lawyer, and papal policies
were firmly based on canonical principles. For good or ill, the
power of the medieval papacy at the peak of its prestige and influence was realized and made effective by canon law. These are
essential reflections in considering the relations between the Roman
Curia and the separate countries comprising the Western Church.

The reciprocal interchange of influence between the English
Church and the papacy is revealed, against this background, in the
crucial matter of ecclesiastical appointments. It was a typical feature of the policies of the reforming popes to foster canonical
elections and to seek an increasing measure of influence over the
selection, or at least to confirm the selection, of ecclesiastical officials. At its highest level, this policy was demonstrated in the papal
promotion of the authority and jurisdiction of primates and
metropolitans, not as representatives of separate *Landeskirchen*, but
as powerful instruments by which the highly centralized government of the Church could be applied in its component parts; and
so the symbolical importance of the pallium was increasingly
stressed, with the requirement that archbishops should receive from
the pope himself this token of their metropolitical office. Papal
concern with the application of these principles to the English

---

[2] The *Pseudo-Isidore*, more generally known as the False or Forged Decretals,
was one of the most decisive works in the history of canon law. Compiled in
Frankish lands, probably at Reims or Le Mans *c.* 847–52, it incorporated both sup-
posititious papal decretals from the early Christian centuries and genuine later
canons. Among its author's motives were the consolidation of clerical privilege in
Christian society and that of papal authority over the whole Church; and for these
themes the collection exercised great influence on subsequent canonical collections.
For further details, see A. van Hove, *Prolegomena ad Codicem Iuris Canonici*, Malines-
Rome (1945), pp. 305–11; W. Ullmann, *The Growth of Papal Government in the
Middle Ages*, Methuen (1955), pp. 180–9; etc.

Church was already evident in the twenty years preceding the Norman Conquest, simultaneously with the exertion of papal pressure, by popes Leo IX and Nicholas II, in the matter of episcopal elections. The anti-pope Benedict X had granted the pallium to the schismatical Stigand of Canterbury; and Nicholas II later granted the same to Ealdred of York, dispatching papal legates at the same time to settle related problems. But, after the Conquest, the process and habit of seeking such papal approbation became an issue of still more importance: in 1071 both Lanfranc of Canterbury and Thomas of York travelled to Rome for their pallia, while Lanfranc had accepted his appointment at the explicit command of the pope. A crisis arose, following Anselm's election, when Rufus obstructed at Rockingham Anselm's request for permission to journey to Rome for papal confirmation with the pallium. Nevertheless, Anselm received the essential symbol from the hands of a papal legate in his own cathedral in 1095, and Rufus's plans were circumvented. For the following century, a few examples only may be chosen from the many to illustrate the continuing interest of this papal prerogative: in Stephen's reign Theobald was elected to Canterbury by royal agreement with the papal legate, Alberic of Ostia; a disputed election to York resulted in the intervention of four successive popes, until William Fitzherbert was deposed in 1147 by Eugenius III, in favour of Henry Murdac, though the papal decision was frustrated in practice by the English king. In the reign of Henry II, Becket consented in 1162 to accept the province of Canterbury at the insistence of the king in agreement with the legate, Henry of Pisa, and English representatives including John of Salisbury and John of Poitiers, later distinguished adherents of Becket in his quarrel with the king, journeyed to the papal court to secure his pallium[3]; his successor, Richard of Dover, was elected in 1174 and travelled to Italy, where he was consecrated at Anagni by Alexander III, receiving the pallium from the pope in person; papal approval, together with the pallium, was freely granted by Lucius III to Baldwin of Ford and Worcester, who succeeded Richard in 1184.

[3] Cf. W. Stubbs, ed., *Radulfi de Diceto Opera Historica*, Rolls Series, 2 vols. (1876), I, 307; John of Poitiers was treasurer of York at that time.

And, most striking instance of all, in the reign of John, Stephen Langton was chosen and consecrated archbishop of Canterbury at Viterbo by Innocent III in 1207, following a disputed election which was quashed by the pope; though it was not until 1212 that John was induced to submit to the papal decision.

It is obvious that royal interests were also deeply involved in these matters. The person selected was normally the choice of the king, and in practice a large measure of co-operation was achieved between both parties. Yet it is significant that in a small number of critically disputed cases the papal action proved eventually the more successful even against the king. On the other hand, in the matter of episcopal elections the principle and practical value of papal approval were increasingly recognized, although the process of such elections provided a focus of recurring conflicts, above all during the investiture quarrel in Anselm's day, and in the Becket dispute over the Constitutions of Clarendon in 1164; and in the mainstream of development the royal will was in general the decisive factor. Nevertheless, papal influence percolated ever more deeply and pervasively through all levels of the English Church with the advance of the century, extending at last to all kinds of ecclesiastical appointments: of deans and archdeacons, of rectors and even monastic officials. The beginnings of the papal practice of granting expectative favours for benefices not yet vacant, the early traces of papal provisions, the granting of benefices to Italian or curial clerics: all these significant trends can be traced in England before the close of the century.[4]

But the problem of canonical elections provoked the use of a sword of two edges, since the legality of papal elections was often itself in dispute in the period. Gradually, through many crises, there evolved the basic canonical rules which were designed to place beyond question the validity of papal elections in the future. In 1059, in the context of ecclesiastical reforms already described, the decree *In Nomine Domini* of Nicholas II confirmed the electoral powers of the cardinal bishops, in consultation with the rest of the cardinal clergy. Yet the following century witnessed re-

[4] These matters are fully discussed in C. R. Cheney, *From Becket to Langton*, Manchester University Press (1956), esp. pp. 75–82.

peated conflicts within the electoral body, reflecting frequently the pressures of secular rulers, with the result that schism became endemic in the Church. After a long and dangerous instance of such confusion, the canon *Licet de vitanda* of Alexander III, in the Lateran Council of 1179, established the principle of a two-thirds majority of the total body of cardinals. Henceforth there could be no uncertainty concerning the legality of a given election; but a further problem arose through the scandal of extended vacancies, when the lawful electors were unable to reach a decision. And so the matter was finally settled in the decree *Ubi periculum* of Gregory X, at the Council of Lyons in 1274, which accepted in canon law the constraints of the conclave.

It follows that the period of this chapter, down to 1179, was one of exceptional danger for the papacy: between 1045 and 1179, no less than thirteen antipopes fractured the unity of the Church, in contrast with ten claimants of doubtful validity in the preceding four and a half centuries, and only one in the following two hundred years down to the outbreak of the Great Schism in 1378. This crisis of authority in the Church sprang in large measure from the conflicts of ecclesiastical and secular interests, as in the Investiture Contest or in the papal-Sicilian issues in the reign of Roger II. But for all secular rulers of the period a problem of choice, and at the same time an opportunity for the advancement of their separate ambitions, resulted. Thus, for England, the German creation of the antipope Clement III against Gregory VII in 1080 provided William I and Lanfranc with an occasion to arrest the promotion of Gregorian claims over the English Church, which fitted in very well with their general concept of ecclesiastical independence; and in the event they adopted a policy at first of hesitation and finally of neutrality. The problem was continued into the reign of William II, when Anselm succeeded Lanfranc, and the question arose of the recognition of Urban II by the English Church; this finally William agreed to approve, while obstructing Anselm's wish to visit the pope in person, as described above. Thereafter, the English Church, with royal agreement, supported the legitimate popes in similar conflicts. Nevertheless, the attitude assumed by English rulers proved of vital concern to the papacy, and frequently of political advantage to the English kings themselves. A difficult period for the Church opened with the double election of Innocent II and Anacletus II in 1130; but Henry I, in common with the French and German rulers, supported the ultimately successful Innocent, whose rival was sustained by forces in Italy and, in an important way, by Roger II of Sicily; and the schism lasted until 1138.

A still more difficult phase began with the death of Adrian IV in 1159, when against the newly and legitimately elected Alexander III, a line of antipopes was inaugurated by Frederick I; and a relentless conflict continued for almost twenty years until 1177: an experience clearly instrumental in provoking Alexander's electoral decree in 1179. In this schism also the English king supported the lawful claimant, refusing to accept Frederick's choice of Victor IV, at the Council of Pavia in 1160. But for many years Alexander was confronted with enormous difficulties: at times in exile from Rome, and even from Italy; often in danger of violent defeat at the hands of his German adversaries; and burdened with great expenses to sustain his fight and compensate for the loss of important revenues. Henry II was able to gain much profit by a diplomatic use of this crisis; and it is a matter of the highest significance that the papal schism covered the period of the Becket dispute in England. At the height of the English conflict, Henry's emissaries John of Oxford and Richard of Ilchester attended the schismatical Diet of Würzburg in 1165, and in somewhat obscure circumstances pledged support for the antipope Pascal III; in addition to which it is known that Henry wrote to the Imperial chancellor in 1166 of the possible transference of his allegiance from Alexander. In this context, Alexander is often accused of having adopted a weak and vacillating policy, of being lukewarm or even reluctant in his support of the English archbishop; but, in assessing his role in the insular conflict, it is vital to recall the problems which pressed more immediately and more persistently on him. The papal-imperial agreement at Venice in 1177 ended the series of crises which had revolved so long round the problem of papal elections. Meanwhile the wheel had turned full circle in England when Henry sought Alexander's support in his own dangerous crisis in the rising of 1173–4, conceding at that moment of peril, according to one admittedly questionable record, even the feudal subjection of his kingdom to the pope.[5]

With some of the major themes of contemporary papal and English ecclesiastical history established, it is feasible now to attempt a chronological sketch of Anglo-papal relations from the Conquest to the death of John. The overall trend is one of gradual extension and ramification of papal influence in England, with many setbacks and against frequent opposition: a gradually rising plane, broken by three peaks of crisis: the first in the time of Lanfranc and more particularly of Anselm, the second in that of Becket, and the third in the days of Langton. At each of these moments a major break-through of papal policy was achieved in dramatic circumstances. The intervening periods were not intrinsically less significant; indeed, in a less spectacular way, it was in those very phases of comparative quiet that the practical working out of ecclesiastical and secular issues was achieved; and, in the event, for the long-term fortunes of the Church and its relationship with secular law and government, these periods were to prove by far the more productive. But it is not possible to believe that the extent of the Church's success within the wider framework could have been achieved without the exceptional effort made in the periods of open conflict.

An earlier view that a radical change in Anglo-papal relations was accomplished by the Norman Conquest is no longer acceptable without substantial qualification. It is evident from the foregoing arguments that a coincidence in time explains, to some extent at least, the participation of the English Church in a wider movement. But more than this, it has also been clearly shown that the late Anglo-Saxon Church was by no means as moribund as

[5] The record of an alleged letter of Henry II written during the crisis is preserved by Peter of Blois, but its authenticity is doubtful. On the other hand, Duchesne's edition of the Life of Alexander III by Cardinal Bozo discusses variant MS readings of the Avranches Settlement of 1172 as found in Bozo MSS. The later MSS attribute to Henry II an undertaking very suggestive of feudal submission to the pope, but Duchesne's judgement is against this version, as being a possible interpolation; cf. L. Duchesne, *Liber Pontificalis*, Paris (2nd ed., 1955), Tome II, p. 426, n.1.

was previously imagined, that it was not at all isolated from contact with the papal Curia, and that the early seeds of reform had already been planted in it. The corollary of this thesis is that certain familiar measures of the immediately post-Conquest period have conventionally received a disproportionate emphasis. A more balanced view, revealing both innovation and continuity, has now been achieved, notably by Darlington and Barlow among more recent scholars.[6] A single example will serve to clarify this point: the *Northumbrian Priests' Law* of *c.* 1020 affords evidence for the existence and operation of canon law in ecclesiastical courts, reducing to some extent the significance of the Conqueror's oft-quoted writ dealing with the separation of ecclesiastical and secular jurisdictions. In the same way, the concern of the reforming papacy with the English Church from the time of Leo IX has already been noticed. Nevertheless, it is true that the Normans conquered the island with papal approval, at a moment when the archbishop of Canterbury was a schismatical supporter of the antipope Clement. They came, moreover, with a tradition of support for ecclesiastical reform on the continent; and there is no doubt that, in spite of the limits which the Conqueror wished to impose on the ideological aspects of papal policy, an important drive forward in the general reform of the Church was the inevitable result of the change of political direction. It is more fitting to speak therefore of a swifter application of reform and advance of the Church as a result of the Conquest, an acceleration of a movement which was already set in motion.

The policies and personalities of the first post-Conquest kings and archbishops require a similar evaluation. The Conqueror is rightly seen as a conscientious supporter of ecclesiastical and moral reform, in contrast with his son, William Rufus, who was disinterested in spiritual and moral questions, a despoiler of Church property and an oppressor of ecclesiastical persons. The deterioration of relations between *regnum* and *sacerdotium* which took place in England with the transition from one reign to the other

[6] Cf. R. R. Darlington, *The Norman Conquest*, Creighton Lecture in History 1962, Athlone Press (1963), esp. pp. 13–18; for the latest detailed study of the immediately pre-Conquest Church, see F. Barlow, *The English Church, 1000–1066*, Longmans (1963).

is partly explained by this altered royal attitude. At the same time, Lanfranc, the Conqueror's coadjutor at Canterbury, was in sympathy with the king's ecclesiastical policies, including his determination to govern effectively his *Landeskirche* in England, to set up the ring-fence round his dominions, to erect a barrier between the island and the continent, and thus to control the interchange both of ideas and of persons between the English Church and the Roman Curia. Whereas Anselm, Lanfranc's successor, was imbued with the very spirit of Gregorian Reform in all its aspects; therefore, for him, the reform of the regional Church in detail, though important, was no longer sufficient, and the denial of the fullest papal claims was an intolerable burden. In these circumstances, the happy co-operation which had existed between William I and Lanfranc was no longer feasible. The change was accomplished by a twofold and contrary transmutation: the royal policy had deteriorated through abuse to corruption, while the archiepiscopal purpose had risen from a moral and merely ecclesiastical level to a full theocratic and ideological programme. There is much that is true and illuminating in this theory, though in several aspects it is an insufficient, and even over-simple, explanation. To mention one obvious example: the papal programme had itself gained further momentum in the meanwhile.

The Conqueror's attitude was unambiguous enough. The judgement of Zachary Brooke seems somewhat generous in the circumstances. For Brooke, William 'was naturally devout and, like his fellow countrymen of Southern Italy, filled with a deep regard for the papal office'; yet his own analysis of William's dealings with the papacy suggests the actions of a ruler of realistic and understandably practical self-interest: the pope's support was useful at the time of the Conquest, and papal legates were necessary in the early transitional stages; but there was no hesitation on William's part in rejecting whatever aspects of papal policy were subsequently unwelcome to him. Gregory urged against him the fullest papal theories, claims which in their origins were retraceable to Gelasius I: 'As I have to answer for you at the awful judgement, in the interests of your own salvation, ought you, can you, avoid immediate obedience to me?' No king, not even a pagan king, Gregory claimed with some exaggeration, had opposed him in William's fashion. The latter agreed to contribute the traditional Peter's Pence to the support of the papacy, but utterly rejected the implications of tribute and feudal subjection which might be inferred from it: his predecessors, he firmly asserted, had not done fealty to the popes, nor had he promised to so do at the time of the Conquest. Therefore, despite his support for the ecclesiastical reforms in detail, the political aspects of reform were obscured in his reign in England: the investiture decrees remained a dead letter in William's dominions, and he ended his reign in easy neutrality between rival claimants for the papal title. Rufus continued the policies of his father, in this respect, in confronting the inroads of papal influence attempted in his kingdom, but without the Conqueror's compensating qualities: he was a persecutor of the Church and no supporter of spiritual and ecclesiastical reformation; and therefore he alienated many who otherwise might have supported him in the more political aspects of the question. But it is clear that Anselm regarded his curtailment of papal authority and his resistance to the developing canon law as the critical issue: Rufus had acted, in Anselm's judgement, contrary to the law of God in arrogating to himself the adjudication of papal elections and in resisting the application of the investiture decrees.

In contrast, the conventional distinction drawn between the policies of Lanfranc and Anselm is both valid and over-simple. It is important to stress the qualities they had in common as well as their differences: both were Italians who came to England as monks from the Norman abbey of Bec; both were great scholars of international reputation whose fame was established independently of their archiepiscopal office; both were imbued with the spirit of the reforms of the time, and acquainted at formative phases in their careers with popes or future popes, members of the papal Curia and leading reformers; both fully accepted the prevailing theories of papal supremacy, even if Lanfranc supported the limitation of the theories at times in practice. Lanfranc was a distinguished theologian and perhaps a product of the law schools of Italy, though an earlier view that he was numbered among the *causidici* in the schools of Roman law at Pavia has now been seriously challenged.[7] His later career as primate of the Church in England reveals his continuing interest in canon law and its general application; no work was more congenial to the promotion of all that the Gregorian reformers stood for than the *Pseudo-Isidore*, whose derivative collection Lanfranc certainly used in England. At the same time, he undoubtedly modified the rigour of some of the reforming policies in detail, such as the absolute insistence on clerical celibacy, without questioning their validity. He likewise accepted in full the right of appeal by ecclesiastics to the papal Curia, but simultaneously distinguished the secular interests which might make an appeal inappropriate. He fully supported the Conqueror's limitation of papal encroachments, and emphasized in particular situations his rights as metropolitan rather than the superior authority of the pope. His attitude was therefore to some extent ambivalent; and the interesting suggestion has been made that his coldness to Gregory VII resulted in part from the latter's earlier obstruction, as Archdeacon Hildebrand, of Lanfranc's project to build up a kind of patriarchate for the British Isles under his own control.[8] No doubt his attitude was compounded of many varied factors, and the common assumption is too facile that his difference of outlook from that of Anselm was largely explicable because Anselm was born a generation later.

But Anselm was more obviously a zealous adherent of the most advanced Gregorian party: a distinguished theologian and, paradoxically, less experienced in legal studies than his predecessor. He displayed in his attitude to the papacy, and on all the main planks of the papal reform programme, a complete acceptance of the Gregorian theories: his conflict was joined with Rufus on such key issues as the papal confirmation of his own election, the receipt of the pallium, and the recognition at the same time of the validity of Urban II's election. In the event, Anselm's resulting period of exile, from 1097, broke down the barriers which the Conqueror

[7] On this see R. W. Southern, 'Lanfranc of Bec and Berengar of Tours', in R. W. Hunt *et al.*, edd., *Studies in Medieval History presented to F. M. Powicke*, Oxford (1948), pp. 27–48, esp. pp. 28–30.

[8] This is suggested by E. Amann and A. Gaudel in 'Lanfranc', *Dictionnaire de Théologie Catholique*, Paris, VIII, ii (1925), col. 2562.

had erected, brought Anselm himself even more directly in touch with the central stream of reform at Church councils in Italy, at Bari and Rome in 1098 and 1099 respectively, from which he returned on Henry I's accession in 1100 determined more than ever to uphold the principles for which he had accepted exile. Meanwhile, with hardly less significance, signs of a wider movement were evident among the English bishops towards the recognition of an effective papal authority over elections, appeals and similar related questions. Herbert of Losinga, bishop of Thetford, travelled to Rome in 1093, resigned his bishopric on the grounds that his election in 1091 was tainted with simony, and accepted it back from the hands of Urban II; the bishops of Hereford and Salisbury, who had previously dissociated themselves from Anselm's actions, now moved over to his side, just as the bishops-elect of Winchester and Hereford later refused to accept investiture from Henry I, and likewise aligned themselves with Anselm.

The Investiture Contest was thus brought into England in the reign of William II; and the beginnings of a grouping of ecclesiastical leaders round Anselm and in support of the most advanced papal programme are clearly seen. It was an advantage to Henry I to receive back Anselm initially into favour, but the investiture issue was quickly resurrected, leading to Anselm's second exile and thus to the compromise worked out finally in 1107. The agreement was in the form of a compact in which each side gained some measure of success: Henry accepted that the symbols of investiture, the episcopal ring and staff, should not be conferred by a layman, but the bishops would nevertheless be elected in his court or chapel; and he ensured in practice that the homage of a bishop-elect would take place before his consecration. In its turn, the Church had secured the formal royal concession of the canonical principle that investiture was in essence a spiritual matter, though it may well be thought that in substance the greater gain was made by the king. The English compromise was accepted by Pascal II, the reigning pontiff, after a long series of difficult negotiations, and foreshadowed the very similar agreement at the papal-imperial level at the Concordat of Worms in 1122. But it would be idle to think that these agreements on the specific question of investitures resolved the basic conflicts of which it was merely symptomatic. The Becket dispute in mid-twelfth-century England, as well as the re-emergence of the papal-imperial struggle in the days of Barbarossa, revealed in a very true sense the posing of the same elemental questions in an altered situation.

Meanwhile, Henry I adopted a position *vis á vis* the Church in England logically transitional between the policies of his father, William I, and his grandson, Henry II. All three were strong kings who moved forward in many areas of mutual co-operation with the Church, yet with varying degrees of success for their plans to limit the extent of papal intervention in their kingdom. The barriers which the Conqueror erected were breached at certain vantage points in the reign of Henry I, but they were by no means destroyed altogether. Recourse was had to Rome for the pallium for Archbishop Ralph in 1114, but in circumstances which provoked the complaints of the pope over lack of consultation and the obstructions which were placed in the way of inter-communication: Pascal II wrote a letter of protest in 1115 with specific reference to papal letters, legates, appeals to the Curia, and the translation of bishops without papal consent. Nevertheless, the practice of appeals later made significant headway, of which the *Liber Landavensis* provides convincing evidence. The appointment of legates assumed a heightened importance. A total of nine legates were appointed during the reign: among these, the legate Anselm was commissioned in 1116, but detained in Normandy for three years; with uncertain results, Henry I sought papal agreement in 1119 to limit the scope of legatine action in England; the commission of John of Crema in 1125 was of outstanding importance, and he held a legatine council at Westminster in that year. A measure of compromise was reached when Honorius II granted the status of legate to Archbishop William of Canterbury in 1126; and William convened a legatine council, with royal approval, in the following year. Throughout the same period, various disputes occasioned the departure of English ecclesiastics for the Roman Curia, with a resulting continuous contact with papal policies at their centre of formulation; the re-emergence of the Canterbury and York dispute over the primacy is a particularly revealing instance. These few examples suggest a tangible advance of papal influence in England in the reign of Henry I, yet they must still be viewed against a general background of royal control over a very wide area of the Church's activities, as in the vital matter of episcopal elections, mentioned above: in Henry's reign, quite apart from his effective voice in the selection of candidates, bishoprics were sometimes kept vacant for long periods, and the practice of simony remained a scandal.

A less qualified judgement is appropriate to the progress made by the English Church in Stephen's reign, for there is no doubt that the desired freedom of the Church, the *libertas ecclesiae*, was approached in decisive strides at that time. Stephen owed much to the Church for its support of his own accession; and in his coronation charter of 1136, which echoed the tenor of that of Henry I, he promised redress of the principal abuses touching ecclesiastical appointments, possessions and jurisdiction. Foremost among these undertakings was the promise that episcopal elections would be canonical and free from taint of simony. It is generally accepted that Stephen at first respected these commitments, but later deviated from them as opportunity arose. Nevertheless, the reception of papal influence was ever more evident. Stephen indeed had acknowledged the papal confirmation of his own election, though it was not until 1138 that Innocent II, harassed by an eight-years' conflict with the antipope Anacletus II, was free to take a more positive line with the Church in England. Then Alberic of Ostia arrived to resume the work of John of Crema in the previous reign, and to hold a legatine council dealing with Church reforms by a clear assertion of papal authority. In the following year the dispute between Stephen and Matilda was argued by their supporters in the presence of the pope at the Lateran Council; in 1139 also, Stephen's brother, Henry of Winchester, was created legate for the English Church, of which he was the dominant figure until his commission lapsed with the death of Innocent II in 1143, to be resumed in the person of Archbishop Theobald until his death in 1161.

These two contrasting figures, Henry and Theobald, were second to none in the application of papal jurisdiction and centralized administration in England. It is no longer possible to accept Henry of Huntingdon's statement that appeals to the Roman Curia were first made under Henry of Winchester, for there is ample evidence of them earlier; but it is possible that papal judges delegate with explicit commissions and mandates can first be clearly traced from this time. The *Liber Eliensis* affords valuable evidence of the operation of ecclesiastical jurisdiction, as in the Stetchworth dispute, involving Gilbert Foliot of Hereford and Archbishop Theobald as ecclesiastical judges. Foliot, who was later to be translated to London with papal approval and to play a leading role in the Becket dispute, was elected to Hereford in 1148, and consecrated by Theobald outside England, without reference to Stephen but at the command of the pope. Nevertheless, the English bishops present at the consecration dissociated themselves from the proceedings, and Foliot himself swore fealty to the king on returning to England. Meanwhile, English prelates had attended the Lateran Council in 1139, and others attended the Council of Reims in 1148. Stephen's intention to prevent the primate from attending the latter was abortive; and, despite their nominal reconciliation, this incident was symptomatic of deteriorating relations between the papacy and influential English bishops on the one hand, and Stephen and his dynasty on the other. The coronation of Eustace, Stephen's heir, was forbidden in 1152 and the Angevin succession in 1154, in the person of Henry II, was greatly facilitated by this alignment of interests.

The problems confronting Stephen in the political sphere, and his resulting weakness compared with the Conqueror and Henry I, as well as with Henry II who succeeded him, have influenced too decisively the conventional views of his reign, since no less significant were the wider developments in the Church as a whole under papal guidance in the period. This factor has been mentioned above in the introductory section, and need only be briefly repeated here. The increasing efficiency of papal jurisdiction through the reception of appeals and the appointment of judges delegate spread evenly through the Western Church at the time, and was in no way peculiar to Stephen's kingdom. The vital developments in papal conciliar legislation, and in the codification and interpretation of canon law, associated above all with the great school at Bologna and with the *Decretum* of Gratian, were destined to infiltrate gradually into all the provinces of the Western Church. Scholars and ecclesiastics from England were increasingly involved in such advances, frequently participating in a creative way. Many English theologians and canonists studied and taught in the schools on the continent: Robert Pullen became cardinal and Chancellor of the Roman Church in 1144; Hilary of Chichester served in the papal chancery in 1146; Bozo was cardinal and chamberlain from 1149; in which year also Nicholas Breakspear was created cardinal, to be raised to the papal throne as Adrian IV in 1154; many of the later protagonists in the spectacular controversy of Henry II's reign were in the early phases of their careers during that of Stephen.

The rapid expansion of the monastic and canonical orders throughout Europe, and within England in full proportion, contributed beyond measure to the increase of papal influence. In this context, the growth of the Cistercian Order, as explained already, was of outstanding importance: the advance of papal power in the mid-twelfth century in the extent of its permeation of the Church was at least in part linked with the higher pitch of religious fervour achieved by the Cistercians. The great moral force of St. Bernard, especially in French society, had its counterparts in England too; and English society was confronted for the first time on a very large scale by an order decisively conceived on a supra-national basis, and markedly detached from the structure of the feudal kingdom. At the same time, the religious orders in general proved the natural and constant allies of the papacy, with which many contracted a special and immediate relationship, and almost all found it useful to seek regular confirmation of their privileges and possessions by the highest ecclesiastical authority. It is now generally recognized that the archiepiscopate of Theobald provided the prelude to the more dramatic events of Becket's career: the advance of canonical learning, mentioned above, was fostered in an important way in Theobald's household; and many of the individual points of conflict which were later to make up the controversy between Henry II and Becket were already exposed in the closing years of Theobald's life. Moreover, Theobald was seen presiding as master of the English Church, as in his legatine council of 1151; and the period witnessed numerous and increasing instances of a two-way traffic between England and the Curia: judicial problems and disputed elections, such as that of Richard Belmeis to London in 1152, were referred to the papal court for a decision. This was itself a measure of the inroads which papal policies had made in England during Stephen's reign and of the extent to which the stronger policies of the Anglo-Norman kings had been dissipated. It was Henry II's objective to attempt to restore the previously-existing conditions, to put back the clock, to reconstitute the conditions which prevailed in the time of his grandfather. But neither in England nor on the continent could the changes of many years be forgotten, and there was something unrealistic in the appeal, however accurate and understandable, to the customs of a superseded period.

It was in this situation that there was fought out one of the most famous conflicts of secular and ecclesiastical forces in Christian history. The strands of English and papal history are so interwoven in Henry II's reign that only a ruthless selection of the most important elements is possible in this chapter. There is no doubt that Henry selected Becket as primate in the expectation that the former association of William I and Lanfranc, to their mutual advantage, would be re-created; and this was natural in recollection of the important political role which had been filled by English prelates down to that time, while contemporaries noted how in a wider canvass the German rulers enjoyed a similar relationship with the archbishops of Mainz and Cologne as imperial chancellors. But this expectation was not to be realized. The conflict which ensued will not be understood if the vision is narrowed to the particular points at issue at any given stage of the controversy. If this were done, it would be possible to argue that personal differences between Becket and Henry were of primary importance; or that material interests, such as the Canterbury properties, dominated Becket's policies; or that primatial notions of prestige and power in the English Church lay at the root of Becket's relations with the English episcopate. All these elements are present in the story and have their importance; but they could not explain why, for instance, Alexander III, despite the difficulties of his own position and his reluctance at times to be committed to the full rigour of Becket's logic, nevertheless associated Becket with Lucas of Gran as the twin buttresses of the Church's liberties.

This is not to make a moral judgement for or against the archbishop or the king: both their policies are explicable in the framework of their thought processes. It is possible in retrospect to sympathize either with the one or the other, while fully accepting and understanding the views of both. On the one hand, there is the background of relentlessly advancing canon law and papal ideology already described, together with the spiritual and religious climate reflected in the dynamic monastic movements of the period; on the other, there are the concepts of medieval kingship and the increasingly self-conscious theories of royal justice and its practical realization. Both these major streams of development were swelling and flowing more swiftly through the century. The intellectual ferment of the age must also be considered, especially the legal and theoretical strands of the so-called twelfth-century renaissance, which was reaching in these respects a peak of achievement in the second half of the century: an intensively creative period in the history of law, whether of canon law and Roman law, or of the regional laws of the various kingdoms. It was virtually inescapable that difficulties, in various forms, would arise as the separate concepts of jurisdiction and legal systems clashed at their many points of overlapping interests.

Henry, in his coronation charter of 1154, had promised to preserve the freedom of the Church. And, while Theobald lived, an open conflict was averted; but there is ample evidence that the aged archbishop was increasingly disquieted by indications of a firmer royal policy. Meanwhile, Henry had thrown his support on the side of Alexander III in the papal schism which opened in 1159; and, in the early phase of Becket's rule, the English Church was seen in harmonious relationship with the exiled pope: both archbishops, of Canterbury and York, attended the Council of Tours in 1163, with a number of English bishops. A widening area of disagreement between Becket and the king rose, however, to a crisis over the question of criminous clerks in 1163, and culminated in Henry's sixteen points programme in the Constitutions of Clarendon in 1164. By these clauses Henry sought formal recognition of the customs regulating relations between royal and ecclesiastical interests as established by the Norman kings. These were the *avitae consuetudines*, the customs of his grandfather; and there is general agreement that his claim was valid on almost all points as to the matter of historical fact. Some of the clauses necessarily involved relations with the papacy, others dealt more specifically with politico-ecclesiastical questions within the kingdom. One vital clause aimed to make the departure of ecclesiastics from England to the continent subject to the king's consent; a further clause cut short the appellate system of ecclesiastical courts at the provincial level, so that recourse should not be had to the papal Curia except at the will of the king; the famous third clause embodied the royal plan to ensure the secular constraint of criminous clerks; yet another clause dealt with ecclesiastical vacancies and electoral procedure. There is no doubt that Henry made a tactical mistake in seeking to extort a sealed acceptance of these requirements, which could not be reconciled with the existing state of the Church's law. He would almost certainly have been able to enforce his will, at least on several points, in practice. Becket, for his part, was adamant in his refusal to agree to such conditions, apart from a temporary vacillation under heavy pressure. For Becket the appeal to custom was quite irrelevant. Echoing directly the words of Gregory VII in the previous century, he argued that Christ had said 'I am the truth'; He had never said 'I am the custom'.

In canon law there is little doubt that Becket was fully justified in the attitude he assumed in opposing the constitutions.[9] But the English bishops, though basically in agreement with him, were not prepared, for various reasons, to support him *in extremis*. The pope, too, was in a perilous phase of his struggle with Barbarossa, and would doubtless have preferred to avoid the English issue alto-

[9] Cf. C. Duggan, 'The Becket Dispute and the Criminous Clerks', *Bulletin of the Institute of Historical Research*, XXXV (1962), pp. 1–28.

gether at that moment. Nevertheless, when confronted directly with Henry's constitutions, he condemned ten outright, while being prepared to tolerate six. The archbishop's exile, his absence in France for six years filled with difficult negotiations and abortive attempts to work out a solution of the quarrel, the final reconciliation and return to England, his martyrdom at Canterbury in 1170, and his canonization by Alexander III in 1173: all these are very familiar details. Relations between England and the papal Curia continued at a high and sometimes anxious level of activity throughout. Alexander's rulings varied in their precision and firmness in some proportion to his own fluctuating fortunes in his struggle with Frederick I; and Henry was not averse to exploiting Alexander's difficulties by the threat of defecting to Pascal III. Constantly, letters were exchanged between both parties in the English dispute on the one hand and the Roman Curia on the other; paradoxically the quarrel increased this intercommunication, which Henry made no attempt to curtail. Meanwhile, Alexander had also to deal diplomatically with the re-emergence of the Canterbury and York dispute, which was brought to a pitch of crisis by Roger of York's coronation of the young king, Henry's son, in 1170 while Becket was still in exile, in derogation of Becket's rights and in opposition to the papal prohibitions. And all the while the routine contacts were maintained, to some extent, between English religious houses and ecclesiastical judges and the papal Curia.

Henry averted the threat of serious papal reprisals for Becket's murder, and his reconciliation with the Church was achieved in two main stages. The Compromise of Avranches in 1172 included royal promises of acts of penance in atonement for the outrage, which Henry swore he had neither wished nor contrived, and policy undertakings in connection with specified points in dispute during the quarrel. He promised to repeal the customs introduced in his time against the Church in his kingdom, though he protested to Bartholomew of Exeter that he considered these very few or even none at all; and he promised also to allow freedom of appeals to the Curia unless injury to his own position was thereby threatened. There was no explicit reference to the Clarendon Constitutions, nor was there mention of the subject of criminous clerks. A letter of Alexander III to Henry, recording the terms of agreement, survives in transcription, from which it is clear that the pope was much concerned to have them officially registered for future reference. Three years later, the legate Pierleoni arrived in England in 1175, and further disputed points were settled by the following year. On this occasion a letter of Henry II to Alexander is extant, agreeing to the elimination of various outstanding abuses touching vacancies and the persons and rights of clerks, and most significantly accepting the principle of clerical immunity from secular justice, with the exceptions of charges relating to lay fees or transgressions of the forest law. Meanwhile, other facets of Anglo-papal relations were revealed by Henry's appeal for papal support in his period of great danger during the rising of 1173–4, and by the young king's dealings with the pope in an attempt to assert his royal position, *vis à vis* his father. In many ways Henry continued to keep a firm grip on the English Church, in spite of several important concessions. Three of his most loyal aides in the contest with Becket were elected to the sees of Winchester, Norwich and Ely in the years of the post-Becket settlement: they were respectively Richard of Ilchester, John of Oxford and Geoffrey Ridel. In such ways as these, Henry was seen to achieve some of the vital objects which he had pursued at Clarendon in 1164. Nor did he faithfully fulfil the promises he had made to the papal legates in 1172 and 1175–6, as the prolongation of episcopal vacancies affords striking testimony.

Historians have variously assessed the results of the compacts between Henry II and the papacy after Becket's martyrdom. For Zachary Brooke, the main theme was a posthumous victory for the archbishop, with the defeat of Henry's attempt to reconstruct the barrier policy of his ancestors, and the opening up of England for the first time to the full impact of canon law after a period of isolation. For Cheney, the Compromise of Avranches settled nothing, in the sense that royal policy seemed not significantly changed by the precise terms of the agreement; and he has adduced impressive evidence in support of the thesis that the period after Avranches was one of 'effective adjustment, with give and take between the two jurisdictions'. For Morey, the importance of the settlement was rather that it permitted the English Church to go forward participating fully in the overall advance of the Western Church, whereas this result might otherwise have been imperilled. In two respects, Brooke's thesis is no longer acceptable, since the English Church had clearly not been isolated before the compromise; and his use of decretal evidence as the main element of proof in his argument is now known to have been misconceived. Apart from this important proviso, the various views are not as irreconcilable as they may seem at first consideration, and are in fact complementary facets of a single whole.

The twelfth century was not an age of unconditional surrender: victory of Church or monarchy on one point did not necessarily entail the same result on others. In this respect, Cheney's view is clearly valid: each side gained some points and surrendered others. It is difficult not to believe that the Church, under papal guidance, gained a great victory in the matter of routine appeals to the Roman Curia: the striking evidence of the decretals which poured into England from the early 1170's (as they did into other countries also) and the ever-expanding jurisdiction of the papal judges delegate prove that the two-way traffic between the English courts Christian and the Curia had now become a constant factor and altogether a matter of course, whatever evidence there may be of royal curtailment of it in specific instances. On the vexed question of criminous clerks, the Church gained recognition of a highly-prized principle, but conceded certain exceptions in return. On other debated matters, the Church failed utterly to establish its position against secular opposition. The question of advowsons, the *ius praesentandi*, affords a significant example of the secular law in practice winning a victory over the law of the Church;[10] and in many other ways, as already indicated, the English king was able to canalize or curtail its full operation. But the canon law in England made dramatic strides forward in the decades following Becket's death: the activities of the English judges delegate and of the canonists in the circles of distinguished English bishops were

---

[10] J. W. Gray, 'The ius praesentandi in England from the Constitutions of Clarendon to Bracton', *English Historical Review*, LXVII (1952), pp. 481–509.

unsurpassed in some respects elsewhere in Europe at that period, of which developments the work of the English decretal collectors provides a major and permanently important illustration. Papal legislation then flowed into England: Archbishop Richard cited Alexander's decretals in his provincial council of 1175; the canons of the 1179 Lateran Council, which English bishops attended, were brought back immediately into England, and transcribed in numerous manuscripts within a year or two of their promulgation; papal decretal letters enforced some of the Lateran rulings in England before Alexander's death in 1181; swift and frequent interchange between the schools of English and continental canonists is abundantly recorded in the manuscripts surviving from the period. Archbishops Richard and Baldwin are frequently judged inadequate successors to Becket, from an ecclesiastical or papal viewpoint, but in the application of canon law throughout the kingdom there is irrefutable evidence of its steady and effective growth throughout their time.

Between Alexander's death in 1181 and the accession of Innocent III in 1198, the Church was ruled by a succession of five pontiffs whose reigns were individually too short to leave any decisive mark on the central government of the Church or on the course of papal relations with the separate countries, yet they can by no means be dismissed as a series of ineffective old men. The papacy then moved forward into a more placid period, the schisms were left behind; new problems arose in connection with heresies, the promotion of a Crusade and many other such matters. But there was no serious interruption or reversal of the trends of papal policies already established: Urban III had been in Becket's circle in the days of his great quarrel with Henry II; and Celestine III had acquired vast experience as a papal legate in his earlier career as Cardinal Hyacinth. Legates continued to arrive in England to deal with special problems; judges delegate were appointed in large numbers to deal with English disputes; several important *causes célèbres*, often involving great religious houses, took English ecclesiastics to plead their cases in the papal Curia. The practice became regular of English archbishops receiving commissions as papal legates by virtue of their office: Richard, Baldwin, Hubert

Walter and William Longchamp were all successively legates in the closing quarter of the century. Relations between the monarch and the papacy also developed further in circumstances of mutual advantage. Transitionally, from the reign of Richard to that of John, the archiepiscopate of Hubert Walter is judged by many historians as a model of the way in which harmonious relations could be maintained between *regnum* and *sacerdotium*. Hubert was at times chief justiciar, chancellor and vice-regent in secular government, as well as primate and papal legate in ecclesiastical affairs; but this was a deviation from the ideal of a Christian bishop in canon law, and it may also be thought that the earlier struggles had helped to make possible the *modus vivendi* as it existed in practice under Hubert, which otherwise might not have been achieved with a comparable balance of interests.

The death of Innocent III in July 1216, and that of John in October of the same year, marked the end of an epoch in the history of Anglo-papal relations, whose final phase was centred on the opening years of Langton's archiepiscopate: in particular on the circumstances of his appointment and its aftermath, and on the triangular relationship between archbishop, pope and king at the time of *Magna Carta*. On the death of Hubert Walter in 1205, the monks of Christ Church elected Reginald, their sub-prior, to the vacant see, to be opposed by John de Gray, bishop of Norwich, the king's nominee. The double nomination passed in due course within the purview of the papal Curia, whereupon Innocent rejected both the rival claimants and consecrated Langton, a distinguished English theologian from the schools of Paris and a curial cardinal at the time of his nomination. In the long quarrel which ensued, a further familiar crisis in English history, issues of critical importance for royal-papal relations were raised, involving not only the principle of canonical elections, but also the specific question whether or not the king could exercise a final veto in the choice of a bishop. The ultimate success of the pope in these circumstances was therefore a development of the utmost significance; and an important by-product of the struggle was the charter of freedom of elections secured in the period between Langton's acceptance in England and his later divergence with the king in the conflict for *Magna Carta*. But these successes were not quickly attained: the king long resisted the papal action and prevented the archbishop's entry into England. Innocent was no less adamant, and it was John's misfortune to be confronted by one of the most resolute and decisive popes in the Church's history. England was placed under interdict in 1208; the king was excommunicated in 1209, and threatened finally with deposition in 1212. And since these developments coincided with a deterioration in Anglo-French relations, which Philip Augustus was ever ready to exploit, John was at length constrained to yield to the pope.

Meanwhile the English Church had been seriously deprived of spiritual guidance at the highest level. In addition to Langton himself, the archbishop of York was also absent from England; the bishops of London, Ely and Winchester left after imposing the interdict; some bishoprics were vacant; further ecclesiastics quitted the country following the more serious penalty of John's excommunication in 1209. Nevertheless, negotiations between Innocent and John were never entirely interrupted, until, finally in 1213, John submitted to the complex of pressures described above, and surrendered his kingdoms of England and Ireland to the pope, receiving them back in return for an annual tribute. The most striking element in the king's submission was the oath of fealty which he took, together with his promise to do homage should he later meet the pope in person. The agreement was formally ratified in St. Paul's Cathedral in the presence of the legate, Cardinal Nicholas, and sealed with a golden bull; and thus the interdict ended in 1214. A paradoxical result was that, when Langton eventually arrived to assume his duties, his former relentless opponent was now in the fullest papal favour, as the feudal dependant of the pope. In the struggle which shortly took place between the king and his magnates, culminating in the sealing of the Charter in 1215, Langton played a leading and moderating role, only to incur in the end the disfavour of Innocent for failing to support the king in this new situation and likewise to condemn his opponents. In the course of this crisis, the issue had been referred to the pope 'since he is lord of England'; and Innocent had declared against the magnates as being conspirators and rebels. But Langton was unwilling to pronounce the sentences of excommunication against them, and was suspended in consequence by the bishop of Winchester and the papal legate. Thus Langton passed into exile for a second period. And, when he returned, both Innocent and John were dead, and papal legates were taking now a dominant part in the government of England in the minority of Henry III.

'That the English Church may be free and enjoy its rights in full and its liberties unimpaired': whatever policy Innocent felt it prudent to pursue in relation to John, his feudal vassal and a committed Crusader, he could not be expected to dissent from this opening clause of the Charter of 1215. But his actions in the English quarrel can be assessed only in the full comprehension of his role as the conscious and supremely confident leader of Western Christendom: Vicar of Christ, mediator between God and men, judge of all men but judged by none, arbiter of all human affairs as well in temporal as in spiritual matters. The universality of his conception, as well as the summit of papal legislative power, was most clearly demonstrated in his great Lateran Council of 1215. It is natural that politico-ecclesiastical aspects of his relations with John should chiefly attract the attention of English historians; but for Innocent these were comparatively small components in an immensely complicated mosaic. On the secular plane, his dealings with a succession of contenders for the imperial title, with the leaders of the various Christian kingdoms, and most particularly his feudal connections with the rulers of Aragon and Portugal, of Sicily and Hungary: all these factors place the English affair in a fitting proportion. But no papal policy was conceived by Innocent on merely secular considerations. If papal intervention was required in the affairs of a secular kingdom, it was because the pope had a duty to act on moral and Christian principles, because a matter of sin or injustice was involved or because peace was endangered. The letters which Innocent wrote to England in condemning the Charter show him proceeding firmly on established canonical doctrines. But quite apart from, and transcending, the major political issues, he was also the supreme judge of all Christian people, the Universal Ordinary to whom every Christian might have direct recourse. The records for England richly reveal Innocent acting throughout his pontificate in this capacity in exactly comparable fashion as he did for all Christian countries: for Ireland and Poland, for Portugal and Hungary, for Italy and Spain. In terms of purely political history, he was a great statesman, the dominant figure of his age, through whose hands passed all the main threads of development in his day. But he was also a great pope and spiritual leader 'devoted to his pastoral task . . . zealous for the faith, strong in legal science and subtle diplomacy, and tremendously active.'

In the interests of simplicity, important strands of Anglo-papal history have been touched on only incidentally in the pages above. Such a question is the primacy of the English Church, contested in the Canterbury and York disputes, for this involved at times the intervention of the pope very decisively. In its origins the problem is retraceable to the letter of Gregory I to Augustine, in which he laid down a scheme for the future organization of the English Church, divided in two provinces under archbishops at London and York, ruling that he should have precedence between these who was consecrated earlier. But, for well-known historical reasons, Canterbury secured the headship of the southern province. The question of primacy, together with various attendant problems such as professions of obedience and jurisdiction over debated dioceses, was swiftly raised by Lanfranc after his elevation, and submitted to Alexander II for adjudication. The pope entrusted the enquiry to the legate Hubert, from whom Lanfranc and Canterbury secured a favourable verdict.[11] But the victory of Canterbury was not destined to remain long unchallenged. Indeed the question of the primacy was raised again as early as Anselm's

[11] The brief account given here of the complex history of the Canterbury-York rivalry is necessarily incomplete. The seminal period from the Conquest to the third decade of the twelfth century is now reviewed in an important study by R. W. Southern on 'The Canterbury Forgeries', *EHR*, LXXIII (1958), pp. 193–226. Southern argues that Lanfranc's success was achieved by his own force of character and persuasiveness, and through the support of the king; he rejects the view that the Canterbury case was argued in Lanfranc's lifetime on a basis of the well-known Canterbury forgeries, which he believes to have been fabricated in or about 1120 and brought forward after January 1121. The intervening period was one of repeated efforts by York to reverse the favourable decision secured by Lanfranc.

consecration in 1093, which occasion Southern notes as the first defeat suffered by Canterbury in the long struggle destined ultimately to cancel the success achieved by Lanfranc in the exceptionally favourable circumstances of his time. And although the papacy supported Anselm's primacy for obvious reasons of mutual interdependence, the altered relations between archbishops and king, after Anselm's death, together with an increasing papal understanding of the English rivalry and its background, led to a more favourable consideration being given by the popes to the claims of York. One curious resulting situation was that Thurstan of York, a former royal servant, vigorously fought for the independence of the northern province, supported now by a series of popes, while the claims of Canterbury were defended by the king. On this occasion, victory was adjudged to York by Honorius II in 1126, by which time the falsity of the Canterbury case had been sufficiently revealed. Inevitably, contacts between England and the Curia were developed in an important way as a result of these extended negotiations, which are recorded in a lively and fascinating version, sympathetic to York, by Hugh the Chanter.

The issue was raised once more in the reign of Henry II, and contested then in bitter fashion between Becket and Roger of York, to be continued by Becket's successors. The problem was complicated still further in Becket's lifetime by the ambitions of Gilbert Foliot, as bishop of London, the foremost of Becket's opponents among the English episcopate.[12] It seems certain that Foliot, a bishop of outstanding ability and reputation, was resentful of Becket's accession to a position for which he might consider himself the better qualified; and there is evidence that the Gregorian plan that London, rather than Canterbury, should be head of the southern province was remembered in Foliot's interests. But there could be no real hope of success in so radical a project. The strife between Canterbury and York reached a heightened crisis with the coronation of the younger Henry by Roger of York in 1170, as explained above, in Becket's absence and in

[12] A critical edition of the letters of Gilbert Foliot is in an advanced stage of preparation by Professor C. N. L. Brooke and Dom Adrian Morey.

defiance of papal mandates of prohibition.[13] This act of derogation of Becket's functions proved in the event the occasion for the final drama leading at last to his murder in Canterbury Cathedral. Alexander III strove to tread his way most cautiously through this tangle of conflicting interests. His support for Becket did not exclude a dispassionate consideration of the rights of York: the diocese, though not the province, of York was explicitly omitted from the legatine jurisdiction which he granted to Canterbury in 1166. Nevertheless, the rivalry was not diminished after Becket's death, and unseemly conflicts continued to mar relations between the two archbishops: the most regrettable incident ending in confusion and physical violence in the legate's presence in 1176; in which year also Alexander once more confirmed the independence of York. A final solution to these difficulties lay only in the very remote future. But the problem left in the meantime a significant trace in canonical history, for certain decretal collections dating from the early 1180's included several papal letters touching the subject, under the title *De preeminentia Lundonensis et Eboracensis*, which some sensitive collectors later diplomatically emended in the interests of Canterbury to *De preeminentia Cantuariensis et Eboracensis*.

A further strand of interest can be traced in the very complex inter-relations between the English monarchy, the papacy and the Celtic peoples of the British Isles. Spiritual and material motives were intermingled in the policies of the Anglo-Norman and Angevin rulers affecting Ireland, Wales and Scotland; and the papal desire for the advancement of legal and administrative reforms, together with the spiritual regeneration of all Christian communities, produced an alliance of royal and papal interests. The work of Irish scholars has established the existence of a two-way traffic between the Roman Curia and Ireland in the eleventh century to a more significant degree than was previously believed. Gwynn in particular has illuminated the subject of papal influence in Ireland in the days of Gregory VII.[14] The reform of the Irish

---

[13] The background and implications of the coronation are discussed by Miss Anne Heslin, 'The Coronation of the Young King in 1170', *Studies in Church History*, II, Nelson (1965: in press).

[14] A. Gwynn, 'Gregory VII and the Irish Church', *Studi Gregoriani*, Rome, III (1947), pp. 105–28.

Church was initiated through a series of important councils, most notably of Cashel in 1101 and Rath Breasil in 1111, convened by papal legatine authority. But it is also clear that Anglo-Norman and papal interests progressed together in Ireland in the days when Lanfranc and Anselm consecrated Irish bishops and dealt with them on terms of implicit superiority. The arrival of the Cistercians, and their influence, diffused under Malachy's guidance, played an important part. A further great council was held at Kells in 1152 under the presidency of the legate John of Paparo, and established the territorial divisions of the Irish Church in four provinces with their suffragan sees.

Both Rome and Canterbury had played their parts in producing the results attained so far. But much remained to be done; and it was in these circumstances that Adrian IV granted to Henry II permission to invade and subdue Ireland, and promote the cause of ecclesiastical reform. The authenticity of the bull *Laudabiliter* of 1155 has been much debated, but its substantial accuracy is now generally accepted: its essential points are recorded by John of Salisbury, who took part in the negotiations, and were later confirmed in the indubitably genuine letters of Alexander III. Both papal authority and jurisdiction and Angevin political rights in the island were reconciled in this policy. The invasion itself was delayed until after Becket's death. And the ecclesiastical results of the conquest were first significantly seen in the legatine Council of Cashel in 1172, under Christian of Lismore, and by the letters exchanged in the same year between Henry II and Alexander III. These letters dealt with the state of the Irish Church and the powers of the English king to govern the island and reform its Church in accordance with the usages of the Church in England. The authority of the English king in Ireland was fully supported by the pope throughout the period which followed; nevertheless, a way was carefully left open by which the rights of the papacy over Ireland, as being within the Patrimony of St Peter, might later be more decisively asserted, and the Irish Church was not subjected to the jurisdiction of English prelates. Thus its integrity and independence were preserved. The Irish Church continued to produce its own characteristic and distinguished members, of whom

St. Laurence O'Toole (†1180) was the outstanding exemplar; but with the appointment of John Cumin to Dublin in 1182 a new type of Anglo-Norman feudal prelate was created with important results for later Irish history.

Meanwhile, Henry's measures for the reorganization and better administration of Ireland went forward with papal support: the legate Vivian reconfirmed the royal rights in a council at Dublin in 1177, in which year also Henry created his son John 'Lord of Ireland' at the Council of Oxford. Later, when John himself was reigning as king, the Angevin policy was more clearly revealed that the native Irish should be excluded, whenever possible, from the Irish sees. The attitude of which this policy was merely symptomatic created a rift between the old Gaelic and the new Anglo-Norman bishops, tending to the weakening and disruption of the Church; and the letters of Innocent III to Ireland show a concern with problems of this kind. In 1202, during a vacancy in the primatial see of Armagh, the papal legate, John of Monte Celio, convened a council at Dublin at which John sought the legate's support against Irish bishops opposed to his methods of controlling the Irish Church, though apparently without success. For Ireland, the period ended, as for England, with formal submission of the kingdom to Innocent and an agreement for the payment of an annual tribute.[15]

For Wales, the interest in this chapter centres on the claims of Canterbury to jurisdiction and primacy over the four Welsh bishoprics, and on their reciprocal claims for independence, together with the increasing efforts of St. David's to establish itself in the primacy of a separate province. It is clear that Anselm exercised an effective control over the Church in Wales from the later-eleventh century, comparable with his policy in Ireland and Scotland at the same time, as when he consecrated Urban to Llandaff in Canterbury Cathedral in 1107. This relationship was effectively maintained by his successors until the days of Theobald, when a notable bid was made by St. David's to assert its

---

[15] Relations between Ireland and the papacy during the pontificate of Innocent III have been greatly clarified by the studies of Rev. Fr. Patrick Dunning: cf. *idem*, 'The Letters of Innocent III to Ireland', *Traditio*, Fordham University Press, XVIII (1962), pp. 229–53, including bibliographical references.

position: in 1140 Bernard of St. David's contested Theobald's right to consecrate Maurice of Bangor and to receive an oath of obedience from him. The significance of this assertion was heightened by the eventual victory of St. David's over Llandaff in a long dispute involving letters and journeys between Wales and the papal Curia; and Urban of Llandaff had actually died in Rome on a visit *ad limina* in 1133. It is in connection with this protracted quarrel that the *Liber Landavensis* affords such striking evidence of papal-Welsh relations from 1119. But St. David's was unsuccessful in the attempt to secure a pallium; and the issue of the primacy between Canterbury and St. David's was decided *in personis* in favour of the former by Eugenius III in 1148, though leaving open the question of right.

Thus, when Becket succeeded Theobald in 1162, the Church in Wales was in legal subjection to Canterbury, with papal approval, at a moment when Henry II was maturing plans for the political subjection of the Welsh princes. The problems arising from these complex relationships were still further accentuated as a result of the Becket dispute, when the exiled archbishop was confronted by the twofold hostility of Henry II in England and Owain Gwynedd in Wales. The Bangor dispute provides a revealing insight into this situation: a troublesome vacancy followed the death of Maurice of Bangor in 1161, and the matter was not finally settled until 1177. Meanwhile, despite the efforts of Alexander III and Becket, Henry and Owain in turn obstructed an acceptable solution, the former preventing a free election in the period *c.* 1167–8, and the latter presuming even to intercept papal letters. Nevertheless, in spite of such vexing problems, Canterbury successfully maintained its metropolitical authority over the Welsh Church throughout the period. But the primacy issue was reintroduced on three further noteworthy occasions: in 1176, at the instigation of Giraldus Cambrensis, at the legatine Council of Westminster; in 1179, in the presence of Alexander III in the course of the Lateran Council; and in 1198–1203, in a most interesting and well-documented fashion, again under Giraldus's guidance, before Innocent III and commissions of papal judges delegate. The case for St. David's was stated clearly in the course of this litigation: it was urged that a metropolitan see in Wales would be to the Roman Church's advantage, and that Peter's Pence would be paid in recognition of this special relationship. Independence for the Welsh Church from the jurisdiction of Canterbury was sought, but neither the primacy nor the pallium was specifically requested. Giraldus hoped, in the event unsuccessfully, that Innocent would confer on the Welsh Church the status of a *filia specialis* which he had granted some years previously to the Church in Scotland.[16]

Affecting Scotland, too, political and ecclesiastical interests were intermingled in English policies. Questions of Church reform and conflicts of jurisdictional authority went hand in hand with the advance of Anglo-Norman and Angevin influence, and naturally attracted the concern of popes. The claims of York in particular for primacy over the Scottish dioceses provided a source of continuing controversy. Lanfranc and Thomas of York had agreed at the Council of Windsor in 1072 that all sees north of the Humber should be subject to York's metropolitical jurisdiction, but without the concurrence of the Church or the king in Scotland. Nevertheless, Calixtus II mandated the Scottish bishops in 1119 to proffer canonical obedience to York. It was therefore all the more significant that Alexander I of Scotland attempted in the following year to fill the vacant see of St. Andrews with Eadmer of Canterbury: a project which inevitably provoked the resentment of York, and was in the event frustrated. This was a phase in which the Scottish kings were clearly anxious to promote the independence of the Church in their realm from external intervention; and a necessary feature of this policy was the attempt to curtail the jurisdictional claims of York, despite the commands of the pope. Nor was the St. Andrews dispute an isolated example: John, bishop of Glasgow, persisted throughout his life in refusing to acknowledge the supremacy of York; and on his death in 1147 his successor was consecrated by Eugenius III in person, and thus the awkward issue was circumvented. The papal favour shown to York was, nevertheless, continued by Adrian IV; and the inter-

---

[16] I. P. Shaw, 'Giraldus Cambrensis and the Primacy of Canterbury', *Church Quarterly Review*, CXLVI (1946), pp. 82–101.

esting point has been argued that, with these claims of York accepted, the ancient Gregorian plan of a northern province of twelve suffragan sees subject to York was now for the first time, if largely theoretically, advanced in practice.

But a point of departure in papal policies may be traced from Alexander III's appointment of William of Moray as papal legate in 1160; and other measures of Alexander III were consistent with a revision in the papal attitude to Anglo-Scottish ecclesiastical relations, though this did not exclude his appointment of Roger of York as legate for Scotland from 1164 until 1181. Meanwhile, a critical period had opened for Scotland with military defeat in the troubles of 1173–4, when William of Scotland participated in the loosely concerted war waged against Henry II by many of his adversaries on both sides of the Channel. The Scottish intervention ended in political disaster with the capture of the king at Alnwick in 1174. The Scottish Church also shared temporarily in this misfortune, since at the treaty of Falaise in 1175 its subjection to the English Church was included in the terms of reconciliation. But the Scottish Church lost no opportunity in reacting against this unwelcome situation, and by 1176 secured the support of Alexander III in disclaiming York's metropolitical authority, which had meanwhile been challenged also by Richard of Canterbury. A phase was now opened when papal legates and judges delegate were more active in Scotland, though not without some hindrance, as revealed very strikingly in the disputed election to St. Andrews from 1178. This vexatious conflict provoked repeated appeals to the Curia and resulting papal mandates, which were successfully resisted by the Scottish king and his nominee, until the former was himself at last excommunicated. More favourable relations were restored by Pope Lucius III and his successors: the St. Andrews dispute was concluded in 1188; and Scotland was freed by the pope from English domination, in secular and ecclesiastical spheres alike, in 1189. Meanwhile, the see of York was itself vacant for a decade, in the years 1181–91, a factor which may well have played some part in favouring Scottish interests. Pope Celestine III declared the Scottish Church a *filia specialis* of the Roman See in 1192, subject henceforth to no one but the pope or his legate *a latere*; and Scottish bishops, free from subjection either to York or Canterbury, attended the Lateran Council under Innocent III in 1215, as did their Irish colleagues.

But Knowles has rightly argued that it is not to the great political issues nor to the papal claims for temporal power that we should look for the most significant contacts between England and the continent in this period, but to the regular and systematic traffic between England and the Curia, accepted as a matter of routine and calling for no particular comment in the contemporary records. And in this respect the archives of the English monastic houses and cathedral chapters provide a source of information second to none in importance in revealing the extent and propagation of papal jurisdictional power. Unfortunately, the papal registers no longer survive for the greater part of our period: between the registers of Gregory VII and Innocent III, at its two extremities, only a brief transcript of an excerpt from the records of Alexander III is now extant. But the cartularies of the individual religious houses and those preserved by some of the cathedral chapters provide a wealth of evidence on which the course of papal policy can be accurately plotted. For England, the records of the religious houses are especially rich and revealing.[17] The spiritual revival associated with the Church Reforms of the eleventh century and the foundation of new religious orders, above all of the great Cistercian Order, as already discussed, and the rapid expansion of the orders of regular canons, blended ideally with the development of papal policies of centralization and universal guidance in spiritual as well as jurisdictional spheres.

It was not a novel idea in the Western Church that religious houses should commend themselves to the papacy in a special relationship, enjoying immediate recourse to the pope, securing papal protection of their rights and possessions, and paying in return an annual tribute; but it was a practice which was enor-

[17] A vast source of information on Anglo-papal relations is supplied by the records of the religious orders: cf. esp. D. Knowles, *The Monastic Order in England*, Cambridge (2nd ed., 1963); J. C. Dickinson, *The Origins of the Austin Canons and their Introduction into England*, London (1950); H. M. Colvin, *The White Canons in England*, Oxford (1951); etc.

mously extended in this period. In the same way, the new religious orders gradually built up a complex of rights and privileges, and found it advantageous to secure papal recognition and guarantees for these. Moreover, both great orders and individual houses plunged increasingly into litigation in defence of their claims, touching spiritual and material interests, in conflict with both ecclesiastical and secular rivals. It became the invariable custom for religious houses and cathedral chapters to seek regular papal reconfirmation of their privileges, particularly on the accession of each new pope or following a definitive ruling resulting from a specific dispute. Transcripts of papal rescripts and formal *privilegia*, papal commissions and mandates to judges delegate appointed to adjudicate between rival claimants: all these were carefully enrolled in the monastic and cathedral archives, and provide the wealth of evidence referred to above. No one has illuminated this aspect of Anglo-papal relations in the twelfth century more significantly than the late Walter Holtzmann, whose three volumes of English *Papsturkunden* include many hundreds of previously unknown papal letters to England. Such records reveal a steadily swelling stream of papal *privilegia* entering England throughout the century, throwing light both on the history of England and of the individual recipients, as well as on the overall pattern in the development of papal justice. Only a minute fraction of characteristic instances can be cited here: no less than ninety-six papal letters relating to the single house of St. Albans were dispatched from the Curia between 1122 and 1198; thirty-seven were sent in connection with the affairs of Bury St. Edmunds between 1123 and 1196; a *regesta* of the Augustinian priory of Kirkham in Yorkshire records the receipt of thirteen letters of Alexander III, privileges and mandates, touching the rights of that single, comparatively insignificant, house between 1159 and 1181. A microcosm of the whole history of the growth of Cistercian privileges and exemptions throughout the Universal Church is clearly provided by the *Papsturkunden* to English Cistercian houses, including the history of the important tithe exemption and of the various immunities from diocesan jurisdiction; the letters to Rievaulx, Byland and a host of other abbeys afford abundant evidence for these developments. No less interesting are the records of papal confirmation of special rights enjoyed by particular houses: letters to St. Albans, Westminster and St. Augustine's at Canterbury, conferring on their abbots the privilege of wearing episcopal symbols of rank; to St. Albans, again, conferring a primacy of honour among all the abbots of England out of respect for the proto-martyr; and so forth. A touching letter of Alexander III to the hermit Godric of Finchale bears witness to the pope's solicitude for his individual subjects in the English Church: he has heard of Godric's holiness, which he commends, requesting in return Godric's prayers for the well-being of the whole Church. It must be said at once, as a point of additional significance, that the *Papsturkunden* for other provinces of the Church provide an exactly comparable record of the scope and pattern of papal influence.

Maitland and Zachary Brooke established two conclusions regarding the medieval English Church which have never subsequently been seriously challenged. Maitland refuted Stubbs's thesis that the medieval canon law was not considered binding on the English Church, and drew the vital distinction between the ideals and teachings of the Church when operating freely in Christian society and the limits imposed on them by secular rulers and local interests: a distinction at no period more necessary to be remembered than when considering the creative phase of canonical developments in the twelfth and thirteenth centuries. Later, Brooke rejected the notion that the medieval terminology used in reference to the English Church reflected a separatist or even national viewpoint, at least in the sources for the eleventh and twelfth centuries which he extensively studied. The concept of an English Church, or *ecclesia Anglicana*, is especially relevant to these considerations, since its existence in this formulation is first discovered in the period considered in this chapter, when it superseded in general usage earlier phrases such as *ecclesia Angliae* or *ecclesia Anglorum*. Brooke rightly argued that the concept of an *ecclesia Anglicana* was in no sense anti-papal, that it was a natural idiom in contemporary papal theory, and that comparable formulations existed for other sections of the Western Church. At the same time, Brooke believed that the phrase was in fact first used by John of Salisbury and was later adopted by the popes; but further evidence now discloses its use in papal documents at an earlier date. No English *Landeskirche* was implied in either the curial or the insular usage.

Such phrases as *ecclesia Anglicana*, *ecclesia Gallicana* and *ecclesia Hibernica* certainly described with aptness the corporate sense and interests of the Churches of the various regions, but they were not designed or understood to imply a separateness from the *ecclesia Romana*. On the contrary, such concepts were commonly used by ecclesiastics to safeguard the rights of the Church against the encroachments of secular rulers: a theory which is nowhere better supported than in Becket's letter *Quae in colloquio* of 1169, in which he argued that no concession should be wrung from him *praeter morem ecclesiae Gallicanae et Anglicanae*, urging elsewhere in the same letter the adoption of policies 'advantageous alike to the Roman and the English Churches', or in the opening clause of *Magna Carta* in 1215, as mentioned above. Moreover, the popes themselves in their decretal letters granted dispensations from the general law in favour of the customs existing in the *ecclesia Anglicana*; and such letters were later incorporated in canonical collections, and canonists referred to the customs of the English Church in their decretist glosses.

It is above all in the reception of canon law by the English Church in the twelfth century that the flow of papal influence into England can be most accurately estimated. A curiously myopic view still survives, even among medievalists, that canonical studies are merely of peripheral or highly specialist interest. So far is this from being a true opinion that the conclusion is inescapable that the canon law deeply affected the lives of all Christians throughout the length and breadth of the Western Church, from birth through life until death, in many of their essential functions in human society. As far as England is concerned, a steady and continuing acquisition of canonical texts is disclosed throughout our period, reaching a climax of extraordinary interest and initiative from the central decades of the twelfth century, and rapidly accelerating after Becket's death. In Lanfranc's day, if not before, the doctrine of *Pseudo-Isidore* was firmly established in England, a tradition so vital for the development of papal ideology and centralized government. Lanfranc's own collection, a derivative from *Pseudo-Isidore*, survives in the library of Trinity College in Cambridge; and many related manuscripts were housed in the libraries of English cathedral chapters in the beginning of the following century. Burchard's *Decretum*, the many collections of the Gregorian reformers, and the major works of Ivo of Chartres: all these were likewise received in England before the mid-twelfth century. The *Decretum* of Gratian, composed at Bologna *c.* 1140-1, came quickly into England: it was certainly known by the canonists in Theobald's household; there is textual evidence of its use by John of Salisbury in 1159 at the latest; and it formed a basis of reference in the Becket dispute from 1163. The foremost Bolognese decretists, with Rufinus at their head, were known to English authors by the early 1170's, possibly even during the Becket dispute itself; and English or Anglo-Norman canonists now began to take an initiative in the various literary exercises which typified the schools of canon law at the time.

A major historical development emerged in the mid-1170's with the beginnings of contemporary papal decretal codification, and English collectors played a dominant role in this work. Of roughly fifty decretal collections surviving in the whole of Europe for the rest of the century, a large proportion are of indubitable English authorship; while of twenty-seven collections of the most primitive and formative phase of composition, no less than fifteen are the works of English collectors.[18] Not only is an original and creative achievement disclosed on the part of English canonists, but a mutual interchange of material between English and continental schools of canon law is also clearly established. English collections were widely disseminated on the continent at least as early as 1179-81; and continental collections, most notably French and Italian, were used in the same period to afforce the English collections built for the greater part from local archives. It must be

---

[18] C. Duggan, *Twelfth-Century Decretal Collections and Their Importance in English History*, University of London Historical Studies XII, Athlone Press (1963).

emphasized that the English works were composed by Englishmen, predominantly from letters addressed by the popes, from the pontificate of Alexander III onwards, to English recipients; and, by the reception of these insular sources into the mainstream of canonical transmission on the continent, a permanently important English imprint was left on the corpus of canon law gradually assembled for the Universal Church at that time, being officially promulgated in the *Decretales* of Gregory IX in 1234. The proportionate English contribution to the total body of canons amassed in the later-twelfth century is truly astounding: of approximately one thousand papal letters preserved in all decretal manuscripts of the period known at present, no less than four hundred were received by English or Anglo-Norman ecclesiastics within twenty years. At no other period in its history did the English Church exert so direct, extensive and lasting an influence on the law of the Church as a whole.

Meanwhile, English canonists continued to play an ever more varied role in the general developments. English clerics studied in large numbers at Bologna, and sometimes taught there, and at the schools of canon lawyers in France and in the Rhineland. Canonical works of all kinds, collections and commentaries, continued to be composed by English authors; and, conversely, the major continental works flowed into England before the close of the century: the leading decretists of the Italian schools down to Huguccio (*c.* 1188–90) were cited with natural familiarity by the 'Oxford School' of canonists in the mid-1190's. The epoch-making *Breviarium extravagantium,* or *Compilatio Prima* (*c.* 1189–91), of Bernard of Pavia was well known to English commentators at the turn of the century; and *Compilatio Secunda* (post 1215) was actually composed in Italy by John the Welshman, on a basis of two earlier collections, also made in Italy, by the Englishmen Gilbert and Alan. By which time it is obvious that English canonists were playing a leading role at the very centre of canonical jurisprudence for the Universal Church.

The quickening of canonical evolution was by no means merely an academic exercise. At the highest level of ecclesiastical legislation, popes in general councils throughout the period laid down

canons applicable to the whole Church. This was an epoch which
may be described as that of 'the popes above the councils', to
underline the decisive papal authority achieved at this stage of
conciliar history. Particularly in the four great Lateran Councils of
1123, 1139, 1179 and 1215, popes were seen presiding with unchallenged authority over mighty representative assemblies, dealing with a vast range of doctrinal, moral, jurisdictional and disciplinary problems. The Fourth Lateran Council is rightly judged
the highest peak of papal legislative achievement in the history of
the medieval Church. But many other papal councils were also
held in the period: the Italian councils of the popes of the Investiture struggle, two Councils of Reims in 1119 and 1148 respectively, the Council of Tours of 1163, and so forth. This papal
legislation was paralleled by conciliar action in England,[19] in
councils held by papal legatine commission or reflecting the work
of the continental assemblies, many of which latter were attended
by English bishops despite the desire of English kings in the period
to control such attendance. The councils of Lanfranc and Anselm
in 1075 and 1076, and in 1102 and 1118, respectively; five legatine
councils in 1125, 1127, 1138, 1143 and 1175, the first and the third
under the presidency of *legati a latere*; the council of Archbishop
Theobald in 1151; the legatine councils of Hubert Walter in 1195
and 1200: all these meetings record the pattern by which a constant effort was made to implement in England the policies and
reforms of the central legislation. Nor was such papal influence
confined to conciliar action. The work of papal legates has been
touched on in numerous contexts above. It is sufficient to add here
that Tillmann has listed sixty occasions between the Conquest and
the death of Innocent III on which papal legates or commissions
were appointed to deal with English questions, or those in which
the interests of the English king were involved; and she has selected
thirty of these for particular mention. The Becket dispute provided
a high-point of such activity: four major commissions of legates
were appointed by Alexander III to negotiate between the parties
in 1167, 1168, 1169 and early 1170, while further legates were

---

[19] C. N. L. Brooke, 'Canons of English Church Councils in the Early Decretal
Collections', *Traditio*, XIII (1957), pp. 471–80.

commissioned to deal with the various stages of the subsequent reconciliation, especially in 1172 and 1175–6.

But no papal agents were more effective than the judges delegate, whose jurisdiction resulted from the rapid upsurge of appeals to the Roman Curia in the twelfth century, which in its turn resulted from the centralization of Church government following the eleventh-century reforms. A vast stream of appeals dealing with problems of all kinds flowed into the Curia, and an equal flood of rescripts, mandates, commissions and decretal letters, issued from the chancery in return. The popes could not hope to deal personally with the immensely increased weight of business; and there were in addition obvious advantages in settling many disputes in their place of origin. The office of the judge delegate was created to deal with this situation: the beginnings of the system can be traced in many parts of the Western Church in the opening decades of the twelfth century; and it was fully matured, with recognized procedures and common form phraseology, within the following fifty years. The delegate's jurisdiction was carefully defined and limited in scope, lapsed on the completion of the issue giving rise to the commission, and was essentially exercised by virtue of papal authority, which was transferred to the delegate for the terms of each single case. England fully shared in the various phases in the development of this system, the records being particularly rich in the decades following Becket's death. Many hundreds of papal commissions and mandates to English judges delegate were certainly issued, and large numbers of these have been preserved in transcription: some in the cartularies of religious houses or cathedral chapters, and many in a very significant way in English decretal collections; but it may be assumed that substantial numbers have also been lost.

It is now clear that the rapid spread of canon law in England from the early 1170's ran parallel with the extension of papal delegated jurisdiction, which stimulated at the same time that unique and creative English initiative in decretal codification which has been mentioned above. The judgement that these remarkable developments were primarily the work of a group of 'papalist' English canonists, supporters for the most part of Becket in the dispute which had just been concluded, has been recently challenged, yet stands firmly rooted in the massive evidence of the English collections, which owed their existence above all to the decretal records of Baldwin of Ford, Bartholomew of Exeter, Roger of Worcester and Richard of Canterbury. Bartholomew and Roger are believed to have been commissioned by the pope more frequently than any other English bishops of their time, and their distinction in this respect is immortalized in Alexander III's description of them as 'the twin lights illuminating the English Church'; Baldwin's personal influence in decretal codification is faithfully recorded in at least one important surviving manuscript;[20] and Richard's archives certainly provided the coherent sequences of Canterbury decretals in many extant collections. Whatever limitations the secular power was able to impose on this species of papal jurisdiction in practice, the reality of its existence and the vast scope of its application present one of the most striking features of the life of the English Church at the close of our period.

An adequate survey of Anglo-papal relations would treat of many matters neglected in this essay, or dealt with only perfunctorily. Events in the Holy Land, the resulting appeals to the West and the negotiations for the promotion of further Crusading efforts; the history of canonization in the context of the papal prerogative of authentication;[21] the history of political ideas, as well as of theology and doctrine, and the contributions of English scholars in these fields; the evolution of papal and episcopal diplomatic, including the increasing skill displayed in the critical examination of official documents; the work of the papal camera and the development of papal fiscal policies: all these are but a selection of the many distinct additional areas of interest in which English and papal history were to some extent intermingled. The pattern of Anglo-papal relations throughout the long period is complex, and no useful purpose is served by its oversimplification.

[20] British Museum MS Royal 10 A.II; cf. Duggan, 'The Trinity Collection of Decretals and the Early Worcester Family', *Traditio*, XVII (1961), pp. 506–26.

[21] Cf. esp. E. W. Kemp, *Canonization and Authority in the Western Church*, Oxford (1948), pp. 53–106.

On the one hand, there are the numberless proofs of the growth of papal authority and influence in the island between the Conquest and the death of John; on the other hand, it would be quite misleading to suggest that movements of thought and policy were pointed in one direction only. It is patent that royal and secular interests were often opposed to the papal progress; and it is no less obvious that the secular power was frequently able to limit or frustrate its application. It was natural that this was so, since the Church of the Gregorian Reform was in a real sense a conscious 'aggressor' against a long-established framework of Christian society, which it considered unjust. The measure of the Church's achievement must be seen against that background: not in the many individual and temporary contests which were waged now with success for the *regnum*, now for the *sacerdotium*, now ending in compromise and the division of the spoils of victory, but in the extent of the ultimate breaches which the Gregorian attack made in a powerfully entrenched existing fortress.

Nor yet were the views of ecclesiastics themselves undivided. Many bishops, while fully recognizing papal authority in theory, accepted willingly the customs which had long governed relations between ecclesiastical and secular activities in practice, considering it reasonable that Christian kings should require and exert a measure of control over the Church in their realms. Some bishops indeed were unlikely to hold a contrary viewpoint, since they were in effect the creatures of secular rulers. On the one side, there were the full papal doctrines, as advanced by Anselm and Robert Pullen, by John of Poitiers, Becket, John of Salisbury and Herbert of Bosham, by the English canonists of the later-twelfth century and by Stephen Langton at the close of the period; on the other side, there were the customs and concepts of an increasingly self-conscious secular monarchy, supported by tradition and by many ecclesiastics who for varied reasons held to a pre-Gregorian notion of the relations between *regnum* and *sacerdotium*: a dualistic ideology, identified sometimes as the Gelasian theory, through misunderstanding of Pope Gelasius's doctrine. The attitude of such bishops in England was perfectly mirrored in the writings and career of Gilbert Foliot, and summed up explicitly during the

Becket dispute in his *Multiplicem*,[22] while a distinctly anti-papal note had been recorded decades previously in the Anglo-Norman tractates, the so-called Anonymous of York, a work of probable Norman origins. But, for this one period of English history, the dominant trend in Anglo-papal relations was in favour of the papal claims in a fullness which had not previously existed, and which would progressively diminish in the following centuries. Knowles has crystallized the matter most succinctly in saying that what had in previous centuries been a union of faith, love and loyalty became now a union of law, discipline and authority while, in the ages which followed, 'though the connection with the continent and with Rome was as close as ever, the time had passed when the external influence of the papacy upon the administration of the Church in England was genial and creative.'

[22] The letter *Multiplicem* is discussed in Knowles, *The Episcopal Colleagues of Archbishop Thomas Becket*, Cambridge (1951), pp. 171–80. Professor D.C. Douglas's *William the Conqueror*, Eyre and Spottiswoode (1964), appeared too late for reference in this chapter. Where not specifically acknowledged in footnotes, my debt to many scholars is indicated in the appendix bibliography.

SELECT BIBLIOGRAPHY

G. Tellenbach, *The Church in Western Europe from the Tenth to the early Twelfth Century, transl. T. Reuter* (1993)

F. Barlow, *The English Church 1066–1154* (1979)

——, *Thomas Becket* (1986)

Margaret Gibson, *Lanfranc of Bec* (1978)

N. Cantor, *Church, Kingship and Lay Investiture in England, 1089–1135* (Princeton 1958)

M. Brett, *The English Church under Henry I* (1975)

R.W. Southern, *St Anselm, A Portrait in a Landscape* (1990)

C.R. Cheney, *From Becket to Langton: English Church Government 1170–1213* (1956)

——, *Innocent III and England* (Stuttgart 1976)

Charles Duggan, *Canon Law in Medieval England* (Variorum 1982)

——, *Decretals and the Creation of 'New Law' in the Twelfth Century: Judges, Judgements, Equity and Law* (Variorum 1998)

L.H. Jared, 'English ecclesiastical vacancies during the reigns of William II and Henry I': *Journl. of Eccles. Hist.* 42 (1991)

Janet Burton, *Monastic and Religious Orders in Britain, 1000–1300* (1994)

Beryl Smalley, *The Becket Conflict and the Schools* (1973)

Julia Barrow, 'Education and the recruitment of cathedral canons in England and Germany, 1100–1225': *Viator* 20 (1989) pp. 178–38

M.G. Cheney, *Roger, Bishop of Worcester, 1164–79* (1980)

THE THIRTEENTH CENTURY

C. H. Lawrence

4

THE THIRTEENTH CENTURY

'As an obedient son, I do not obey, I contradict, I rebel.' These words, with which Robert Grosseteste refused a canonry in Lincoln cathedral to a nephew of Pope Innocent IV, have often been quoted. It has not always been remembered that the man who wrote them, a famous Englishman who possessed one of the most versatile and subtle minds of the thirteenth century, was one of the most thoroughgoing papalists of his age. In another letter, written to his own dean and chapter, he enlarges on the theme of the pope's fullness of power over the Universal Church: the pope alone has received from God the fullness of power to root out and pull down, to destroy and throw down, to build and to plant. It is from him that the authority of every bishop over his own diocese is derived. His type in the Old Testament is Moses seated in judgement over the people of Israel who, on Jethro's advice, chose subordinates to help him carry his burden without diminishing his power. The sun cannot light the whole earth simultaneously, so it illumines the moon and stars which reflect light upon the darkened side of the earth, 'so is the Lord Pope, in respect of whom all other prelates are as the moon and stars, receiving from him whatever power they have to illumine and fertilise the Church.'

The doctrine of the pope's plenitude of power in the Church, which Grosseteste is stating here in its most extreme and uncompromising form, had already a long history of evolution behind it by this period. It had received articulate formulation by the popes and canonists of the previous century and to this process of definition Englishmen had made an important contribution. Its translation into the concrete terms of Church government was the work of Innocent III (1198–1216) and of a series of legally minded popes who followed him. They were helped in this task by the new collections of canon law which the popes now, for the first time, directed and officially promulgated. For this is the age of the *ius novum*, the New Law, of which the pope alone is the universal sovereign law-giver. It is law which, like the Common Law of England, is made *judicialiter*; apart from the decrees of general councils, it consists solely of decretal letters, of rescripts, that is, containing judicial sentences given by the pope. The rapid and vast increase of this papal 'case-law' created an urgent need for authoritative codification. Innocent III took the initiative in 1210 by publishing an official collection of his own decretals, but in 1234 this was superseded by the comprehensive collection drawn up on the instructions of Gregory IX and now known as *The Decretals of Gregory IX*. The interpretation of these new law-books by the great Bolognese glossators of the classical age, men such as Hostiensis, Bernard of Parma, Innocent IV, and Durandus the Speculator, played a vital part in building up the edifice of papal sovereignty.

Grosseteste's simile of the sun, moon and stars, is no rhetorical eulogy. He is stating in terms of Aristotle's cosmology a doctrine which we find clearly enunciated in the letters of Innocent III: that the pope has not merely a super-eminent jurisdiction over all bishops, but that he is the sole source from which all episcopal jurisdiction is derived. The bishop is the ordinary judge in his own diocese, but the pope is the 'universal ordinary' to whose tribunal all men, even the humblest clerk or layman, may have immediate access. It is true that, because of the vast number of his subjects, he delegates his authority to inferiors, the bishops, but in so doing, he in no way abdicates or diminishes his own. This was a dynamic principle upon which to found a highly centralized system of Church government. Its possibilities were inexorably realized throughout the later Middle Ages.

The care of all the Churches could not be concentrated in the Apostolic hands without the help of bureaucracy. As papal sovereignty over the Church materialized in a multitude of different ways, it took on gross and palpable shape in the Roman Curia. Until the pontificate of Nicholas III (1277–80), the normal habitat of the papal court, when the pope was in Rome, was the Sacred Lateran Palace. Here, already in the twelfth century, significant changes had taken place. The antiquated and rudimentary organs of papal government had been replaced by new offices and new techniques modelled upon those used in the court of the German emperors. Some contemporaries observed these developments with mixed feelings. An Augustinian canon, Gerhoch of Reichersberg, complained to Eugenius III (1145–53) that in place of the Roman Church without blemish men now found the Roman Curia, and he goes on to derive the word 'curia' from blood (*cruore*) or, alternatively, from trouble (*curis*). With the thirteenth century the great and ever-growing recourse to Rome by petitioners, the increasing centralization of ecclesiastical patronage, the rise of papal taxation of benefices and clerical incomes, all called for a large and complex mechanism of government and the papal Curia expanded rapidly to meet this demand.

The papal chancery, or secretariat, became a great office organization of many departments, bound by elaborate rules of procedure, and employing a carefully graded hierarchy of notaries and writers, and having its own tribunal, the Audience of Contradicted Letters, where draft rescripts were read out before the attorneys of interested parties. The financial department, the Apostolic Camera, similarly expanded and in the thirteenth century we find that it has its own college of clerks and its own judicial organization. In the earlier years of Innocent III's pontificate the humble petitioner was still expected to present himself in person at the Curia and many a litigant heard the pope himself discuss his case in consistory and had the chance of addressing the pope, as did Gerald of Wales. But after 1215 these days were gone. The papal audience was for most purposes replaced by a tribunal staffed by cardinals or papal chaplains. The ordinary person, whether he was a litigant or simply petitioning for a privilege, required the expert services of a professional proctor to steer his business through the Curia.

Curialism, that is the direction of local Churches and the appropriation and deployment of their resources by the central government of the Church, was the practical realization of the thirteenth-century doctrine of the plenitude of papal power. It integrated the Western Church as never before into a single centralized administrative and legal system. The same period saw the accomplishment of a change which had been coming over the government of the Church during the previous hundred years and which was more fundamental than any administrative expedient. This was the emergence of the college of cardinals as governors of the Church in partnership with the pope. Already in the eleventh century Peter Damian had likened the members of the *presbyterium* of Rome to the senators of the ancient city. In the thirteenth century the cardinals share in every important act of papal government. They subscribe all solemn privileges; they give advice on decisions of high policy and their formal assent is recorded in the written acts which embody the pope's decisions. It was, for example, with the advice and assent of his brethren that Innocent III, after a secret consistory, awarded the empire to Otto of Brunswick in 1202. It is they who choose and assist in the dispatch of legates *a latere*, or papal plenipotentiaries, and give continuing advice to emissaries on the conduct of legations; or, to take a very different example, they participate at every stage in the developing process of canonization and in the final judgement. They share, in fact, in the highest acts of papal sovereignty, as well as taking an active part in the day-to-day government of the Church. Their constitutional importance was given practical recognition by Nicholas IV in 1289 when he permanently allocated to the Sacred College a half of the revenues of the Roman Church. The great thirteenth-century canonist, Hostiensis, wrote of the cardinals and pope together as forming a single 'supreme and excellent college', so that 'possession of the plenitude of power includes not the pope alone, but the cardinals also'. According to this view the headship of the Church was, for practical purposes, not monarchic, but oligarchic. Of course, Hostiensis was himself a cardinal and his opinion represents only one strand in canonistic speculation about the papal headship, but it was a significant attempt to erect a doctrinal superstructure on the foundation of current practice.

Faced with these developments, Englishmen often complained, as did Grosseteste, but like him they accepted without question the principles upon which the system rested. They acknowledged the fact that Latin Christendom was an organic and indivisible unit of which the pope was the spiritual sovereign. Within this body the English Church constituted two provinces. It had its traditions and its saints, but it neither had, nor claimed, any separate juridical identity.

While Grosseteste tells us how the pope's plenitude of power presented itself to the mind of an English churchman in the middle years of the thirteenth century, as a learned and zealous pastoral bishop, he also reflects in himself the other aspect of the papacy of that age as the mainspring and co-ordinator of ecclesiastical reform. In this respect, too, the pontificate of Innocent III inaugurated a new epoch. The path had been laid by the councils of the previous hundred years, but the great Lateran Council—*maximum et celeberrimun concilium*—convoked by Innocent in 1215, enacted a comprehensive programme of disciplinary reform which was to stimulate and guide the efforts of Church leaders for many decades to come. The two English archbishops, Stephen Langton and Walter de Gray, and nine other bishops from England and Wales, attended the council and nothing illustrates so clearly the influence of the papacy upon the English Church as the efforts made by English bishops during the following seventy years to implement the conciliar programme.

We shall cast an eye first at the central government of the Church and see how Englishmen gained access to the Curia and sought means of influencing curial policy. We shall then look at the various agencies through which papal jurisdiction operated in thirteenth-century England. Finally, we shall examine some of the ways in which the papacy influenced the internal life of the English Church and affected the attitudes of the ordinary Christian.

To the governed, the ascendancy of the Sacred College was a fact that had to be taken into practical account. Access to the fountain-head of papal favour lay through the cardinals. The English chancery enrolments show that in the thirteenth century royal envoys to the Curia were always given letters commending them and their business to members of the Sacred College. How far were national interests represented there? Numbers were often low; at one point, on the death of Alexander IV in 1261, they sank as low as eight; but the Italian element seems never to have comprised less than half of the total. If we take, for example, the creations of Gregory IX (1227–41) and Innocent IV (1243–54), we find that Gregory created in all thirteen new cardinals, whose national distribution was as follows: seven Italians, four Frenchmen, one Spaniard and one Englishman. Innocent IV created fifteen cardinals, of whom eight were Italians, four were Frenchmen, one was a Savoyard, one a Hungarian and one an Englishman. Between the death of Robert Curzon in 1219 and the elevation of Robert of Somercotes in 1239, there was no Englishman in the Sacred College. After Somercotes there were three English cardinals, John of Toledo, Robert Kilwardby, and Hugh of Evesham, who followed one another at intervals of only a few years. But after the death of Hugh of Evesham in 1287, there was again a long gap of sixteen years before another English cardinal was appointed.

English interests did not necessarily suffer because there was no English cardinal at the Curia, but it was obviously a help to an English petitioner arriving at the papal court if he could turn to a compatriot who was in a position of power. We can see this from the activities of Cardinal John of Toledo on behalf of his countrymen. We know nothing of his early life. It was probably from the schools of Toledo that he borrowed his name as well as his medical expertise. It was as abbot of the Cistercian house of L'Épau, in the county of Maine, that he presented himself at the Curia in 1244, after escaping from an imperial prison. Innocent IV made him his personal physician and created him cardinal priest of St. Laurence-in-Lucina. In 1261 he was raised to the cardinal bishopric of Porto by Urban IV. For over thirty years he was in a position of power and influence at the papal court and he was constantly used by his countrymen and by his own order as a channel to papal favour. Royal proctors were constantly commended to him. Often it was at his petition that royal clerks received provision to benefices. The English postulators of the canonization of St. Edmund of Abingdon, when the cause got becalmed at the Curia, turned to 'the English cardinal' for help. On at least two occasions he rendered important political services to the English court. The first of these was in 1261, when Henry III was trying to rid himself of baronial domination. He sent his proctors to the Curia to obtain absolution from the oath which he had taken to abide by the baronial plan of government. The business was a delicate one as the baronial party also had their representatives at the Curia working in the opposite sense. It was through the influence of Cardinal John that the baronial proctors were held at bay. The king's protagonist in this diplomatic battle of wits was Master Roger Luvel, who, as well as being a royal clerk, was one of the cardinal's chaplains. Again, when the king's brother Richard of Cornwall, had been elected to the empire, Cardinal John exerted all his efforts to get him elected to the senatorial office at Rome. He had emptied his treasury, as he wrote rather sadly, and denuded his chapel, on the earl's behalf, but he had not as yet received reimbursement. He urges the earl to make haste to Rome if he cares to wear the imperial crown.

Several members of distinguished ministerial families, like Roger Luvel and John of Lexington, were to be found under the English cardinal's roof, as well as men who were to achieve high preferment in the Church, such as Richard Gravesend, the future bishop of Lincoln. Such a household offered a useful foothold for the English petitioner seeking access to a largely foreign Curia. Englishmen were rarely to be found in curial offices. Master Robert of Somercotes had been at the Bologna law schools and for a short time before he was made a cardinal he held the important office of auditor of contradicted letters in the papal chancery. 'The Lord has placed you like a John [the Baptist] at the Curia,' writes Stephen of Lexington to him. 'You will restore the talent of familiar acquaintance, entrusted to you by the Lord, with gain, if you labour to open the way to Peter . . . ' But Master Robert was an isolated case. In the thirteenth century the papal chancery was ruled and staffed almost wholly by Italians.

The English court, English bishops and ecclesiastical corporations, who frequently needed to smooth the path to Peter, did so by creating ties with the permanent curial staff. So we find Master Marinus of Eboli, vice-chancellor to Innocent IV, occupying a canonry in Salisbury cathedral and, at the king's request, being provided to additional English benefices to the value of two hundred marks a year. Marinus' family, too, shared in the royal benevolence: in 1251 his nephew was knighted by the king, who provided the young man with a robe for the occasion. Naturally, as permanent head of the papal chancery, Marinus did not reside in England. He owed his benefices to the fact that the king and the bishop of Salisbury thought his friendship to be worth cultivating. Considerations of this sort lay behind many (though not all) of the provisions of Italian curialists to English benefices.

The problem which faced the English petitioner at the Curia was more than a difficulty of language. The growing complication of the chancery process and its increasing formality made it harder for the non-expert to conduct his own business. Heads of State and other notables could rely upon advice from cardinals or from chancery officials, but the less elevated petitioner, who had no friends at the Curia, needed the services of a professional who knew the ropes, who had friends among the office staff, who knew how to draft his supplication in the acceptable form and would see it through the various stages for him. It was to meet this need that a class of professional proctors arose in the early years of the thirteenth century. Almost all Italians, these men resided on the fringe of the Curia and offered their services for hire.

As time went on, even the mighty found it useful to retain the services of a permanent proctor to act for them and to watch over their interests. From 1255 we find Henry III using a Master Finatus and a Master Robert de Baro for this purpose. In 1259 royal envoys engaged the services of a more influential attorney in Master Angelus of Rome, a papal notary—one of the top men in the chancery—who took an oath of fealty to the king and received an annual pension of forty marks at the Exchequer. Angelus proved a most valuable acquisition to his English master in the critical negotiations of the year 1261. He was taken over from Henry by Edward I, but King Edward was a notoriously bad paymaster and we have a series of letters written to the king and Burnell, the royal chancellor, in Master Angelus' own elegant notarial hand requesting the arrears of his fee. A similar commission was given by Edward to Master Stephen of San Giorgio, a scriptor of the papal chancery and chaplain of the English cardinal Hugh Atratus; the king made him a member of his Wardrobe staff, so Master Stephen had a permanent foothold in both the royal and papal courts. Few ecclesiastical corporations could have afforded the expense of a permanent proctor and when they wanted help at the Curia, they fell back on the 'proctorial pool', but they naturally resorted, where they could, to a man who had served them before, like the proctor Roffredus who was employed by Holy Trinity, Aldgate, on various commissions in the years 1264–74.

The benefits of ecclesiastical government cost money no less than those provided by the State. Those who served the Curia ate meat like other men. This truism was not always appreciated by thirteenth-century writers who attacked the venality of the papal bureaucracy. *The Holy Gospel according to the Silver Mark*, a vitriolic satire of the twelfth century, was refurbished in this period to include the activities of the cardinals:

> At that time, the first day at evening, being the first day of the week, when the doors were shut and the cardinals were there assembled according to the rite of the prelates, came the Lord Pope and stood in the midst of them, and said unto them, 'Peace be unto you,' and they replied 'and on earth peace to men of good fortune and wealth.'

He advises them how to deal with suitors to the Curia and they applaud, saying:

> He hath done all things well: he hath filled the rich with good things and the hungry he hath sent empty away.

The ordinary expenses of chancery were met by the payments that petitioners were required to make for papal letters. These payments were regulated by a fixed tariff and assessed by a chancery officer called the Distributor. The tariff was relaxed for those who were allowed to sue *in forma pauperis*, but most petitioners had to pay the necessary sum into the Distributor's office before their letters were delivered to them. Besides the recognized fees, the payment of *douceurs* in order to smooth the way to Peter was common practice, especially on the part of the great in Church and State. The lavish scale of royal 'tipping' can be gathered from the *Liberate Rolls*, which record money issued to the king's envoys bound for the Curia. A more modest case is that of Thomas of Cantilupe, bishop of Hereford. In 1281 he appealed to Rome against the jurisdiction of Archbishop Pecham. He wrote to his proctors at the Curia explaining that he was sending them a hundred pounds in the form of letters of credit, addressed to the merchants of Pistoia,

> which sum, though it seems small, can nevertheless be useful if it is carefully distributed. This in the opinion of some people could be done in the following way: namely, that the Lord Hugh, the English cardinal, should have 30 marks; the Lord Gerard, the cardinal, our auditor, 10 pounds, and his household 5 marks; the Lord Matthew Rufus, the cardinal, 10 marks; the Lord John, the cardinal, 10 marks; the Vice-chancellor 15 pounds; the Auditor of Contradicted Letters 10 marks; Berard of Naples and the other excellent notary, who is in the pope's special confidence, 20 marks in equal portions; the chamberlain of the Lord Pope 10 marks; the doorkeeper of the Lord Pope 40 shillings. Others consider that 5 marks could be subtracted from the amount allocated to the Vice-chancellor. . . . Others consider that it would be a good plan to give the pope a consideration of 40 or 50 marks, as the archbishop against whom we are appealing is a close acquaintance of his; but our view is that the path of discretion is more profitable and honourable, provided that, if real need arise, the pope should receive something to please him, on whom it is known that all favour depends.

Cantilupe died before his case could be decided, so it is impossible to say whether or not his money was wisely spent. In any event, there was another side to the picture. A bishop engaged in litigation with his metropolitan may have thought it expedient to try and sweeten his judges, but there is also evidence to suggest that the humbler suitor of small means did not find the door closed to him. The Curia had its defenders, such as Gerald of Wales and Henry, the schoolmaster of Würzburg. Gerald relished the story of the learned Master Simon of Tournai, who was stricken speechless for life, because, when he could not get access to the pope, he shouted angrily before the papal chancellor, 'There is no admittance to Simon Peter except through Simon Magus'. Master Henry wrote a dialogue on the subject in Virgilian hexameters. On his way back from the Curia a clerk named Geoffrey encounters Aprilis, a Spaniard, travelling in the opposite direction. The Spaniard explains that he has studied at the schools for fifteen years and is in consequence very poor. He seeks at the Curia no more than some little prebend (prebendula). The Lord Pope will surely help him: he enriches those with little knowledge and so 'perchance he will shake the dust from my burden too'. He wonders how things are done at the Curia. 'Are you taking anything with you?' comes the terse reply. But Geoffrey goes on to deny the slanderous allegations that litigation dries up for want of money. Contrary to popular opinion, the proctors are honest and reliable. The poor scholar is reassured; he will find his business promptly dealt with—about four days should see it through, and he need not worry: the Curia won't put him to much expense. Master Henry wrote in the 1260's and he knew his way round the Curia.

The effective working of the pope's plenitude of power in the Church represented an extraordinary triumph of doctrine over the facts of medieval geography. By the normal land route the journey from England to Rome took fifty days. To the ordinary tribulations of medieval travel were added the hazards of international politics. Abbot Samson of Bury St. Edmunds' liked to remind his monks of his adventures on the way to Rome during a papal schism 'when all the clerks carrying letters for the Lord Pope Alexander were seized and some of them imprisoned, some hanged, and others sent to the pope with their lips and noses lopped off, to his great dishonour and confusion. But I pretended that I was a Scot. . . . And when those that met me asked who I was, I answered nothing save 'Ride, ride Rome, turne Canterbury', and so he carried it off. The incident adds some colour to the complaint made to the papal legate by the Berkshire rectors in 1240. They objected to paying a subsidy for the pope's war against the emperor, because if they did, they would expose themselves to the risk of arrest and death when crossing imperial territory on the way to the Curia. Moreover, the Curia had often to be sought outside Rome. The hold of the popes over their turbulent capital was precarious until Nicholas III imposed his iron rule upon it, and the papal court often resided at one of the cities of the Campagna or Roman Tuscany.

In the thirteenth century the central government of the Church surmounted these difficulties of communication by developing powerful agencies in the provinces. Most litigation was delegated to local judges. An English plaintiff had only to obtain a papal rescript and his case would be heard in England before English judges specifically appointed for the purpose. Papal revenues which accrued in England were collected by permanent resident collectors. The papal chapel itself underwent an extraordinary development at the hands of Innocent IV, by which papal chaplains, men known to, and trusted by, the Curia, were appointed in cathedral and other collegiate churches, and even at the royal court. Legates *a latere*, who wielded almost all papal powers, operated more freely in England during the thirteenth century than at any other period before or after. To understand the working of papal jurisdiction through these channels, it is necessary first to look at the close relations which existed between England and Rome at the political level.

When King John made his submission to the legates of Innocent III in 1213 and surrendered his kingdom as a fief to the Roman See, he was acting with his own immediate needs in mind. He hoped by this means to ward off invasion from France and to gain the help of the pope against his rebellious subjects. For these advantages he pledged himself and his successors to pay to the Roman Church an annual tribute of a 1,000 marks. But the course of events invested his act with greater practical significance than he may have intended. John died in 1216 in the midst of civil war, leaving as his heir a boy of nine. In virtue of his father's act, the boy king Henry III was a papal ward. Accordingly, the papal legate, Cardinal Guala, took the lead, rallied the loyalists round the young king and presided at his hasty coronation in Gloucester abbey. The rebels and the invading French were placed under the ban of the Church. The support of the pope, effectively exercised through his legate on the spot, was invaluable in getting rid of the French and pacifying the country. But the legate's services did not end there. During the long minority of the king, Guala, and a succession of legates after him, played an active part in the council or regency. Thus, during this difficult and dangerous period, the nominal overlordship of the papacy was converted into a political reality.

After Henry had declared himself of age in 1227, he never forgot what he owed to the papacy and relations between the English court and the Roman Curia remained close and cordial. In times of political difficulty, he was inclined to fall back upon the papacy as he did in 1236-7, when he obtained the dispatch to England of the legate, Cardinal Otto Candidus. To a man of Henry's romantic and volatile temperament this close *entente* was not without its dangers. By accepting the crown of Sicily for his son Edmund, he foolishly allowed himself to be drawn into papal plans for ousting the Hohenstaufen dynasty from South Italy. The financial side of the agreement was disastrous. Henry underwrote the debts which the papacy had already incurred in the war and so pledged himself to Alexander IV for the payment of a fantastic sum. The chief part of the burden fell upon the English clergy, whose income was taxed for five successive years. This aroused bitter resentment both against the king's ineptitude and against papal policy. 'The clergy and laity of England are oppressed,' write the representatives of the Lincolnshire clergy, 'because at the suggestion of certain traitors the king's simplicity has been circumvented in the matter of his bond concerning the kingdom of Apulia, to the scandal of the Roman church and to the grave prejudice of the king's person. We protest,' they go on significantly, 'that we are willing in virtue of our obedience to give financial support to the Roman church on lawful occasions.'

In the end, Henry was unable to meet his commitments and was forced to turn to the baronage to extricate him. This brought on a complete political collapse and the seizure of power by a baronial council. In the years of turmoil that followed, diplomatic activity between England and Rome was intense. The baronial council tried during its brief period of power from 1258 to 1261 to win papal approval. But they found themselves outmanoeuvred at the Curia by the king's proctors. Alexander IV abandoned all hope of getting an English prince on the Sicilian throne, but the popes continued to give Henry steady support against his domestic opponents. In November 1263 the cardinal bishop of Sabina, Guy Foulquois, was dispatched as legate to strengthen the king's hand. But this mission misfired. While he was on his way to England, civil war broke out and the king's forces were heavily defeated by Montfort at Lewes. King Henry became a helpless political prisoner. The cardinal arriving at the French coast in the late summer of 1264, was refused admission to the kingdom by Montfort's regime and, after weeks of fruitless negotiation, he had to content himself with launching sentences of excommunication and interdict against the rebels from the French side of the Channel.

The thorny task of the English legation passed to Cardinal Ottobuono Fieschi, who set out in the summer of 1265 armed with powers to preach a crusade against the English rebels. When he reached Northern France, he received the news that Montfort had been defeated and killed at Evesham. The way was now open and he was able to join the king and begin the long and difficult work of pacification. Ottobuono's legation was the last great political service that the papacy rendered to Henry III. The legate's primary task was to deal with those members of the higher clergy who had thrown in their lot with the rebels. This he performed, but this was the least significant part of his work. It was due to the wise counsel of this shrewd and humane man that the king was persuaded to moderate his desire for revenge and to grant reasonable terms to those who had helped the losing side.

Relations between the English court and Rome were never again so close and warm as they had been in the reign of Henry III. Edward I, who succeeded his father in 1272, was a man of very different temper. Imperious and autocratic by nature, he was a realist in his attitude towards the papacy as towards all else. His personal relations with the pope were generally cordial. He had met, and liked, the future Pope Gregory X while on Crusade, and on his way home from the East, early in 1273, he passed some weeks as a guest of the papal court at Orvieto. But it was clear from the start that there was to be no return to the political dependence of his father's reign.

A rough and ready barometer to the diplomatic climate between the English court and the Curia is provided by the payment of the annual tribute to which John had bound his successors. This had been paid promptly each year by Henry until he ran into serious financial difficulties in the 1250's. Even after the civil war Henry paid off his arrears. The fact that payment ceased for the last five years of the reign is probably a sign of the increasing influence of the Lord Edward in the affairs of government. After his accession, he instructed the English delegates who attended the Council of Lyons in 1274 to lodge a protest against the feudal bond as being contrary to the king's regality. Edward did not, however, take the drastic step of repudiating it. Arrears of tribute were paid at spasmodic intervals, when the king was seeking concessions from the Roman Curia. The last payment was made in 1289, when he was negotiating to secure the levy of a tax on the English clergy for his own use. Thereafter, repeated requests for payment fell upon deaf ears. For the remaining seventeen years of Edward's reign the tribute was unpaid.

Although papal government operated in England in the same manner and through the same agencies as it did elsewhere, the close entente between the English court and Rome entailed particular consequences for the English Church. One of these was the heavy incidence of papal taxation upon the English clergy, who found themselves being mulcted under papal auspices in order to finance the king's policy. Another consequence was the protracted residence at various periods of papal legates, who made a mark of their own upon English ecclesiastical affairs.

Papal taxation, as it developed in the thirteenth century, revealed the most parasitic aspect of curial government. Nothing did more to alienate clerical feeling. A direct tax on the income of ecclesiastical benefices was an expedient devised by Innocent III to finance the Crusade, but his successors ruthlessly exploited it in order to pay for their Italian wars in defence of the papal states. The first step in this direction was taken by Gregory IX in 1228, when he called upon the clergy to subsidize his struggle against Frederick II. The papal tax of the year 1250 established a pattern that became increasingly familiar. Innocent IV granted King Henry a tenth of the income of the English clergy for three years to finance a royal crusade. But Henry did not go on crusade. When, in 1255, the agreement over the Sicilian crown had been clinched, the king was authorized to appropriate the yield of the clerical tax for this purpose. It was in vain that the Lincolnshire clergy protested that they were under no legal obligation because their original consent had been to a crusading subsidy, not to a war tax for use in Apulia. The combination of their spiritual and temporal lords was irresistible.

The same procedure was repeated under Edward I, but with a significant difference. The Council of Lyons in 1274 levied a tax of one tenth on all clerical income for six years for the relief of the Holy land. Edward sought, and eventually obtained, this money by the device of taking the crusader's vows, which he never honoured. The tax was used by Edward entirely for his own ends. The king entered into the field which the pope had ploughed for him and reaped a bumper harvest. The same fate befell the crusading tenth levied by Pope Nicholas IV in 1291. Although Edward should have forfeited the grant by failing to take the Cross, the spoils were in fact divided between him and the pope.

The frequent levy of taxes necessitated new machinery for assessment and collection. In the course of the century three valuations of English benefices were made on papal instructions as a basis for tax assessment. The first of these, made in 1254, was called the Valuation of Norwich, after the bishop of Norwich, Walter Suffield, who was the chief assessor. A large fragment of the returns survive. They show that the valuers, moved by obvious regard for their own order, substantially undervalued the incomes of their colleagues. Accordingly, in 1276 a new valuation was ordered, this time 'according to the true value' (*iuxta veram valorem*). But this assessment too was found to be over-indulgent, and in 1291 Pope Nicholas IV ordered a third to be made 'according to the truest value' (*iuxta verissimam valorem*). The feelings of the clergy in face of these successive re-ratings are succinctly voiced by the annalist of Barnwell priory: 'The first pricks us, the second wounds us, the third flays us to the bone.'

In the middle years of the century the discontent of the clergy was focused upon the diversion of ecclesiastical wealth into papal policies which they did not approve. In a list of grievances presented by the rectors of churches in the archdeaconry of Berkshire it is suggested that the pope's Italian policies should be financed from the pope's own patrimony, that is, from the revenues of the papal states. It is true that all the churches pertain to the pope, but, they argue, this means that he has the care and solicitude of all the churches, not that he is their owner and landlord. Churches have been endowed by kings and nobles and the other faithful to support the sacred ministry and to provide for the needs of the poor. If they are to be taxed for the purposes of the Roman Curia, these services will no longer be rendered and patrons will be defrauded and will demand back the endowments.

In the later years, the diversion of papal taxes to meet the pressing needs of the State may have somewhat disarmed this criticism, but it is doubtful whether it reconciled the clergy to the system. Royal taxation by papal mandate eliminated the principle of consent and enforced payment by spiritual penalties. In addition to papal income taxes, the clergy were subject, like the laity, to periodic royal demands for subsidies. An escape from this two-pronged fork seemed to be offered in 1296 by the bull *Clericis laicos*, which forbade the clergy to grant lay subsidies without papal consent. Boniface VIII issued the bull at the petition of the Cistercians in France, but it had an immediate relevance to the situation in England. Edward I, who had a war with France on his hands, was demanding a large subsidy from the clergy. Archbishop Winchelsey rallied convocation behind the new papal prohibition. This, however, involved the clergy in a head-on collision with the king. Edward reacted violently. The temporalities of bishoprics were seized and the clergy were placed outside the protection of the law. Resistance began to crumble and Winchelsey, though taking his personal stand on the papal constitution, felt obliged to leave the issue to the consciences of individuals. A way out of the impasse was provided by an additional bull *Etsi de statu*, published July in 1297, which allowed the clergy to grant a subsidy to the secular power in a recognized case of 'urgent necessity'. In the autumn the rout of the English army by the Scots at Stirling Bridge provided just such a case and convocation freely offered a subsidy. But Winchelsey's un-flinching stand had saved the principle for the time being. Edward made no further attempt to tax the clergy directly. It was easier to do it through the pope.

The growth of papal taxation brought in its train a new species of curial agent, the resident papal collector. In the fourteenth century permanent collectorates were established all over the Western Church, but it was in thirteenth-century England that the office made its first appearance. The collector was appointed by the papal *camerarius* and was accountable to him. He had a general commission to collect not only income taxes, but all the many and varied sums to the Roman Church from England, including the annual tribute, the ancient offering of Peter's Pence, and the census paid by monasteries which enjoyed the papal privilege of exemption. From the appointment of Stephen of Anagni in 1228 it is possible to trace a continuous list of resident collectors in England. They bore the style of nuncio. They were almost all Italians who had been trained at the Curia; many were university graduates and papal chaplains. They were typical and not unworthy representatives of the curial service, generally per-forming their unamiable duties with tact and reasonable con-sideration. The arrogant and high-handed Master Martin sent by Innocent IV in 1244 was exceptional. It was probably because of the hostility that he aroused that Innocent appointed Englishmen as his two immediate successors.

The history of the financial dealings of the papacy with the English Church in this period is not a happy one. Given the great expansion of centralized Church government, the development of some regular system of subsidy was inevitable. It was equally inevitable that, once the rich seam of clerical income had been opened, the king would be drawn into the field. The clergy were ground between the competing claims of their two masters. They sought escape either by invoking the rights of their lay patrons against the pope, or by invoking papal authority against their lay lord, but before a combination of the two they were powerless. A sense of bitterness and grievance was created which was directed against the papal Curia more than against the king, who was, in the end, the chief beneficiary of papal taxation.

The resident papal tax collector was a new kind of agent created to deal with a new situation. For centuries past the omni-competent agent of Rome had been the papal legate. In the twelfth century the papacy had from time to time conferred legatine powers on individual archbishops of Canterbury and in virtue of these privileges they came to claim that the papal lega-tion was a permanent adjunct of their primatial office; in the phrase consecrated by Innocent IV, they were *legati nati*. The Curia seems neither to have admitted nor to have disavowed the claim which, for practical purposes, does not appear to have amounted to very much. Certainly no thirteenth-century arch-bishop of Canterbury was able to exercise in the Northern province, or even in his own, the wide powers which the canonist Durandus assigns to a *legatus natus*. Pecham attempted to exercise the judicial powers of a legate over the subjects of his suffragan bishops, but this provoked a storm of protest and led to an attempt to draw a clearer line of demarcation between the arch-bishop's primatial and legatine rights. If the Roman Curia was not greatly disturbed about these archiepiscopal pretensions, it was because it had in its armoury a weapon by which they could be easily and effectively neutralized: all other legatine powers were superseded by the coming of a *legatus a latere*, the agent *par excellence* of papal sovereignty.

The legatine office was at its zenith in the thirteenth century. 'It seems', writes Durandus, 'that the *legatus a latere* can do any-thing that the pope has not specifically reserved to himself, for he acts as his vicar.' He can summon councils, he can suspend bishops, he can confer benefices over-riding the rights of ordinary patrons, he exercises the plenary jurisdiction of the papal court. He is, as it were, clothed in the pope's person, a fact which was outwardly demonstrated by his wearing the scarlet mantle and other insignia of the pope. A formidable agent of the papacy at the height of its hierocratic power, he reflected in many ways the structure of the Roman Church. He was the emissary not of the pope alone, but of that 'supreme and excellent college', the pope and cardinals. At an earlier period it had been quite common to entrust a legation to papal chaplains, but after the middle of the thirteenth century it was the custom of the Roman Curia, as Durandus tells us, to grant the style of *legatus a latere* only to cardinals. An *ordo*, or ceremonial book, of the Roman Church, written at the beginning of the fourteenth century by Cardinal James Caetani, describes the ceremonies which surrounded the dispatch of a legate. The pope first consults the cardinals in consistory about the expediency of granting a request for a legate. The emissary is then chosen in consistory. Before leaving, the legate is expected to visit each of the cardinals singly in his own house and on the day of his departure the Sacred College assembles outside the city walls to see him off. Likewise, on his return, he is met by the cardinals and escorted to the Lateran palace and in the next consistory he is required to make a report on his legation.

These ceremonies are more than merely picturesque; they express the corporate responsibility of pope and Sacred College for the legation. The same conception is apparent in the close contact which was maintained during the legate's tour of office. A stream of correspondence passed to and fro over the Alps between the Curia and its legates in England, France and Germany. A small portion of the letter register kept by Cardinal Ottobuono during his English legation of 1265-68 has survived and we find him writing to the cardinals of the Curia to report on his progress and on the state of his mission following the death of earl Simon de Montfort and requesting them for orders and advice. It is probable that the Curia was never again so closely and accurately informed on English affairs as it was when it was receiving regular bulletins from this detached and shrewd observer.

The legations of the cardinal deacons Otto and Ottobuono during the reign of Henry III constitute the high-water mark of the resident papal legation in England. Both men were sent at the king's request to help him out of his political difficulties. It

was inevitable, therefore, that they should incur some of the unpopularity which resulted from his maladroit policies. This was
so with Otto, who arrived in July 1237. Contemporary annalists
viewed his coming with misgiving; one writer, at least, believed
the reasons for his mission to be purely fiscal. It was probably
this disagreeable image which lay behind an ugly incident the
following year at Oseney abbey, outside Oxford, where the legate
was staying. A brawl broke out between a group of Oxford
scholars, who had come out to present a petition, and some of the
cardinal's domestics. There was a sharp fight in which the
cardinal's cook was killed; the legate himself was hurried off by
the frightened canons and locked for safety in the abbey tower.
He emerged unscathed and the inevitable reprisals followed:
Oxford was laid under interdict and the fugitives were pursued
relentlessly by the king's writ from shire to shire. The incident
suggests, apart from local xenophobia, that the legate was not a
popular figure, but it would be a mistake to see in it a projection
of his relationship with English churchmen in general.

The most impressive thing about Otto's legation is the fact
that, despite the political handicap under which he worked, he
succeeded in gaining the confidence of the English bishops and
clergy, and that his jurisdiction and authority were everywhere
accepted, as were those of the pope. In part this may be explained
by the tact and restraint with which he wielded his great powers.
He was a modest and gracious man—even such an implacable
critic as Matthew Paris conceded so much—and he was careful
to avoid even the appearance of partisanship. He consistently refused to interfere in contested episcopal elections or in other
domestic disputes of the English Church unless expressly required
to do so by papal mandate. It was typical of him that, while doing
his best to mediate between Archbishop Edmund of Abingdon
and his rebellious cathedral chapter, he declined to impose a
solution on the parties by force. On the other hand, through his
chancery and his court he discharged all the routine tasks of papal
jurisdiction in England. Whether he was staying at Durham Hall,
the London residence assigned to him by the king, or moving
about the country, clerks of all ranks and the agents of monas-

teries and ecclesiastical corporations pressed ceaselessly upon him for the many and various favours which the papal court had to bestow, confirmations of privileges, dispensations, indulgences and, above all, litigation. His court was especially attractive to litigants as it offered the advantages of papal judgement without the expense and delay of getting letters from Rome. English monastic and cathedral records contain numerous references to legal actions in the legate's court, many of them, necessarily, delegated by Otto to subordinate judges.

In his routine administrative work Otto was simply performing the multifarious functions of the papal Curia; the detailed matters which came under his eye illustrate the immense scope of curial government in the thirteenth century. But it was the other side of his work, in which he reflected the mind of the reforming papacy, that left a most enduring mark upon the English Church. A few years before, he had enacted a series of important canons for the Churches of North Germany and Denmark. In November 1237, within only four months of his arrival, he convened a council of both provinces of the English Church for the same purpose. The assembly was held in St. Paul's and was attended by the two archbishops and the bishops and higher clergy. The main business was the publication by the legate of a collection of statutes bearing on questions which had preoccupied papal and episcopal reformers for the previous twenty-five years, ranging from such matters as the ordination and residence of vicars and the proper administration of the sacraments to such humdrum administrative details as the keeping of seals and archives. As can be seen from the multiplicity of manuscripts, these constitutions, together with those issued by the legate Ottobuono in 1268, were widely disseminated and held a position of unrivalled authority in the English Church in the later Middle Ages; they inspired much of the diocesan legislation that followed and were subsequently absorbed into the Church law of Scotland and Ireland. On many points, Otto's legislation did no more than apply the enactments of the third and fourth Lateran Councils to English conditions, and in this sense it did not break much new ground, but there is evidence in the bishops' registers to show that it provided new and effective armaments to English Church leaders in their struggle against abuses.

Otto's statutes were, with a single exception, directed to reforming abuses and improving the pastoral effectiveness of the secular Church. In the following year he summoned a general chapter of the Benedictine abbots of both provinces to meet him in London and enacted a series of constitutions concerned with monastic discipline. Here too he drew upon the legislation of Pope Gregory IX as well as upon the experience of provincial chapters and monastic visitors. Both these assemblies give us a vivid glimpse of papal authority in action through the most powerful agency of central government: only a legate could bring together the two provinces of the English Church into a single synod and inspire a concerted effort to implement the conciliar programme of reform. If the practical results of all this effort were, in the long term, disappointing, much of the blame rests with the Curia itself. In 1239 war broke out between pope and emperor and Otto was given the less agreeable job of raising a clerical subsidy. Thus he had painful experience of the deepening dilemma between the pastoral interests of the Church and the political expedients of the Roman Curia.

We turn now to a less spectacular, but more normal and pervasive agency of papal jurisdiction. The most astonishing achievement of medieval papalism was the great fabric of law and legal administration which it erected. This achievement would not have been possible without the practice of delegating jurisdiction. The courts of judges delegate were a vital part of the judicial system of the medieval Church; they brought papal justice within the geographical and financial reach of every man. With the growth of legal recourse to the Curia, the workings of such courts claimed a growing place in canon law: in the first book of *The Decretals of Gregory IX* the whole of the twenty-ninth title is devoted to the office and powers of the judge delegate, and it is not without significance that, of the forty-three decretals cited in the title, sixteen relate to English cases.

Throughout the thirteenth century the number of litigants

who sought legal redress from the Curia, both in the first instance and by appeal from the sentence of a lower court, continued to increase. The Anglo-Irish canonist William of Drogheda, in his famous *summa* on legal procedure, which he wrote in 1239 for the benefit of his Oxford pupils, takes it for granted that they will find the larger and more remunerative part of their practice in the courts of papal judges delegate. Much of the litigation that 'went to Rome' was, in fact, contentious litigation of a pedestrian, sometimes of a quite trivial kind. Its staple commodity, to judge from our surviving records, was questions of tithe and advowson. In 1275 we find the Augustinian abbey of Oseney suing the rector of St. Peter-le-Bailey, Oxford, before papal judges, for the right to bury one of his parishioners in the monastic cemetery. What made litigants in such cases prefer a papal court to the consistory court of their bishop, which was more readily accessible? There were many reasons. Exempt monasteries were chary of inviting episcopal jurisdiction for fear of bruising their hardly won immunity; the discovery that a case was rarely terminated by a sentence in the bishop's court, since the loser would appeal to Rome, encouraged litigants to seek papal justice in the first instance; but above all, the papal system of delegation had its own peculiar attractions.

When a litigant wanted to start an action before a papal court, he had to begin by asking his proctor at the Curia to get him a rescript. This was in the form of a commission addressed to judges in the locality concerned, instructing them to summon the parties and witnesses and to hear and determine the case, further appeal being debarred. The persons appointed in such commissions were, in general, drawn from the ranks of the higher clergy, bishops, cathedral dignitaries, archdeacons, and heads of monastic houses. Now the procedure had two great advantages from the petitioner's point of view: he was permitted to nominate the judges whom he wanted and also to name a convenient place where the action might be heard. The law allowed either party to object to a judge at any stage before the pleading began, but the prudent defendant would have his proctor ready briefed at the Curia itself. When the draft rescript was read out in the chancery tribunal called the Audience of Contradicted Letters, the defendant's proctor could object to the judges proposed. If, as was most often the case, the proctors of the two parties were unable to reach an agreement on the names of the judges, the auditor of the tribunal imposed a solution. Each party was invited to nominate one judge and the auditor named the third; the rescript was then redrafted accordingly.

At first sight the procedure had the unusual advantages of being swift and conclusive. The judges, on receiving the rescript, summon the parties and witnesses into court, using canonical penalties to ensure attendance. A litigant who fails to appear after a third summons will be suspended and will lose his case. The exclusion of the right of further appeal made the proceedings conclusive. In practice, however, the system was as exposed as any other to malversation and abuse. Until Cardinal Otto's constitution of 1237, the responsibility of serving the summons on the defendant rested with the plaintiff, and William of Drogheda describes a classic dodge for doing the poor man down: three serving boys are employed to serve the summons; two of them place it upon the altar of the defendant's church and depart; the third then quietly removes it and absconds. The first two report to the judges that their errand has been accomplished and the unwitting defendant, on failing to appear in court, is suspended for contempt. The judges were not always tractable. Their task, which involved time and travel, was often unwelcome to them. The law allowed them to sub-delegate to subordinates and they very frequently did so. A complex case might have to pursue its course before a whole series of sub-delegates. Again, the clause *appellatione remota*, which should have given finality to the proceedings, was in fact subject to so many qualifications that it was almost wholly ineffective. In general, it seems that the system worked tolerably well, but that it was not proof against the determination of rich and powerful litigants. Its weaknesses were exposed by such a case as the Durham *versus* York contest of the 1280's.

In March 1281, William Wickwane, archbishop of York, proposed to make a metropolitan visitation of the chapter and diocese of Durham. The bishop of Durham and the cathedral chapter, mobilized by the prior, Richard Claxton, determined to resist and appealed to Rome. Disregarding their appeal, Wickwane attempted to visit the cathedral priory in June, only to find his way forcibly barred. He therefore excommunicated the chapter and the bishop and placed Durham under interdict. The matter was thenceforth in the hands of the lawyers. The first group of judge delegates appointed to hear the case consisted of the abbot of Waltham and the chancellor and dean of Lincoln. The court opened at Stamford in February 1282. The chancellor of Lincoln was not present, but was represented by two sub-delegates; the Durham chapter objected to the presence of the dean of Lincoln on the bench because he held benefices in the archbishop's diocese and he was forced to retire. The archbishop, apparently misliking the new look of the court, failed to send his proctors and, after several adjournments, the abbot of Waltham (the judge chosen by the chapter) gave sentence in favour of Durham. Meanwhile, the dean of Lincoln, who refused to resign his commission, held a court elsewhere, in which he was represented by three sub-delegates. This court quashed the sentence of the abbot of Waltham, found in favour of the archbishop and imposed a heavy fine on the bishop and chapter of Durham. Both parties sought confirmation of sentence at Rome. These were only the opening salvos in a duel of heavy guns which went on for five years through six successive courts, involving, in all, twelve different judges delegate and sixteeen sub-delegates as well as a multitude of papal rescripts. In the end, after both the bishops involved had died and prior Claxton had resigned, the parties yielded to royal pressure and accepted a compromise. In this case, the Durham chapter thwarted a definitive sentence largely by the device of making a continuous stream of appeals.

The York-Durham case displays the defects of the delegate system writ large. At a humbler level, litigants often found it expedient to agree on a compromise rather than to allow the full rigour of the law to run its ruinous course, for the expenses of the case were assessed by the judges and levied on the losing party. Such were the series of tithe agreements made between the priory of St. Gregory, Canterbury, and the rectors of the churches of Chartham, Harbledown and Lenham, in the years 1238–40. The priory opened proceedings before three different sets of papal judges, but in each case agreed to a composition to which the judges put their seals. Nevertheless, the widespread recourse to papal justice by litigants of all ranks suggests that the system could, and did, work. However imperfect—and it was hardly more so than any alternative medieval judiciary—it realized in an impressive way the canonists' conception of the pope as the 'universal ordinary' and of Rome as being, for law, 'the common fatherland of all men'.

Let us shift our viewpoint from the agencies through which the papacy operated to the body upon which it acted. One of the points at which the papacy touched the life of the English Church most intimately was appointment to ecclesiastical office at every level, from bishops down to rectors of parish churches. The principle that the bishop was freely elected by the cathedral chapter had long since been established in law, but what prevailed in practice was a fragile compromise between the canonical procedure, as laid down by the canon *Quia propter* of the Lateran Council, and the traditional claims of the king to nominate. Within this framework the canon law admitted a number of occasions calling for direct papal action. On the pope devolved the scrutiny and confirmation of elections to metropolitan sees as a matter of course. In other cases, where the candidate suffered from some canonical disability, where, for example, he already held a bishopric and would have to be translated, or where he was under the canonical age, then the chapter could not make an election, they could only postulate the pope to act.

In the course of the thirteenth century the scope of papal intervention in episcopal elections was enlarged. Where an election was contested, it was morally certain to find its way to the Roman Curia and this certainty was made absolute by Alexander IV, who reserved all such cases to the papacy. On occasion, the pope would take from the metropolitan the duty of scrutinizing an election and discharge it himself; Gregory IX did this with the election of

Walter de Cantilupe to Worcester in 1236. Commonly, electoral disputes arose from the unwillingness of the chapter to accept a royal candidate, and in these instances the popes threw their weight behind the canonical electors and usually clinched the matter by consecrating the bishop-elect at the Curia, as Innocent IV did in the case of St. Richard of Chichester in 1245. It was in this period, too, that the papal plenitude of power achieved a startling advance in practice by reserving whole groups of cathedral and collegiate churches to the pope's collation. This step was taken by Innocent IV in Germany and Sicily for political reasons; Clement IV extended the practice to England in 1265, so as to ensure that, after the turmoil of civil war, vacant sees should only be filled on the advice of the legate Ottobuono.

The expanding influence of the pope over episcopal elections was reflected in the character of the English episcopate. Such outstanding bishops as Walter de Gray of York, Richard le Poore of Salisbury and Durham, William Blois of Worcester, and Alexander Stavensby of Coventry-Lichfield, all owed their promotion to acts of Innocent III and Honorius III during the minority of Henry III, when the popes supervised elections most carefully. The most striking mark of papal influence is to be found in the succession of men who occupied the see of Canterbury during the thirteenth century. As the scrutiny of the election in this instance fell to the Curia, it allowed free scope to the papal viewpoint. The king's interest in the election of the primate was no less keen, and a royal candidate was invariably proposed, but after the Great Interdict the royal claims were never pressed to the point of open conflict with Rome. The result was that, of the seven archbishops chosen in the thirteenth century, six were in effect designated by the pope. In one case, before the election of St. Edmund of Abingdon in 1233, three previous candidates, all of whom had received the royal assent, were set aside by Gregory IX. It is interesting to consider the character of these men who were regarded by the papacy as suitable instruments of its policy. All six were Schoolmen and five, Langton, Edmund, Kilwardby, Pecham and Winchelsey, were theologians of eminence; all had incepted and taught in the schools of Paris; all were profoundly involved in the religious movements of their time and treated their pastoral responsibilities with the utmost seriousness; one was canonized and another was the subject of canonization proceedings. A list of the rejected candidates would be hardly less significant. Royal administrators always accounted for a proportion of the bishops, but the king's natural desire to promote one of his servants to the primacy was thwarted. Edward I twice postulated the pope, each time in vain, to provide his chancellor, Robert Burnell, to Canterbury. The only successful royal candidate was Boniface of Savoy, who probably owed his favour at the Curia to his Savoyard relatives. Similarly, repeated efforts by the monastic chapter of Christ Church to obtain a monk as archbishop were defeated. The men, upon whom the pope's choice fell, represented the most vital tendencies in the thirteenth-century Church: they were seculars or, in the case of Kilwardby and Pecham, Mendicant Friars; they were men filled with the reforming zeal of which the papacy was still a source, and they were drawn from the newly fledged universities, which the popes assiduously nursed with their favour and protection. They mirrored the mind of a papacy which was still a creative, as well as a subduing, force.

The influence which the papacy exerted upon the English Church through the conferment of lesser benefices is more controversial and less easy to assess. The practice of provision, by which the pope presented a clerk directly to a church, overriding the claims of the normal patron, or instructed an ecclesiastical body to present a clerk to the next vacant benefice in their patronage, had its beginnings in the last decades of the twelfth century. It realized in yet another way that plenitude of papal power in the Church, which, as Clement IV (1265–68) expressly stated, included the full and free disposal of all churches and benefices. Under Innocent III, at the beginning of the thirteenth century, direct papal provision to prebends and parish churches was an occasional expedient, but under Innocent IV and his successors it grew into a large and well-defined legal system. In particular, expectatives, which entitled the holder of a papal mandate to a future vacancy, were issued in an uncontrolled flood. The dimensions of the problem thus created can be gathered from the constitution *Execrabilis,* issued by Alexander IV in 1255, which revoked many of the rescripts granted by his predecessor on the ground that in some Churches as many as twenty expectants were awaiting provision, while in others, the number of expectants exceeded the total number of prebends that the Church possessed.

In England, as in France, this concentration of patronage in the hands of the Curia evoked a rising volume of protest which reached a peak in the time of Innocent IV. Hostile criticism was directed not so much against the system itself as against what was felt to be an abuse of it, namely the provision of alien clergy to English livings. In 1231–2 a Yorkshire knight named Robert Tweng organized bands of masked raiders who attacked Italians on the roads and plundered the barns of non-resident Italian clergy. Tweng, whether he was airing a personal grievance or was the agent of more powerful interests, clearly represented a significant body of opinion. In 1241 a royal inquiry was held; English bishops were required to make a return of benefices in their dioceses to which Roman clerks had been provided by the pope or legate. We no longer have the returns to this inquest, but the English delegation which attended the Council of Lyons in 1245 presented a remonstrance against 'the Italians, whose number is now infinite', who had been provided to English benefices and they complained that in some churches 'Italian succeeds Italian'.

The actual incidence of provisions in this period, particularly of those in favour of aliens, is hard to assess, because systematic evidence is lacking. Only a fraction of the provisions issued were registered by the papal chancery and no doubt many of those that were granted failed to take effect. Recent studies have thrown a kindlier light upon the system. They have stressed the impersonal legality of the procedure and have pointed out that it brought positive benefits to the Church by offering educated clerks, who lacked local patrons, the chance of getting a benefice. English clerks certainly made full use of the system and the greater lay patrons, from the king downwards, used it to obtain benefices for their servants. It was not against aliens, but against English clerks armed with provisions, that Archbishop Walter de Gray sought and obtained papal protection in 1239. The chief complaint came from ecclesiastical patrons, from bishops, cathedral chapters and monasteries, who found their patronage being steadily taken over by the Roman Curia. Lay patrons were hardly touched, for, although the canonists insisted that the pope had equal rights over livings in lay patronage, in practice he generally left them alone.

Most of the Italians who were provided were, of course, members of the Curia. The pasturing of its personnel on the Universal Church was a natural outcome of a highly organized system of central Church government. Even idealists like Grosseteste accepted in practice the axiom that public services were a legitimate charge upon the endowments of the Church. In using benefices to support his administrators, the pope was doing no more than was done by kings, bishops and lay magnates. Most of the curial clergy were planted in the richer kinds of benefice; prebends in cathedral and collegiate churches were most favoured; the incidence on parish churches seems to have been comparatively slight. Taking, for example, the Institution Rolls of Bishop Hugh de Wells for the huge Lincoln diocese, covering the years 1209–35, we find that out of some 2,400 institutions to benefices, only 31 are in favour of aliens, of whom 16 are members of the Roman Curia or relatives of cardinals. Although they are incomplete, these figures, taken from the Midland counties at a time when Tweng's activities were attracting much attention, are suggestive. On the other hand, a list of prebendaries from Salisbury cathedral made in 1226, for the purpose of taxation, indicates a more serious problem. There were 52 prebendaries, three of whom were French abbots, whose presence is explained by the structure of the chapter's estates, and five were Italians. Doubtless most of the latter were pluralists, like the cardinal deacon of St. Adrian, who also held a prebend in Lincoln cathedral. This is a substantial proportion at such a relatively early date, though it but faintly foreshadows the situation at Salisbury a century later when fourteen of the prebendaries were Italians, including the dean and the treasurer, who were both cardinals residing at the Curia.

The complaint of the English that 'Italian succeeds Italian' suggests a significant attempt at wedge driving on the part of the Curia. The constitution *Licet ecclesiarum*, issued by Clement IV in

1265, by reserving to the pope all benefices vacated at the Curia, ensured that this result would follow. It is easy to understand the concern of ecclesiastical bodies in the face of this procedure; they felt that a prebend which had once been conferred upon an Italian was in danger of slipping permanently from their grasp. There is a marked stiffening of resistance on the part of ecclesiastical patrons about the middle of the thirteenth century, which may be explained by this anxiety. In 1246, for example, the bishop and chapter of London received a papal mandate to induct Master John of Asti, a papal chaplain, to the prebend in St. Paul's formerly occupied by Benedict, another papal chaplain. Two years later, Master John complained that he had not received Benedict's prebend nor, although many prebends had been subsequently vacated, had he received anything from the bishop and chapter. A fresh rescript is issued, appointing the dean of Wells (also a papal chaplain) as executor, to cause Master John to be provided with an income equal in value to the first prebend that fell vacant after the receipt of the previous mandate; the income is to be levied upon the goods of the bishop of London annually until Master John is found a benefice of equivalent value.

It seems that growing numbers of Italian clergy, who had obtained provisors, were unable to make good their claim except by protracted litigation, or were permanently bought off for a pension. John of Camezano, for instance, a nephew of Pope Innocent IV and auditor of contradicted letters (an important office in the papal Chancery), attempted to make good his provision to the church of Lenham, which was in the patronage of St. Augustine's, Canterbury, but in May 1253 he agreed before a papal judge to a compromise, by which the abbot and convent undertook to pay his agents an annual pension of eighteen marks until such time as they had found him some other church in the Canterbury diocese. Five years later the abbot and convent had still not found him a church and were still paying the pension. He found equal difficulty in prosecuting a claim to a rich church in the patronage of St. Albans; here again the monastery secured release from the mandate in return for an annual pension of twenty-five marks. Another Italian, John of Vercelli, who held a prebend in

Lincoln cathedral, fought a long and ultimately unsuccessful litigious duel lasting from 1236 to 1245 against Matthew of Stratton, archdeacon of Bucks, for possession of the church of SS. Peter and Paul, Buckingham.

It would be a mistake to assume that all, or even the greater number, of the curialist clergy provided to English benefices were regarded as unwelcome intruders. We do not know how many of them obtained their letters of provision, like Master Marinus, the papal vice-chancellor, at the request of king or bishop, but it was obviously advantageous to a cathedral body to have a senior officer of the Curia or a cardinal among its members. Some of the nine relatives of Innocent IV who were beneficed in England probably owed their churches to this fact. Moreover, not all the 'Romans' in possession of English livings were Italians. Many provisions were issued in favour of English clerks serving at the Curia as chaplains to English cardinals. The impact of the alien providee upon standards of pastoral care was probably slight. By the middle of the thirteenth century the typical parish church in England, as elsewhere, was served not by its rector, who was generally non-resident, but by a perpetual vicar or a stipendiary chaplain. It cannot have made much difference to the rustic parishioners whether their absentee rector was a royal clerk, a monastic body, a bishop's officer, or a writer in the papal chancery. Papal provision was only one element in the exploitation of parish endowments. The exploitation was, no doubt, unfortunate in its long-term effects upon the Church, but its roots were entwined in the foundations of medieval society.

It was this involvement with the social structure that eventually rendered fruitless much of the effort that was made in the thirteenth century to eradicate abuses. The growth of plurality is a case in point. Enlightened bishops like Richard le Poore and Grosseteste struggled to implement the canon of the Fourth Lateran Council forbidding the tenure of more than one benefice with cure of souls, but they found the ground cut from under their feet by the Roman Curia itself, which granted dispensations with increasing freedom to 'sublime and literate persons'. The issue was kept alive for much of the century. Gregory IX was prevailed upon to strip the bloated Rufinus of most of his English benefices, and the anonymous Paris preacher of the 1230's, who invoked the curse of Habakkuk upon those who multiplied prebends, found an echo in the heart of Pope Gregory X. But in the end good intentions were smothered by social pressure and administrative convenience.

The pervasive influence of the papacy upon the parish life of the English Church is indeed hard to assess, and nowhere is this harder than at the intimate level of religious practice and piety. The rural parishioner, who confessed annually to his parish priest in obedience to the decree of the Lateran Council, and his unlettered confessor, chaplain or vicar, who struggled under his bishop's lash to equip himself for the exacting task laid upon him by the council, were both acting in fulfilment of a programme conceived in the mind of Pope Innocent III. The legal sources provide ample evidence of such a programme, but they offer little guidance to performance. The canon of the council requiring every person to confess at least once a year to his or her parish priest set a new minimum standard and it demanded the provision of a better instructed parish clergy to implement it. The proliferation of schools in the twelfth century and the rise of the universities had created a well-educated *élite*, but had left almost untouched the problem of the unlettered peasant priest living in a predominantly oral society. The English bishops of the thirteenth century wrestled with the problem in a variety of ways. They used diocesan synods to bring home the conciliar canons to their clergy and to train them in the duties of their office. They licensed, or on occasion, commanded individual clergy to attend the schools; some even supplemented these expedients by the provision of humble manuals of pastoral instruction, like the *Templum Domini* composed by Grosseteste and the anonymous *Manuel des péchés* written in Anglo-Norman verse.

Innocent III must be counted among the promoters of a more personal sacramental piety in virtue both of the Lateran Council and also of his own treatise on the Eucharist which influenced later scholastic writers on the subject. But the roots of the great changes in religious sentiment which took place in the twelfth and thirteenth centuries lie much deeper than this. An intense personal devotion to the humanity of Christ and a compassionate regard for the sufferings of the Crucified, expressed alike in ascetical writing, religious art and popular devotion, are the marks of a re-orientation of Western piety which had its origins in the monastic spirituality of the eleventh century. It was largely through the teaching of the Franciscans that in the thirteenth century it emerged from the cloister and became part of the religious experience of the ordinary Christian. The legislative programme formulated by the thirteenth-century popes reflected rather than impelled this profound movement of the spirit. Perhaps the most important contribution made to this development by the papacy was the decision to loose upon the Church the New Mendicant Orders: in England, as elsewhere, the preaching friar reached a public with which the established hierarchy of the Church was still poorly equipped to deal.

We may end with an example of papal activity in which the juridical apparatus of papal government came into most immediate contact with popular devotion, namely the process of canonization. This in many ways epitomized the papal primacy of the thirteenth century. Recourse to Rome for canonization had grown step by step with the advance of the *plenitudo potestatis*; although the canonization of Edward the Confessor by Alexander III in 1161 is the earliest English case, there already existed in England and elsewhere by that date a widespread belief that only the pope could authorize the cultus of a new saint. This claim was expressly formulated by Innocent III in the bull of the year 1200 announcing the canonization of the empress Kunigunde. The canonical collections of Innocent III's pontificate consider it an established axiom that canonization is a judicial act reserved to the papacy, and in 1234 this principle was embodied in the official law books of the Church. With the establishment of papal control came the development of the papal process of canonization. Already in the twelfth century a commission of inquiry had normally preceded the act by which the pope inscribed a person in the catalogue of the saints; by the beginning of our period the regular process is taking shape. In form it is judicial: in response to petitions the pope issues a rescript appointing commissioners, usually three in number, drawn from the local clergy, to collect evidence and interrogate witnesses; these commissioners will draw a procès-verbal of their proceedings, including the depositions of sworn witnesses, and will submit it to the Curia; there it will be examined by a tribunal of one or more cardinals, who will interview the witnesses afresh; if this tribunal pronounces favourably, the pope will lay the matter before the cardinals in consistory; if all are agreed, a day will be fixed on which the pope will pronounce the solemn judicial sentence. In the course of the thirteenth century this final act was, as befitted a supreme act of the *plenitudo potestatis*, clothed with a splendid ceremonial.

The development of the process enables us to glimpse the operation of papal jurisdiction in England in a peculiarly vivid way. In the course of the thirteenth century seven causes were postulated at the Curia by the English Church. Five of these were successful; one, that of Cantilupe, was brought to a successful conclusion in the following century; and in one case, that of Grosseteste, the postulators failed in their efforts to get a commission of inquiry appointed. In these cases we can see the process taking shape according to the new and astringent rules of evidence formulated by the popes of the period. In 1201 the promoters of the cause of St. Gilbert of Sempringham, the earliest process of which we have any details, had their dossier set aside; depositions containing the *ipsissima verba* of witnesses were called for and the prelates were required to send selected witnesses to the Curia for examination. Thus the Curia began to play a more active role in the proceedings; the work of the local commission increasingly came to acquire a preliminary character. The case of St. Edmund of Abingdon illustrates this development. Two commissions of inquiry were set up in 1244 by papal letters, one in France, consisting of the archbishop of Armagh, the bishop of Senlis and the dean of Paris, and one in England, consisting of the bishops of London and Lincoln. The report of both commissions, when submitted to the Curia, was adjudged insufficient, and a fresh inquiry was ordered. In England a new commission was appointed, consisting of Richard Wych, bishop of Chichester and formerly St. Edmund's chancellor, the prior of Canon's Ashby, and the

Dominican Master Robert Bacon, who was also an old associate of St. Edmund. This report reached the Curia, which was then residing at Lyons, in November 1245. Its examination was delegated to a tribunal consisting of three cardinals, the bishops of Lincoln and Cambrai, the canonist Vincentius Hispanus and the theologian Alexander of Hales. Consideration of the case now continued at the Curia for a further year. Witnesses of miraculous cures were with difficulty induced to leave their peasant tenements in England and go to the Curia, where they were summoned to the houses of individual cardinals for interrogation. On the 15th December 1246 the matter was laid by Innocent IV before the cardinals in consistory and the following day, in Lyons cathedral, he proceeded to pronounce the sentence of canonization.

These proceedings, for which parallels could be drawn from other countries, illustrate the participation of the English Church in the most up-to-date developments of papal sovereignty. They show the increasing part played by the Curia, gathering into its hands unique control over the cultus of the saints; they show too, in the litigious form of the process, the dominion of law over an important part of medieval religious experience; most clearly of all, they illustrate the inter-play of different interests at the Curia. The chief promoters of St. Edmund's cause were the Cistercians of Pontigny, to whom he had given his body for burial. They were seconded in their efforts by an energetic English pressure group which had its centre in the household of the dead archbishop. The attitude of the king was negative, but his rich and powerful brother, Earl Richard of Cornwall, was actively interested. The ultimate success of the business was due chiefly to the efforts made at the Curia by the English Cistercian cardinal, John of Toledo.

In the thirteenth century the English Church was incorporated into the huge legal organism which had been brought into being by the doctrine of papal plenitude of power. But this is only one aspect of the medieval Church, even if it is the face most plainly turned to the historian. It was not only the lawyers who thought of Rome as 'the common fatherland of all men'. Men went to plead and found themselves pilgrims. Giraldus, after staying three times at the Curia on business resolved to make his fourth visit a pilgrimage 'to the threshold of the Apostles'. Beyond the jostle of litigants, the cries of the money-changers, and the cosmopolitan babble of the proctors touting for custom in the forecourt of the Lateran, there was the great basilica and palace which recalled a gift made to a pope by the first Christian emperor. In the inner sanctuary of the papal chapel men looked with awe at the weird and venerable relics, the ark of the covenant, the seamless robe of Christ, and the linen with which he dried the feet of the disciples. The pope was the Vicar of Christ and supreme pontiff, the bridge between the temporal order and eternity, and in his house the apparatus of both was strangely mingled and confused.

SELECT BIBLIOGRAPHY

W. Ullman, *The Growth of Papal Government in the Middle ages* 2nd edn (1963)

C. Morris *The Papal Monarchy: The Western Church 1050–1250* (1989)

J.A. Watt, *The Theory of Papal Monarchy in the Thirteenth Century* (1965)

Jane Sayers, *Papal Judges-delegate in the Province of Canterbury 1198–1254* (1971)

——, *Papal Government and England during the pontificate of Honorius III, 1216–17* (1984)

——, 'Proctors representing British interests at the papal court, 1198–1415': *Monumenta Iuris Canonici series C, Subsidia IV* (Vatican City 1971), pp. 143–63

R. Brentano, *York Metropolitan Jurisdiction and Papal Judges-delegate, 1279–96* (Berkeley, California 1959)

A. Paravicini Bagliati, Cardinali di Curia e familie cardinalizie dal 1227 al 1254: *Italia Sacra, Studi e Documenti* 18 (Padua 1972)

G. Barraclough, *Papal Provisions* (1935)

W.E. Lunt, *Financial Relations of the Papacy with England to 1327* (1939)

M. Gibbs & J. Lang, *Bishops and Reform, 1215–72* (1934)

C.R. Cheney, *English Synodalia of the Thirteenth Century* (1941)

E. Kemp, *Canonization and Authority in the Western Church* (1948)

C.H. Lawrence, *The Life of St Edmund by Matthew Paris* (1996)

——, 'The University in State and Church': *The History of the University of Oxford*, vol. I, ed. J. Catto (1984), pp. 97–150

F.M. Powicke, *Stephen Langton* (1928)

R.W. Southern, *Robert Grosseteste, The Growth of an English Mind in Medieval Europe* (1986)

Decima Douie, *Archbishop Pecham* (1952)

N.C. Vincent, *Peter des Roches, An Alien in English Politics, 1205–38* (1996)

THE FOURTEENTH CENTURY

W. A. Pantin

5

THE FOURTEENTH CENTURY

THE fourteenth century saw a remarkable combination of the centralization of the Church on the one hand with well-developed nationalism on the other, and it is the coexistence and interplay of these two factors that make the period so interesting. It is a mistake to think of this as a period of 'decline and fall' for the medieval papacy as an institution, as is sometimes popularly done; if the Avignon popes were undoubtedly weaker than Innocent III at a purely political level, the papacy and the papal Curia in terms of ecclesiastical government and administration were stronger and more highly organized than they had ever been before. At the same time the strength of nationalism showed itself in the power of the English king (as of most other kings) and the way in which he had learnt to get his way in ecclesiastical matters, and national sentiment showed itself in such varied ways as the vernacular writings of the English mystics, the half-mystical, half-political aspirations and anguish of Piers Plowman, and the protests of the Good Parliament against the 'sinful city of Avignon'.

The Avignonese popes enjoyed great power, prestige and splendour, and they were at the head of a great bureaucratic machine, with all the unpopularity that a bureaucracy always engenders; and the costly and luxurious papal court in its exile at Avignon became a source of scandal to many; few popes have been so violently criticized as the later Avignonese popes were by such contemporaries as St. Brigit of Sweden or Petrarch. At the same time, it must be remembered, in contrast, that this was not an age of 'bad popes' and that the Avignonese popes were personally all men of good life; their failings, like the weakness of Clement V or the aggressiveness of John XXII, were political rather than personal; and some of them, like Benedict XII and Urban V, were men of austere and even saintly life. These popes also illustrate how profoundly the rise of the universities had by now affected the Church; it is equally characteristic of the age that all these popes were university graduates, including the three who began life as monks, and that those who were doctors of theology (Benedict XII and Clement VI) were heavily outnumbered by those who were legists (Clement V, John XXII, Innocent VI, Gregory XI and Urban V).

It is worth looking briefly at the personalities of these popes, if we want to understand how they were likely to act and how they would appear to contemporary Englishmen with whom they came into contact. Clement V (1305–14) was the first of the French popes, though he did not reside at Avignon. He and his family have left their mark in the fine castles that they built, in the neighbourhood of Bordeaux; he was a Gascon and therefore in his early career a subject of the English king, and probably of all the fourteenth-century popes he was on the most friendly terms with the English crown. He showed his complaisance towards Edward I by suspending Archbishop Winchelsey, who had been such a valiant champion of the rights of the Church; it was this same weakness which he was to show, even more tragically, in his dealings with Philip the Fair of France. John XXII (1316–34) was a very different person, a good deal more interesting and attractive. He could be vigorous and aggressive, as in his dealings with the Emperor Lewis the Bavarian and the rebel Franciscans. He is not to be dismissed merely as a dry legist and organizer; he was an intellectual, with a well-trained mind, and he saw that theology and law were not abstractions but had practical bearing. He was quick tempered but could show personal charm. He was authoritarian and bold, and he had a taste for controversy without perhaps fully realizing the difficulties involved. It was this that led him into his well-known theological *faux pas* on the subject of the beatific vision; he had however the grace to retract and on occasions he was ready to consult commissions of theologians, among whom some Englishmen served. It was probably just as well that this very masterful pope coincided with the weak king Edward II and with the youthful Edward III, and he shows himself at his best in the letters of friendly and fatherly advice which he sent to these two kings, advising Edward II, for instance, to get up early and avoid imprudent friends and keep on good terms with Thomas of Lancaster; and it was to John XXII that Edward III, when a boy of eighteen and virtually a prisoner of his mother and her paramour, addressed his famous secret letter, explaining that when he had a genuine request to make, he would write the pass-word 'Pater sancte' at the foot of the letter.

Benedict XII (1334–42) is again a contrast; a Cistercian monk and a trained theologian, he was preoccupied with religious and theological matters. He legislated for the reform of the Cistercians, the Black Monks and the Augustinian Canons, and characteristically encouraged the sending of monks to the universities. He tried hard to introduce some austerity into the Curia and to moderate papal provisions; he built the first instalment of the palace of the popes at Avignon, in a style austere enough, but by so doing he firmly anchored the papacy there for another forty years.

Clement VI (1342–52) was another monk and theologian, but again a contrast in personality. He had the tastes, the generosity and the extravagance of a great lord, as is reflected in his splendid additions to the papal palace. He used up the savings of Benedict XII and was more lavish than ever in papal provisions. But he was a man of intellectual prowess as well; he projected a reform of the calendar; he had made a reputation as a teacher at Paris, and the Oxford scholar Walter Burley rededicated to him his commentary on Aristotle's *Politics*, because he had so much admired the style of Clement's lectures. In spite of the accusations of Petrarch and others, he was not an evil liver, but he lacked the deep seriousness of Benedict XII; he left the papacy more Frenchified, more settled at Avignon than ever, and he did much to confirm the general impression of worldliness and extravagance that made the Avignon Curia so unpopular in England as elsewhere. In particular his reign saw the height of opposition to papal provisions in England, the statute of Provisors, and the first English successes in the Hundred Years War. Innocent VI (1352–62) lacked the brilliance of his predecessor, but was capable of taking a strong line; he repudiated an attempt by the cardinals to secure an oligarchical control, he seriously prepared for the return of the papacy to Italy, and he made attempts at reform. But if he spent less on display, he spent more on war in Italy, so he could do little to lessen the unpopularity of the papacy. Urban V (1362–70) was another monk, but more in the manner of Benedict XII than of Clement VI; he was a legist, not a theologian; he was noted for his piety, and five centuries later was beatified. He was a particularly generous patron of students. Urban was interested in reviving the idea of the crusade, and he succeeded in returning to Rome for a short time, though he came home to Avignon to die. Gregory XI (1371–8) was the nephew of Clement VI, whom he resembled in his love of display and in his intellectual liveliness; he was a friend of Petrarch and had humanist tastes. It was he who brought about the permanent return of the papacy to Rome; this was indeed followed by the tragedy of the Great Schism in the papacy, with rival lines of popes in Rome and Avignon, but it at least enabled Englishmen to feel that they now had popes who were no longer living in the pocket of their hereditary enemy, the French king; they could in fact feel a national pride in supporting the legitimate Roman line of popes in contrast to the schismatical French and Scots, and even Wyclif at first welcomed 'our Urban'. The weak position of the popes during the schism was calculated to make them more anxious to please, as is shown by their readiness to translate bishops for political reasons during the ups and downs of Richard II's reign, though a more intransigent line was temporarily taken by both pope and parliament in the years 1388–93, when the statutes of Provisors and Praemunire were re-enacted. On the whole, however, Anglo-papal relations were better at the end than they had been in the middle of the century. The efforts of the later Avignonese popes to return to Rome had been a severe strain on their resources, and this led to financial claims on England—a demand in 1365 for the arrears of tribute due from King John's submission, and a demand in 1372 for a 'charitable subsidy'; these were not surprisingly refused, but there followed negotiations lasting from 1373 to 1377 which led to an abortive attempt at a concordat. Anglo-papal relations throughout the century present a curious mixture of high and intransigent claims with a constant readiness to negotiate.

Finally it should be noted that the later Avignon popes came under the fire and the influence of two great mystics, the Swedish princess St. Brigit and the humble St. Catherine of Siena; both bombarded the papacy and the Christian world with advice and denunciation of abuses. These two mystics represent the admirable capacity for outspoken criticism which is a feature of this century and the remarkable power which women have from time to time wielded in the government of the Church and in spiritual direction. These two women, it may be noted, had ardent followers and admirers among the English; William Flete, an Austin Friar and bachelor of theology from Cambridge, went out to be a disciple of St. Catherine in Italy, and wrote home to his brethren urging reform and loyalty to Pope Urban VI; St. Brigit had a great admirer and defender in the English Benedictine cardinal, Adam Easton; in a later generation, her order was introduced into England by King Henry V as one of his chief contributions to monastic reform; and when a devout woman like Margery Kempe visited Rome as a pilgrim, she made a point of visiting St. Brigit's house and interviewing the maid who had attended on her, some forty years before. Rome had always had two great functions, as a centre of pilgrimage and a centre of Church government, and English pilgrims continued to visit Rome, while the Curia was in exile at Avignon; in 1362 the English Hospice in Rome (later to become the English College) was founded, and from the records of the Hospice have been compiled a list of some English residents in Rome from 1333 onwards, including a number described as rosary-sellers.

Paradoxically, the period of the popes' apparent humiliation during the 'Babylonish captivity' at Avignon was also the period when the papal Curia, and the departments into which it was divided, came to be most highly organized; and this was partly because it was at Avignon that the Curia became for the first time for centuries firmly fixed in one place; it was at Avignon that the papacy found, so to speak, its Westminster or Whitehall. The administration had never before had such splendid accommodation as it had in the palace of the popes at Avignon. In earlier centuries the popes had sometimes been driven out of Italy, and more frequently had moved round between such residences as Rome, Anagni, Orvieto, Viterbo. All royal courts in medieval western Europe were ambulatory, and this must always have entailed some inconvenience; but whereas for a secular ruler there was some compensatory advantage in being able to travel round and visit the different parts of his kingdom in person, for a pope there was no such advantage, since his rule was over a world-wide Church, which had to be governed by correspondence and embassies.

It would be difficult to overestimate the importance and power of the cardinals; they were the pope's councillors, with whom he would discuss all important business in consistory, including canonizations and heresy; the pope might administer justice in conjunction with the cardinals in consistory, or he might depute individual cardinals to act as judges in his stead. The cardinals were all resident in the Curia, for the practice of distributing cardinals' hats to distinguished metropolitans or diocesans did not develop until the fifteenth century, and Simon Langham, for instance, had to give up the see of Canterbury on being made a cardinal in 1368. Compared with the large size of the college of cardinals in modern times, the fourteenth-century cardinals were a very small body, only about twenty or so; and this probably made them all the more powerful as an oligarchy. It is not surprising that the English king set great store by good relations with the cardinals; he would give them pensions, and fiscal privileges; and when he wanted to get something done, such as getting a man promoted to a bishopric or a cardinalate, or having an Englishman canonized, the king would write round to each of the cardinals as well as to the pope. Conversely, the cardinals valued the English king's good opinion. After the election of Pope Urban VI in 1378, which was to prove so controversial, Cardinal Aigrefeuille eagerly asked Adam Easton what the king of England's reaction would be.

About half the cardinals were university graduates, and as with the popes, the lawyers outnumbered the theologians, which was not surprising, in view of their judicial and administrative functions.

The majority of the cardinals created by the fourteenth-century popes came, like the popes themselves, from southern or central France. This worked well enough for English interests at first, for Clement V's cardinals were, like him, Gascons, and so had ties with the English king. Things were more difficult with the development of the Hundred Years War and the predominance of more purely French cardinals; cardinal Elie Talleyrand de Perigord was denounced as England's worst enemy. When there were only about twenty cardinals, one could hardly expect England to be represented by more than one cardinal at a time, yet even this was lacking during most of the century. At the beginning of the century there were indeed appointed three English Dominican cardinals in rapid succession, all holding appropriately enough the title of S. Sabina: William of Macclesfield, created cardinal in 1303; Walter of Winterbourne, cardinal 1304–5; Thomas Jorz, cardinal 1305–10; Winterbourne and Jorz had been confessors to King Edward I. After these there was a gap for over fifty years until Simon Langham, a Benedictine and archbishop of Canterbury, who was made cardinal in 1368 and died in 1376; he was followed by another Benedictine, Adam Easton, who was cardinal from 1381 to 1397.

In addition to the papal household, the Curia was by the fourteenth century divided into several departments: the papal chancery, dealing with the papal letters; the apostolic penitentiary, dealing with such matters as ecclesiastical censures and matrimonial dispensations; the apostolic chamber, dealing with finance; and the administration of justice, done, as has been said, sometimes by the pope in consistory, sometimes by individual cardinals, but also increasingly by a body of judges or auditors of the court known as the tribunal of the Rota. Among the personnel of the Curia in general, as with the cardinals, Frenchmen predominated, though there was a fair proportion still of Italians; as might be expected, Englishmen formed only a minute proportion (about 2%) of the traceable officials, and the majority of these Englishmen (22 out of 24) were concentrated in two departments: the penitentiary (where English-speaking officials would naturally be needed) and the auditors of the Rota (where a knowledge of English conditions, especially in dealing with benefices, would be needed). Some of the English auditors were men of great distinction, like Thomas Fastolf and Simon Sudbury, as will be noted below.

If Englishmen were few among the curial officials, they must have been more in evidence among the throngs of suitors and proctors engaged in litigation or seeking provision to benefices, and the great pillared waiting hall under the chapel of Clement VI in the papal palace must have been all too familiar to them. One would like to know more about these English suitors and proctors, who they were, how they lived, where they lodged. There may be more evidence to be found about them in monastic or other archives, like the letters from Durham which give such a lively picture of litigation at the Curia at the end of the thirteenth century. There survives a very full account of an English embassy sent to Avignon in 1344 to treat with French; this gives us a good view of the papacy acting as an international arbiter and of the discussions and correspondence involved. One of the English envoys, the dean of Lincoln, wrote home describing some uncomfortable interviews he had with Clement VI; the pope complained bitterly of the English king's attacks on the Church's rights and of the ill-treatment of the cardinals' proctors, with historical references to St. Thomas of Canterbury and Innocent III and King John. When the dean pointed out that the English opposition was due to excessive grants made to certain cardinals, and that the pope's remedy was to exercise more restraint, the pope replied that the popular clamour was being craftily engineered by certain persons (including some clerics whose names he had); he had created cardinals up to a certain number, and as it was necessary that they should have their livelihood by the ordinance of the Church, he had apportioned them for their keep among the provinces and kingdoms, and nowhere had he found resistance, save only in England. If the king of France had done against the Church what the king of England had done, the pope would have proceeded against him long ago; but for the pope's zeal for making peace between England and France, he would not have put up with these injuries. It is interesting to see how diplomatic and ecclesiastical issues and negotiations got intertwined.

In general there is an interesting contrast between the constant elements of papal authority and the now fully organized Curia on the one hand, and the changing personalities of the individual popes on the other. One might have expected that the oligarchy of cardinals or the bureaucracy would have the advantage; but I do not think that any fourteenth-century pope was a prisoner of his own Curia, and the marked personal character and policy of the pope made themselves felt in each successive pontificate.

In examining the relations of England and the papacy, one useful line of approach will be to analyse the various functions of the papacy and to see how these affected or were affected by Englishmen or English affairs. First one may ask what was the influence of the papacy in doctrinal and intellectual matters in the fourteenth century? We shall not expect to find the papacy initiating doctrinal speculation or intellectual movements; quite apart from the papacy's long tradition of theological gravity and prudence, the unfortunate example of Pope John XXII putting forward, as a private theologian, his peculiar views about the beatific vision was enough to discourage such incursions into the theological arena. The papacy's role was rather to moderate and where necessary to define, rather like the presiding master in a scholastic disputation. To initiate and develop theological speculation and trends was rather the function of the theological schools—those schools, the absence of which in the nineteenth century John Henry Newman so much deplored. The schools in the fourteenth century meant in practice the universities and to a rather lesser extent the cathedral schools and the schools of friars; all of these were institutions which the papacy had in the past done so much to encourage, so that their scattered and localized activities in the fourteenth century may nevertheless be regarded as the long-term effects of earlier papal policy. In the mass of local disputations and controversy, England had its full share. The methods of the schools naturally bred controversy; the three duties of a doctor or master, *legere, disputare, praedicare*, were all capable of being controversial, and naturally this was specially true of disputation, by its nature. But it was precisely the wealth of constant disputation and controversy that made controversy seem so respectable and harmless.

There were many degrees of intensity in these controversies, ranging from friendly and even routine disputes to serious accusations of error or heresy, which might have to be referred to the archbishop of Canterbury (as with Uthred of Boldon's dispute with the friars over grace and justification) or to the papacy itself (as with William of Occam and Wyclif). A man like Wyclif must have seemed at first just one among a host of controversialists, and this helps to explain why some people at least took so long to see the full danger of his views and why it took so long to get him condemned. When an English Austin, Friar, Adam Stocton, copied into his notebook an anti-papal treatise by Wyclif in 1379, he described the author as *venerabilis doctor*; it was only a year or two later, when Wyclif's eucharistic teaching had become more openly heretical, that he crossed out these words and wrote *execrabilis seductor*. Perhaps also the theological controversies of the age may have been coloured by contemporary litigation; this was a very litigious age, and men were familiar with everlasting and rather inconclusive lawsuits, like those between the monks of Durham and their metropolitan or bishop. Theology and canon law had much in common; papal bulls and canons of councils might deal with both; and when we come to something like Archbishop FitzRalph's quarrel with friars, carried up to the papal Curia, it is rather difficult to say whether it was a canonical dispute about the friars' privileges, or a theological argument about the part to be played by bishops and priests, religious and popes in the life and work of the Church. And like some of the lawsuits, this particular dispute seems to some extent inconclusive; it would be hard to say who really won, though the pope confirmed the friars' privileges.

In view of the great mass of theological controversies in the fourteenth century, it is remarkable that the official pronouncements of the papacy were comparatively few and limited to certain themes, especially if we contrast them with the number and variety of papal encyclicals in modern times. Denzinger-Bannwart's *Enchiridion Symbolorum* lists about a dozen papal pronouncements for the period 1305–78: the condemnation of the errors of the Beguins and Beghards, on the state of perfection, and of the Franciscan Peter John Olivi (at the Council of Vienne, 1311); of the Fraticelli (1317); and of Jean de Pouilly, on confession to the friars (1321); on the doctrine of the poverty of Christ (1323); the condemnation of Marsilius of Padua and John of Jandun, on the constitution and powers of the Church (1327); of the errors of Echard, the German mystic (1329); on the beatific vision, determining the controversy begun by John XXII (1336); the condemnation of the philosophical errors of Nicholas of Autrecourt (1348), and of the Franciscan Denis Foullechat, on poverty (1368). To these may be added what amounted to condemnations of William of Occam (from *c.* 1325) and of John Wyclif (1377). The fourteenth century saw two lines of attack on the classic system of theology and Church government as it had evolved in the thirteenth century: on the one hand there were the open attacks on the authority and powers of the Church, especially in relation to the lay powers, and the growth of what has been called 'l'esprit laïque', of which Marsilius and Wyclif are outstanding examples; on the other hand, there were the deeper and more subtle philosophical and theological movements, of which William of Occam was a prime example, dissolving the thirteenth-century synthesis. Thus the papacy had among its leading opponents two Englishmen, with rather contrasting careers: the Franciscan William of Occam, who spent most of his career abroad, in alliance with the Emperor Lewis the Bavarian; and John Wyclif, an Oxford don supported, for a time at least, by the English government. It will be noted that the papacy in its official pronouncements was quicker to deal with the more practical topics of Church polity like the Franciscan theories of poverty or the attacks of Marsilius than with more speculative philosophical or theological trends.

What was the fourteenth-century papacy doing for the education of the clergy, and how did this affect Englishmen? In the past the universities had owed much to papal encouragement and protection; the first privilege that Oxford University is known to have received came from a papal legate in 1214, and as late as 1318 we find John XXII confirming Cambridge as a *studium generale*. And the universities had been notably successful in producing an ecclesiastical *élite*. Throughout the thirteenth century the papacy had secured the promotion of leading scholastic theologians, like

Langton, Kilwardby, Pecham and Winchelsey, to English bishop-rics. But this policy was not fully sustained in the fourteenth century; we do not get bigger and better schoolmen in English sees. For one thing, John XXII, himself a canonist, generally preferred canonists to theologians, and provided six lawyer bishops to English sees between 1317 and 1325. More important still, the English kings and popes came to a practical arrangement about filling English sees, and this made for a predominance of royal servants and administrators. It must be remembered that an increasing proportion of these administrators were graduates as well, and if they were not exactly 'men with fire in their belly', some of them made excellent diocesans, like Archbishop Islip at Canterbury or Archbishop Thoresby at York. We cannot altogether blame pope and king for playing for safety with well-educated administrators. A fire-eating theologian like Richard FitzRalph, the hammer of the friars, seems attractive to the his-torian of ideas, but he would have made an embarrassing arch-bishop of Canterbury.

Apart from promotion to bishoprics, however, the papacy was an important patron of English scholars. This is shown by the rolls of deserving scholars sent up by the universities to the pope, and by the universities' protests, later, against the restriction of papal provisions. An English friend at the Roman Curia, writing to John Lutterel, chancellor of Oxford, c. 1317–22, urged him to come out to the Curia if he wanted preferment; he would find favour not only with Pope John XXII, but with the king of Sicily, a lay connoisseur of theology; if Lutterel made a couple of disputations in the Curia, in some good matter of theology, well planned and thought out, he would carry off more profit and honour than he ever got from all his acts in the schools. The Roman Curia was important to English scholars not only as a source of patronage, but also as an intellectual centre and a meet-ing place for men and ideas. This can be illustrated from the careers of several English scholars. The Dominican Nicholas Trevet (c. 1258–1328) was commissioned to write a commentary on Seneca's tragedies by a fellow Dominican, Cardinal Nicholas of Prato, who had already read and appreciated Trevet's commentary on Boethius; a few years later Trevet was commissioned by Pope John XXII himself to write a commentary on Livy. These men wanted someone to make the classics intelligible to busy but interested administrators who were already feeling the first ripples of humanism at Avignon, at a time when Petrarch was still a boy. Trevet's connection with the Curia is the more remarkable since there seems no evidence that he ever visited Avignon himself, though he studied at Oxford and Paris; it was perhaps at Oxford that he met Cardinal Nicholas of Prato. Thomas Waleys (d. *c.* 1349) is a dramatic example of both the opportunities and dangers of a connection with the Curia. After an Oxford career he was sent to the Curia in 1318, probably to represent his order in their struggle with the university of Oxford; here he may have got to know Cardinal Nicholas de Prato. After another spell at Oxford, he was sent to lecture at the Dominican *studium* at Bologna, and by 1333 we find him as chaplain to another Dominican cardinal, Matteo Orsini, at Avignon. Waleys would have found himself on the side of the pope in his struggle with the Franciscan extremists. But it was just at this time that John XXII put forward his view that the blessed would not enjoy the beatific vision until the day of judgement. The theologians were divided; Waleys attacked the pope's view, and in a sensational sermon denounced the pope's supporters as flatterers actuated by the hope of gain: their favourite text was *Fiat, Fiat*— the formula used for the papal grant of a benefice. Waleys was charged with heresy, not indeed in the matter of the beatific vision, but on other points, and kept in prison probably till 1342. The disturbing part of this story is not that Waleys' quick temper should have got him into trouble, but that his enemies should have kept him in prison long after the opposition to John XXII had been vindicated by Benedict XII's bull on the beatific vision. After his release, Waleys found another patron in Theobald Orsini, archbishop of Palermo, a cousin of his former cardinal-protector; and finally in 1349 we find Waleys old and paralysed, being looked after by a friend, whom he petitions the pope to provide to a benefice in Wiltshire. Richard FitzRalph, Dean of Lichfield, and Archbishop of Armagh, was another visitor to the

Curia who, coming on business, repeatedly found intellectual stimulus there. He first visited the Curia in 1334–5, at the height of the controversy over the beatific vision, and was consulted by the dying pope John XXII and probably by his successor—a surprisingly large number of Englishmen appear on theological commissions at the Curia at this time. He next visited the Curia from 1337 to 1344 to represent the chapter of Lichfield; it was then that he underwent a conversion from philosophy to theology, and it was then too that he was commissioned by the pope to write his great *summa* explaining the Catholic faith to the Armenian envoys—thus an Anglo-Irish schoolman becomes linked up with negotiations in the East for reunion with Rome. These negotiations were part of the remarkable process by which the East was being opened up to Europe in the late thirteenth and fourteenth centuries. FitzRalph was again at the Curia *c.* 1349–51, representing the king of England; this time, in company with a Dalmatian archbishop, he became involved in controversy with the friars, a controversy which lasted the rest of his life, caused him to write his great treatise *De pauperie Salvatoris*, and brought him again to Avignon to spend his last years defending himself against the friars. FitzRalph's story shows the extraordinary number of lines that crossed at the Curia: Ireland, England, Dalmatia, the Armenians and the friars.

Yet another example is the Benedictine monk scholar from Norwich, Adam Easton (*c.* 1325–97). After a distinguished career at Oxford, Easton went to the Curia, apparently as *socius* to another Benedictine, Simon Langham, newly created cardinal, in 1369. He acted as proctor at the Curia for the English Benedictines, and it was probably he who was responsible for getting Wyclif condemned by the pope in 1377; he must have been one of the few Englishmen to know the political writings of Dante, Marsilius and John of Jandun, and he saw at once Wyclif's unconscious resemblance to Marsilius's attacks. If the Curia could sometimes be cautious and slow to condemn, here was a case where it could be perspicacious and act quickly. In 1381 Easton was made cardinal by Urban VI, perhaps as a reward for writing his *Defensorium ecclesiastice potestatis*. This vast work, of which only a fragment survives, was an elaborate defence of the highest claims for papal and ecclesiastical superiority; it was dedicated to Urban VI as 'monarch of the world'. In order to prepare for this work, Easton had taken up the study of the Old Testament, and this in turn entailed learning Hebrew from a Jewish scholar, an interesting sideline for an official at the Curia. Among Easton's other interests was the enthusiastic support of St. Brigit, the Swedish mystic who had come to the Curia and pressed so hard for reform; here again residence at the Curia opened up unexpected vistas. Like Waleys, Easton experienced the dangers as well as the rewards of the Curia; he was one of the cardinals imprisoned and tortured by the suspicious Urban VI, but was reinstated in 1389, and enjoyed a wide range of benefices, being among other things Archdeacon of Shetland, Provost of Beverley and Precentor of Lisbon. His tomb in his titular church of St. Cecilia in Trastevere, proudly displaying the leopards and lilies of England and France, is one of the loveliest memorials of Anglo-Roman relations.

So far we have been considering the education of an ecclesiastical *élite*. What was the papacy able to do to help the education of the rank and file of the clergy? How to provide a sufficient number of people with a sufficient amount of education has always been a pressing problem and is (*mutatis mutandis*) a very pressing one today. Setting up chairs of Hebrew, Arabic and Chaldee at Paris, Oxford, Bologna and Salamanca, as ordered by the Council of Vienne, was excellent for missionary purposes, but would not be much help to the ordinary parish priest. In pre-Carolingian days clerics had been trained in the bishops' households; in post-Tridentine times they have been trained in seminaries. The Middle Ages never really solved the problem of the mass training of the clergy; that was the reason for the chronic ignorance and indiscipline that was so often found among the clergy. The universities, which, as has been said, owed so much to papal encouragement, represented one possible, partial solution to the problem, but only in so far as they could be made accessible to a sufficiently large number of clergy. This brings one to another perennial (and still topical) problem, how to provide for the maintenance of scholars at the schools. One solution was of course for scholars to be maintained by their parents or friends or patrons (who were often bishops or abbots); about this medieval students' letters have much to say, like the splendid series of letters from the scholars maintained by Henry of Eastry, prior of Christ Church, Canterbury, at Oxford, Paris, Bologna and Orleans; and it was out of this maintenance of scholars by patrons that the colleges of Oxford and Cambridge may be said to have developed. The other alternative was for a scholar to maintain himself at the schools by holding a benefice. This was how some of the most eminent and respectable schoolmen supported themselves, and it was also how some less eminent and less respectable scholars lived; the two scholars whose alleged riotous behaviour sparked off the massacre of St. Scolastica's day at Oxford in 1355 were both beneficed clergymen, rectors of west country churches. The system could support the just and the unjust, as always at the universities; *sinite utraque crescere*. But was it right that even a respectable beneficed scholar should be away at the schools and leave his sheep encumbered in the mire? Two important principles of Church reform thus got across each other: the drive for more clerical education and the drive against non-residence and pluralism. Papal decrees against non-residence such as the decree *Licet canon* of 1274 were making it more difficult for beneficed clergy to go to the schools. It was here that Pope Boniface VIII came to the rescue with the constitution *Cum ex eo* in 1298, which had a profound effect on clerical education in the fourteenth century. Pope Boniface pointed out that existing legislation was discouraging able young men without private means from taking benefices, at a time when the Church most needed learned men; he therefore gave all bishops the power to dispense beneficed clergymen from the obligation to take priest's orders and reside on their cures, for a period of up to seven years, for the purpose of study, provided that they committed themselves to a clerical career by taking subdeacon's orders and provided a deputy to do their parish work. The effect of this constitution can be seen in fourteenth-century English bishops' registers, where incumbents are given leave of absence for study at the rate of up to twenty a year per diocese, and a bishop's zeal for the education of his clergy can be measured by the number of such dispensations he grants. The constitution *Cum ex eo* was an intelligent and generous measure, but it was nevertheless limited in its effect. On the one hand it could only benefit those clerics who were fortunate enough to have benefices; it could do nothing to help the vast clerical proletariate of unbeneficed, stipendiary priests who in fact did most of the Church's pastoral work. And on the other hand, it may be wondered how far the university education it made available was really suitable for practical purposes for parish priests. Seven years would enable a scholar to complete the arts course, and absorb a great deal of Aristotle, but it would only bring him to the threshold of the theological course. With the best will in the world, the medieval university could not really be made to provide the strictly vocational training that a seminary gives.

Another way in which the papacy affected the English Church was in its legal and judicial function, as the apex of the system of canon law. Freedom of appeals to Rome, free application of canon law to England: these points had been the great issue in the twelfth century in the struggle between Henry II and St. Thomas. They had long been conceded in general principle, and no one denied that the English Church was part of a universal system of canon law; such checks as there were on the working of canon law, such as writs prohibiting Church courts from dealing with advowsons, or the statute of Praemunire, came from the lay power, not from English churchmen. In the classical period of the canon law, English ecclesiastics, by the cases they submitted to Rome and the questions they asked, had played a very large part in the making of law. How far can England be said to have continued to play its part in the manufacture of canon law in the fourteenth century, when papal centralization and papal jurisdiction may be said to have been at their height? This is not easy to answer. By 1234 the classic period of the production of canon law was over. The publications that followed, the Sext, published by Boniface VIII in 1298, the Clementines, published by Clement V, 1314–17, the Extravagants of John XXII, and the *Extravagantes communes*, seem to be based now less on particular cases than on general constitutions issued by the popes, either by themselves or in the general councils of Lyons (1245 and 1274) and of Vienne (1311); so we have less chance of tracing English influence. There is, however, one good example of the old method of basing a general law on a particular *cause célèbre*, at the beginning of the century. The monks of Durham claimed that when their bishop wanted to make a visitation of their community, he must come unaccompanied by any secular clerks, and they engaged in an expensive lawsuit over this point with their masterful bishop, Antony Bek, at the Roman Curia. Boniface VIII gave his decision in 1302, in the constitution *Debent*, which was afterwards embodied in the law book *Extravagantes communes*; he ruled that while the monks' objection to clerks accompanying the bishop was indeed based on custom, it was nevertheless unreasonable and against the public utility, and should therefore be overruled.

Another source of canon law which was coming into being in the fourteenth century was the decisions made by the auditors of the court of the Rota at the papal Curia. Several collections of these decisions were published at various dates between 1336 and 1381, and it is interesting to notice that the first of these collections was edited by an English canonist, Thomas Fastolf, member of the well-known Norfolk family, auditor of the Rota *c.* 1340-8, and afterwards bishop of St. David's, 1352-61. Some of these decisions were based on real cases, including a few English ones, but many seem to be discussions of hypothetical cases by the judges. On the whole the English do not seem to have made a great contribution to canon law in the fourteenth century; there were many Englishmen who graduated and practised in canon law, but few of them wrote on the subject, and the English commentaries that survive are on the whole rather derivative or jejune. There are a few exceptions, particularly those canonists who wrote on subjects where canon law and pastoral theology overlapped, such as William of Pagula, who wrote the well-known treatise *Oculus sacerdotis* (*c.* 1319-23) and probably did more for the education of the clergy than any professed theologian of the period, and the anonymous author of the *Memoriale presbiterorum*, a manual for confessors

containing a remarkable analysis of the sins of all classes of contemporary society; this is said to have been written by an English
canonist at Avignon in 1344 and may have been the work of a
man like Fastolf.

English lawsuits might come to the Roman Curia in two ways;
they might come by way of appeal from lower courts; or alternatively any case might be brought to Rome in the first instance,
by reason of the pope's jurisdiction as 'universal ordinary'. When
a case was referred to Rome, it had often been the practice for the
pope to appoint as judges delegate local ecclesiastics (generally
three in number), who would decide the case on the spot, from
local evidence, in the pope's name; the *plenitudo potestatis* was thus
delivered on one's doorstep, and interminable and expensive delays at the Curia were (in theory) avoided. This procedure was
very popular from the late twelfth century until the beginning of
the fourteenth century at least; the Oseney cartulary, for instance,
records about fifty such cases in a hundred years. But in the fourteenth century there seems to be some falling off in the use of local
judges delegate; it may be that cases get recorded less frequently
in documents or chronicles, but I think there may have been a real
falling off, for one or two reasons. In the first place, the procedure
did not in practice prove necessarily quicker or cheaper; it might
involve endless sending back and forwards of messengers, proctors
and evidences; half the battle was getting favourable judges appointed; and it might be quicker to get a good auditor in the Curia
and have the case heard there. That for instance seems to have
been the experience of the prior of Durham in his legal battle with
the archbishop of York at the end of the thirteenth century. We
can still read the prior's anguished outbursts in his correspondence
with his proctors at Rome: 'cases in the court of Rome are like
things immortal and only with difficulty come to any effective
end. . . . And for the passion of Jesus Christ, act so circumspectly
that we may have at least two judges in whom we can have confidence in these matters. And please bear in mind how the dean of
Lincoln deceived you and us.' Secondly, besides this dissatisfaction with the use of delegates, there was probably by the fourteenth century an improvement in procedure at the Curia, in the

expediting of causes. While centralization was maintained, in fact there was devolution of the actual work of hearing and judging. Innocent III had heard cases in person, and law-students found going to hear his judgements better than attending lectures in the schools. Since then judicial work had been increasingly delegated, first to cardinals, and then to the 'auditors of the sacred palace' or auditors of the court of the Rota, who became a properly constituted body of judges in the Avignon period. The auditors of the Rota, as we have seen, were one of the few departments of the Curia where Englishmen were to be found in appreciable numbers; the auditors were all important and experienced men, and several of the English auditors were promoted to bishoprics, like William Bateman, Thomas Fastolf, and Simon Sudbury (who became archbishop of Canterbury). It is significant that two of the best documented lawsuits of our period, that between the monks of Canterbury and John Wyclif and others, over the possession of Canterbury College, Oxford, and that between Thomas Sotheran and Cockersand Abbey, over the church of Mitton (1369-70), were both heard in the Curia itself and not by local judges delegate; and both seem to have been regarded as sufficiently important to be heard by cardinals rather than by auditors of the Rota; this is not surprising in the Canterbury College case, since it involved among other people Simon Langham, himself a cardinal at the Curia. Another possible contributory factor in the decline of judges delegate may have been an improvement in local ecclesiastical courts in England. English bishops who had served as auditors in the Roman Curia may well have raised the standard of procedure at home; and several successive archbishops of Canterbury made elaborate rules for the guidance of the Court of Arches.

What were the relations between the papacy and the religious orders in England? The relationship was naturally most direct with the orders that were most highly centralized, that is to say with the Mendicant Friars. The papacy had from the first welcomed the friars as an instrument of reform and improved pastoral work in the Church, and therefore protected the friars when they came into conflict with other bodies. Thus Boniface VIII in his bull *Super cathedram* in 1300 made a statesmanlike settlement between the friars and the secular clergy, which allowed the friars to preach in their own churches and elsewhere by invitation and allowed panels of friars licensed in each diocese by the bishops to hear confessions. In 1321 John XXII condemned Jean de Pouilly's attack on the right of the friars to hear confessions; and in the great controversy between Richard FitzRalph and the friars, *c.* 1350–60, the pope finally upheld the friars' privileges. Similarly in the struggle between the friars and the universities of Oxford (*c.* 1303–20) and of Cambridge (*c.* 1303–6) the papacy secured a reasonable settlement in favour of the friars.

The Franciscans presented a peculiarly difficult and stormy problem. There was the century-old controversy within the order between the 'spirituals', with a more extreme interpretation of poverty, and the 'conventuals' or moderates. The papacy, which was interested in seeing the friars function as a body of well-organized, well-educated evangelists, had ever since 1245 allowed a compromise by which the property of the Franciscan order was vested in the papacy as a kind of trustee. With characteristic ruthlessness John XXII who had protected the pastoral rights of the friars against Jean de Pouilly rejected this compromise in two bulls, *Ad conditorem canonum* (1322) and *Cum inter nonnullos* (1323); he renounced the papal ownership of the Franciscans' property, and condemned as heretical the doctrine that Christ and the apostles had owned no property. This caused a split in the order, and the minister general of the order, Michael of Cesena, went over and joined the pope's enemy, the Emperor Lewis the Bavarian in 1328. The English Franciscans, who had a tradition of strict observance without being extremist, seem to have been less disturbed than those on the Continent; they produced some pamphleteers on both sides, but most English Franciscans accepted the pope's ruling, and it is interesting to find an Italian Franciscan regent master at Oxford, Ludovico de Castiglione, *c.* 1344 lecturing in support of John XXII, while testifying to the virtues of the rebel Michael of Cesena, and he performed this with the approval of the whole university, so we are told by one of his disciples. The pope had indeed ordered his agent in England to distribute copies of his

writings against Michael of Cesena to the bishops and the universities. But there was one English Franciscan who went over to the
pope's enemies, with momentous results, namely William of
Occam. Occam, who had been summoned to Avignon to answer
for his alleged philosophical and theological errors, escaped from
the city in June 1328, in company with Michael of Cesena, and
joined the emperor; in his later writings Occam was to become
probably the most dangerous opponent, next to Marsilius and
Wyclif, that the fourteenth-century papacy had to face. This was
a remarkable and unforeseen result of John XXII's intervention in
the poverty controversy.

   With the older religious orders such as the Black Monks (the
older type of Benedictines, as distinct from the Cistercians) and
the Augustinian canons, the problem facing the papacy and the
orders themselves was very different; not one of excess of zeal but
of endemic inertia. In particular two major problems had become
evident in the thirteenth century and were still being wrestled
with in the fourteenth century, and on both the papacy had
something important to say. In the first place both the Black
Monks and the Augustinian canons, who between them accounted
for such a large number of houses in England, including the most
wealthy and illustrious ones, had originally not been an order at
all, but a collection of isolated, disconnected houses which happened to follow the same rule, and temporary attempts at unity
and uniformity, as under St. Dunstan or Lanfranc, had tended to
evaporate in time. By a stroke of genius Innocent III in the Lateran
Council of 1215 had imposed upon the Black Monks and Augus-
tinians a federal solution, similar to that already evolved by the
Cistercians; while the essential autonomy of each community was
maintained, the houses were controlled by attendance every three
years at a general chapter of each province, which made legislation
and appointed visitors. Monasteries were thus subject to a double
set of visitations, by the bishops (unless they had exemption) and
by the visitors from the general chapter. Everything of course
depended on the vigour with which this system was carried out. It
would seem that the general chapters were more successful among
the Black Monks in England than in most countries. During the

late thirteenth century, and especially *c.* 1277–9, the general chapter of the Canterbury province carried through some important reforms, such as a pruning of the time devoted to the liturgy in favour of more study, and the setting up of a common house of studies for their monks at Oxford; in the latter case in particular it was no small feat to secure the collaboration of some fifty or sixty independent-minded prelates. But this achievement seems almost to have exhausted the energies of the order. In the early fourteenth century attendance at the chapters became extremely bad; in June 1319 the presidents were in despair and threatened to give up holding chapters and to write explaining their action and its reason to the pope, John XXII, who, they added, had for some time been watching the order and himself intended to carry out the reform which they were neglecting. It is interesting to note that the energetic John XXII seems to have intended the monastic reform that was in fact carried out by his successor Benedict XII; no doubt Pope John was diverted from this by the spate of controversies connected with Franciscan poverty, the beatific vision and the Emperor which occupied his later years. The other big problem facing the older orders was the rise of the universities and of scholastic theology, both external phenomena which threatened to leave the monasteries in an intellectual backwater. It was to prevent this isolation that the monasteries started sending monks to study at Oxford and imported or trained lecturers to teach arts and theology to the monks in the cloister; this practice was well established at least in some of the English monasteries by the early fourteenth century.

In 1336 Pope Benedict XII, himself a Cistercian, issued his bull *Summi magistri*, later known as the Benedictine constitutions, for the reform of the Black Monks. This overhauled the existing system of general chapters; in England there was now to be a single chapter for the whole country instead of one for the province of Canterbury and one for the province of York (which only contained four Black Monk houses); and above all the constitution made it obligatory for all monasteries to provide claustral lecturers and to send one in twenty of their monks to the university. In other words Benedict XII made obligatory throughout the order the system which the English Black monks had in fact been practising voluntarily for over half a century; this is characteristic of the way in which papal legislation was so often based on well-tried experience. The general chapters had been faltering, as we have seen, and Benedict XII put new life into them; the general chapters and their visitations continued to function regularly right down to the dissolution of the monasteries. The effectiveness of the system naturally depended on the vigour of the men working it. It was perhaps at its most effective when the authority of the general chapter could be backed by the king, in his capacity of patron of the chief monasteries, as when Abbot Thomas de la Mare of St. Albans visited Eynsham, Abingdon, Battle, Reading and Chester, *c.* 1362–6, while at the same time (1366) Uthred of Boldon, the notable monk scholar of Durham, was visiting the collapsed monastery of Whitby; this seemed to be the best way of putting the fear of God into corrupt or incompetent superiors. The connection of the monasteries with the universities, which Benedict XII had the good sense to take up and enforce, was enormously important for the Black Monks, as well as for the Augustinian Canons and the Cistercians, throughout the later Middle Ages; if it did not produce great schoolmen of the same intellectual stature as those that the friars produced, it did train an *élite*, the monk-graduates, who came to play a leading part in the government of their houses and of the general chapters. The years that such men spent together at Oxford or Cambridge (as we know from surviving correspondence), as well as in the work of the chapters, must have done something to break down parochialism and create a common spirit in the order.

Finally, there was one tragic and deplorable way in which the papacy made an impact on the religious orders, namely when Clement V, a sick man, under great pressure from King Philip the Fair of France, suppressed the Templars in 1312; there could not be a better illustration of the fact that the chief fault of the later medieval papacy lay not in its intransigence but its compliance. The English Templars were apprehended in 1308, and although the use of torture was theoretically authorized in their trial, the northern prelates at least protested against this, and England was spared the revolting cruelties that accompanied the suppression in France. The Templars' property went to the Hospitallers, though Edward II and his queen managed to have their cut.

I have left to the last the most prominent feature of Anglo-papal relations—the disposal of benefices, great and small, from bishoprics downwards. It is this that looms largest in the calendars of papal registers, sometimes accounting for about two thirds of the documents recorded; and the prolonged dispute between the English crown and the papacy over papal provisions is undoubtedly the best known episode in Anglo-papal relations in the fourteenth century. That this should be so may seem at first sight to suggest the prevalence of a cynical attitude; but it would be unfair to infer that fourteenth-century men were so preoccupied—to quote Chesterton's poem—with 'the pews and steeples And the cash that goes therewith' that they had no time for the 'souls of Christian peoples'. In the nature of things administrative machinery and records are mainly concerned with tangible legal rights and financial interests. Moreover, one cannot measure the effect of documents quantitatively, as through a computer; a single papal document like the constitution *Cum ex eo* about the education of the clergy, or the constitution of Benedict XII for the reform of the Black Monks must have had more effect than thousands of letters about benefices.

In order to understand the impact of papal policy on benefices, one has to bear in mind two important factors. One was the widespread exploitation of all classes of benefices, from bishoprics and cathedral dignities down to parish churches, for purposes not directly connected with the cure of souls. The Church was the largest property owner in the country, and some benefices were often richly endowed; hence it seemed to almost everyone that if one could hire a deputy to do the necessary pastoral work cheaply, it was reasonable to siphon off the superfluous revenues of a benefice to support some important person in the service of Church or State, or some deserving institution like a monastery or a college. Pluralism and non-residence were thus erected into a system. Bishop Grosseteste in the thirteenth century had been one of the very few people to put the cure of souls first and to object totally to this exploitation of benefices, but if few were prepared to go as far as this, there was at least a desire to regulate and control the system and make it less irresponsible. We have already seen how a papal decree against non-residence in 1274 was sufficiently effective to come into conflict with the encouragement of study at the universities. Three fourteenth-century popes issued decrees against pluralism, Clement V (1305-14), John XXII in 1317 and Urban V in 1366. John XXII in his decree *Execrabilis* laid down that in future no one (except cardinals and king's sons) should hold more than two benefices, one with cure of souls, one without, under pain of forfeiture; and since the forfeited benefices lapsed to the pope, there was a strong motive for enforcing the law, which, as Maitland pointed out, was enforced by the royal courts (to the king's advantage) as well as by the ecclesiastical courts. Although some dispensations still continued, there was between the mid-thirteenth century and the mid-fourteenth century a real improvement in the control and rationalization of pluralism, in which papal legislation played an important part. This improvement can be illustrated from the careers of three clerics who successively owned the large house in Oxford called La Oriole which was afterwards occupied by Oriel College. The first owner was Bogo of Clare, a younger son of the Earl of Gloucester, who died in 1294. In 1272 he was reported to be holding thirty benefices (most of them with cure of souls) without adequate dispensation, and although he had spent some years studying at Oxford, there is no evidence that he ever performed any useful function in Church or State; he represents the extreme form of uncontrolled, irresponsible pluralism. The next owner was James of Spain, an illegitimate son of King Alfonso X of Castile and a nephew of Queen Eleanor, wife of Edward I; he died in 1331. A graduate by 1292, he collected a good many benefices, and by 1300 held six prebends in various cathedral and collegiate churches, but only two rectories; and he was for years a clerk in the king's service, employed in the exchequer and the king's chamber. Thus while he clearly owed his advancement to his royal blood, her performed some useful functions, and only held two benefices with cure of souls. The third owner was Adam de Brome, who died in 1332. He held six rectories (in succession, not concurrently), an archdeaconry and two hospitals; he was a very active and successful king's clerk, serving mainly in the chancery; and he was the virtual founder and first head of Oriel College, to which he secured the appropriation of one of his rectories (St. Mary's, Oxford) and one of his hospitals. He represents a type that appears repeatedly in medieval English academic history—the successful royal servant who exploits his position to further the cause of learning, and he represents pluralism in its most rational and respectable form. A generation or two later, a return of pluralists throughout England in 1366 tells much the same story of controlled and rationalized pluralism. In the diocese of London, for instance, there were 169 pluralists, but a third of their combined wealth was held by three outstanding pluralists; two royal servants, the great William of Wykeham (holding an archdeaconry and ten prebends) and David of Wollore; and a papal envoy, Hugo Pellegrini. At the same time, a large number of the pluralists were in fact comparatively poor men, trying to make both ends meet with two or three small benefices.

Thus the papacy at least helped to control this system of the exploitation of benefices, and it was perhaps asking too much that it should abolish the system altogether. One cannot help sympathizing with the dilemma that faced medieval kings, popes and bishops; they had to provide for their servants, and this must have seemed the only way. Nevertheless it was not a wholly honest or equitable system. On the one hand, it meant a wholesale raiding of Church endowments for secular purposes; a man like William of Wykeham was really a civil servant disguised in clerical dress in order to draw a clerical income; and his vast wealth and power indicated not the Church's strength but her weakness and subservience to the state. And on the other hand, the system kept up the division of the Church into 'two nations': an *élite*—admittedly more a meritocracy than an aristocracy—which took all the spoils, and a clerical proletariate which did the bulk of the work. In this as in other matters the papacy was too ready to compromise, though it did do something to mitigate the evils.

The other factor to be borne in mind is the system of patronage which pervaded the Church at every level. All parochial benefices were in the gift of patrons, either secular lords, from the king down to the local squires, or bishops or abbots. Prebends in cathedral churches were in the gift of the bishops. The bishops themselves, though in theory elected by their cathedral chapters, were, as we shall see, usually in fact nominated by the king or the pope or by both. Only the superiors of religious houses remained truly elective. Patronage affected the unbeneficed clergy also; the army of stipendiary priests who in fact did so much of the pastoral work of the Church were the employees either of the incumbents whom they assisted or for whom they deputized, or of the local lords whose domestic chapels they served. Everyone therefore who wanted promotion or even the merest foothold in the Church had to attach himself to some master. Conversely, all lords were anxious to use the maximum amount of patronage to promote their dependants; the king used the patronage of vacant bishoprics and abbeys; the king and other lords were constantly bombarding the pope or other ecclesiastical patrons to promote their protégés. Nothing could illustrate better the strength of patronage and the respect for vested interests than the career of John Wyclif; though accused of heresy by the English bishops, by the university of Oxford and by the papacy, he none the less remained until his dying day not only unpunished but in possession of his benefice, the parish priest from whom the parishioners of Lutterworth were in theory, one supposes, bound to receive the sacraments every Easter (though we know that in fact he employed a curate) and this mainly because he had once enjoyed the patronage of the king and the Duke of Lancaster.

These two factors, the exploitation of benefices and the exercise of patronage, are important if we are to understand the effect of papal provisions, which involved the clash of two rival systems of patronage and exploitation, papal and royal or local, though it must be remembered that the same man might owe his promotion at one stage to the king, at another stage to the pope. Papal provision was essentially the centralization of ecclesiastical appointments in the hands of the pope, analogous to the centralization of ecclesiastical justice. By the fourteenth century the theory and practice of papal provisions had been worked out thoroughly. In theory the pope had the right to dispose of all benefices throughout the Church. In practice the pope exercised the right over certain categories of benefice. Thus if a man died at the Roman Curia, or was promoted to a higher office by the pope, the pope had the disposal of all the benefices thus vacated. This could mean that a valuable benefice could be almost permanently earmarked for a succession of papal provisors. In practice too the pope was careful not to interfere with the rights of lay patrons. But since the king not only used his own patronage, but claimed to use the patronage of vacant bishoprics and abbeys by the so-called 'regalian right', this often brought him into conflict with the papacy.

The system of papal provisions is commonly thought of as filling English benefices with foreigners. But it is important to remember that a papal 'provisor', that is to say some one provided to a benefice by the pope, could be either an Englishman or a foreigner, and that the overwhelming majority of papal provisors were in fact Englishmen, even when papal provisions were at their height, as under John XXII and Clement VI. Alien provisors were unpopular, not because they were numerous, but because a few of them, notably the cardinals, tended to monopolize some of the most valuable benefices. As one might expect, the cardinals and curial officials benefited by papal provision, and these would be mostly foreigners. There were two classes of Englishmen who benefited by papal provisions: royal officials and university graduates. As we have seen, the universities sent up long lists of requests to the pope: and one of the disappointments in John Wyclif's life was when, instead of receiving provision to a prebend in the great cathedral chapter of Lincoln, he only received a small prebend in a very minor collegiate church at Westbury near Bristol.

Of all the various types of office or benefice in the English Church, it was the bishoprics that were most completely affected by papal provision. In theory, bishops were canonically and freely elected by their cathedral chapters, but in spite of King John's grant of free elections, there had always been a good deal of royal pressure in bishop's elections, which the need for a *congé d'elire* and royal confirmation made easy; and there had been some examples of papal provision of bishops in the thirteenth century, and also disputed elections which had to be referred to Rome. Even such a strong king as Edward I had been unable to get his chancellor Robert Burnell made archbishop of Canterbury and had to accept a papal nominee, the Franciscan John Pecham, instead. In the early fourteenth century, bishops were still sometimes elected by their chapters, but royal and papal pressure steadily increased, and there was sometimes a trial of strength between the two. Sometimes the king got his man appointed, sometimes the pope, the honours being about equally divided; but when the weak king Edward II overlapped with the strong pope John XXII, it was not unnaturally the pope's will that tended to predominate. It was in the course of the reign of Edward III that pope and king settled down to a working compromise that lasted till the Reformation; by this in effect the pope provided the bishop, who was generally the man that the king asked for. Bishop Trillek of Hereford (1344) seems to have been the last bishop not provided to his see by the pope. The courtly pope Clement VI is reported to have said that if the king of England asked him to make an ass a bishop, he would do so. On the other hand, his successors Innocent VI and Urban V sometimes demurred at the king's nominees for their lack of learning—one of them, Robert Stretton, the Black Prince's nominee for Lichfield in 1360, was twice examined and twice 'ploughed', once at Avignon and once in England, and Edward III had great difficulty in getting through the appointment of William of Wykeham to Winchester. But even in such cases the king got his way in the end. About a quarter of the bishops under Edward III had served the king in some capacity, either in administrative departments or as royal envoys and so forth. The climax of papal complaisance came in the reign of Richard II, when the pope (weakened by the Schism) duly promoted or demoted bishops for political reasons at the request of whichever party, the Appellants or the king, happened to be in power. In general then the system of papal provision to bishoprics worked well for the king; perhaps only too well, for the papacy may be thought to have missed the opportunity of providing outstanding men like Pecham or Kilwardby, though, as has been pointed out, the royal administrators sometimes made good bishops. It is perhaps hardly necessary to point out that papal provision did not mean that English bishoprics were filled with aliens; there were only two foreigners appointed to English bishoprics in this century, both in the reign of Edward II: Lewis de Beaumont, a relative of the king, to Durham in 1318, and Rigaud d'Assier, a papal collector, to Winchester in 1320.

It was the cathedral chapters, with their deaneries and other dignities, archdeaconries and prebends, that provided what Maitland has described as 'the staple commodity of the papal market'. These were particularly suitable for papal provision; many of them, especially in the three great chapters of Salisbury, Lincoln and York, were extremely lucrative; canonries were held to involve no cure of souls, and only a minority of canons were expected to reside. Cathedral chapters were therefore very heavily affected by papal provisions, including the provision of cardinals and other aliens. At Lincoln the archdeaconries of Oxford, Buckingham and Leicester were held by aliens for two thirds of the time between 1300 and 1370. At Salisbury in 1320–1 fourteen out of twenty-nine non-resident canons were foreigners. Many of these foreign beneficiaries were cardinals, whom the king was always anxious to favour, provided they did not compete for a particular benefice with one of his own protégés. On the whole, the flooding of cathedral chapters with alien provisors probably did not do a great deal of practical harm to the working of the English Church; and it was always useful for any institution to have a friend at the Curia. It was more unfortunate that archdeaconries were treated as sinecures, to be worked by deputies, since the well-being of the Church demanded that archdeacons should keep a firm hand over the swarm of minor ecclesiastical officials, summoners and apparitors and the like, against whom there is so much accusation of corruption and extortion in contemporary literature, whether it is Chaucer's *Canterbury Tales* or a manual for confessors like the *Memoriale presbiterorum*. It was here that absenteeism and pluralism probably had their worst effects, though it is only fair to remember that royal and papal nominees were equally responsible. At least one cardinal archdeacon got more than he bargained for; when Cardinal Gaillard de la Motte, nephew of Clement V, and archdeacon of Oxford, tried to wrest from the university of Oxford some of its jurisdiction, including the valuable right of proving wills, he was involved in a struggle for twenty years (*c.* 1325–45), in which the university won; the king, it may be noted, supported the university, for if he valued cardinals, he valued the university even more.

Thirdly there was the large class of minor benefices, the parish churches; these were least of all affected by papal provisions; in particular the proportion of alien provisors to Englishmen must have been infinitesimal, being about 1·4 per cent in the diocese of Durham, for instance. It would be only a few particularly rich benefices that would be seriously affected, and these would probably fall to absentees in any case. In general I think one may conclude that the effect of papal provisions on the English Church was much less drastic than might be expected; a great many Englishmen benefited by provisions, for whom this was just one of several possible avenues of promotion, and indeed several types of patronage might be combined, as when the king or a magnate petitioned the pope to provide for a protégé. A few highly favoured aliens, such as the cardinals, enjoyed a few rich benefices, as has been said.

What were the reactions of Englishmen to the system of papal provisions? One's first impression is of a sustained and clamorous opposition. This is largely the result of a succession of documents such as the petition of the lords and commons to the parliament of Carlisle (1307), the letter of Edward III to the pope in 1343, and the preamble to the Statute of Provisors in 1351. These give a highly coloured picture of the evil effects of papal provisions throughout England: divine worship and the cure of souls are neglected; church buildings fall down; alms and hospitality are withdrawn; learning is discouraged; the founders' intentions and the rights of the crown and other patrons are undermined; the kingdom loses its counsellors, its secrets are betrayed and its treasure exported to its enemies. The picture becomes rather different if we analyse it in more detail. The most vociferous opposition came from the lay lords and the commons, who in fact suffered least directly from papal provisions; it was to some extent part of a long-standing hatred of foreigners, which had already been very strong in the thirteenth century, and reached a climax in protests in the Good Parliament of 1376 against the 'brokers of benefices in the sinful city of Avignon'. The clergy were those who suffered most directly, especially the bishops and abbots, for it was their patronage of prebends and rectories that was most often raided for the benefit of papal provisions; but at the same time it was they who found it most difficult to protest officially, for they were bound to admit, as Grosseteste had done, that in principle the pope had a right to dispose of all benefices, and they felt bound to dissociate themselves officially from lay attacks on papal rights. But in practice the bishops could and did make dignified protests to the pope, as Bishop Mortival of Salisbury did to John XXII, and Bishop Grandisson of Exeter did to Clement VI, pointing out how their churches were burdened with a multitude of provisors, so that they could not themselves adequately provide for their own servants or for theologians to lecture and preach in their cathedrals. Some of the chroniclers express themselves even more strongly, like the so-called 'monk of Malmesbury' (who was probably in fact a canon and a legist who had been disappointed of a bishopric); after telling how the pope had agreed with the king to set aside the virtuous and learned Thomas Cobham and appoint instead the king's favourite Walter Reynolds to the see of Canterbury, he bitterly denounces the exactions of Clement V: 'legates come and depoil the land, men armed with papal bulls come and claim prebends . . . Lord Jesus, either take away the pope from our midst or lessen the power that presumes to exercise over the people.' But whatever the complaints of commons or chroniclers, what mattered most was the attitude of the king, and this was complex and interesting. Neither the king nor the pope would ever, in theory, give up any of what they regarded as their lawful rights, and the king would point out that he was bound by his coronation oath to maintain his royal rights; if a royal official and a cardinal found themselves claiming the same prebend, litigation might be relentlessly pursued for generations; 'no time runs against the king'. On the other hand, the king was in fact always ready to do business with the pope, to ask him to promote the king's servants, to grant pensions and privileges to the cardinals; the system of papal provisions, as we have seen, meant that on the whole the pope gave the king the bishops he wanted, while pope and king went shares over the greater benefices; in a word, the king found he could get more by diplomacy than by bullying.

It is against this background that we must see the famous statutes of Provisors (1351) and Praemunire (1353). By the first statute, papal provisors could be imprisoned, and if the normal patron or elector was afraid to fill a post because of a papal provision, the king could step in and fill the vacancy himself—a useful addition to royal patronage. It was important to prevent a baulked provisor from pursuing his quarrel in the Roman Curia; and for this purpose the statute of Praemunire forbade anyone, under severe penalties, to take out of the realm cases cognizable in the king's courts, such as advowsons. It was not intended as a frontal attack on papal authority or jurisdiction. That Edward agreed to these drastic statutes was due to parliamentary pressure, for, as we have seen, it was the commons who were most opposed to papal provisions. By a typical manoeuvre, Edward agreed to the statutes and then proceeded to ignore them as much as he liked; he was not much interested in them, because he could get what he wanted from the pope by diplomacy, but the statutes remained a useful threat in dealing with the pope. It would be a mistake, however, to regard the statutes as ineffective, for there seems to be evidence that the amount of papal provisions did lessen in the second half of the fourteenth century. And it should be noted that the provision of aliens to English benefices was almost unknown after 1400, so that this unpopular practice cannot be regarded as a contributory cause of the breach with Rome in the sixteenth century. Twice in the later fourteenth century attempts were made to establish a formal concordat between the English crown and the papacy, first between 1373 and 1377, and again in 1398, but in each case the agreement was still-born, first through the death of Edward III, and secondly through the deposition of Richard II. The concordat of 1398 would in the main have simply recognized the existing practice whereby king and pope collaborated to appoint bishops and shared the cathedral chapters and collegiate churches, though it gave the pope a larger share of lesser benefices. That neither concordat came to fruition did not perhaps matter very much, since the practical arrangement between king and pope, especially in the appointment to bishoprics, seems to have continued to work to the king's satisfaction to the end, as the attitude of most Tudor prelates was to show. Whether it worked for the well-being of the English Church is another matter. However, it should be remembered that St. John Fisher, Wolsey and Cranmer were all provided to their sees by the same time-honoured machinery, which went back to the fourteenth century; it was a machinery which could be used for better or for worse.

How far can Anglo-papal relations in the fourteenth century be said to have fulfilled the promise of earlier centuries, when free intercourse between the English Church and the papacy had been such a vital issue? Or to put the problem in a different form: Robert Grosseteste, himself a thoroughgoing supporter of the papal *plenitudo potestatis*, had nevertheless complained that the papal Curia was itself the fountainhead of those abuses like pluralism and non-residence that wrecked the cure of souls; was this a valid accusation in the fourteenth century? Were conditions better or worse? It must be admitted that the fourteenth century showed a lack of saints and men of really great stature, like Gregory VII or Anselm, Innocent III or Langton, whether in England or at the Curia. At the same time it seems also to have lacked the more fantastic figures that had once disgraced high places in the Church, like Ralph Flambard or Roger Norreys, though there was still probably much corruption among minor officials; even comparatively harmless ecclesiastical drones like Bogo of Clare seem to have become rarer in the fourteenth century. The Avignon popes were respectable, well-intentioned men, controlling a much better organized machinery of government than their predecessors had had, but by some law of diminishing returns they seem to have less influence in the last analysis than they deserved or than might have been expected. Perhaps this was due more than anything else to a readiness to compromise, to their acceptance for instance of the system of exploitation of benefices for non-pastoral purposes, their failure to use papal provisions as an instrument of reform. The greatest and most durable achievements of the thirteenth-century papal and conciliar reform had perhaps been in the intellectual and spiritual movements that carried on into the fourteenth century and produced writers, preachers and mystics like Bromyard, William of Pagula or Hilton, and devout lay people like Henry of Lancaster or Margery Kempe. These were regions where perhaps in the nature of things Anglo-papal relations could have little direct impact; although, as we have seen, the papacy could do something to encourage clerical education, and the Curia might provide an intellectual stimulus or opportunity to scholars like FitzRalph or Adam Easton.

SELECT BIBLIOGRAPHY

G. Mollat, *The Popes at Avignon 1305–78* transl. J. Love (1963); for fuller bibliography see the 10th French edn. (1965)

Y. Renouard, *The Avignon Papacy 1305–1403*, transl. D. Bethell (1970)

W.A. Pantin, *The English Church in the Fourteenth Century* (1955)

A. Hamilton Thompson, *The English Clergy and their Organisation in the Later Middle Ages* (1947)

Katherine Walsh, *Richard FitzRalph in Oxford, Avignon and Armagh* (1981)

E. Perroy, *L'Angleterre et le Grand Schisme d'Occident 1378–99* (Paris 1933)

E.F. Jacob, *Essays in the Conciliar Epoch* 3rd edn (1963)

——, 'Petitions for benefices from English universities during the Great Schism': *Trans. of the Royal Hist. Soc.* 4th ser. xxxvii (1945), pp. 41–59

W.E. Lunt, *Financial Relations of the Papacy with England 1327–1534* (Cambridge, Mass. 1962)

Margaret Aston, *Thomas Arundell* (1967)

J.A. Watt, *The Church and the Two Nations in Medieval Ireland* (1970)

J.J.N. Palmer, *England, France and Christendom 1377–99* (1972)

R.N. Swanson, *Universities, Academics and the Great Schism* (1979)

F.R.H. DuBoulay, *The England of Piers Plowman* (1991)

R.L. Storey, 'Papal provision to English monasteries': *Nottingham Medieval Studies* 35 (1991), pp. 177–91

THE FIFTEENTH CENTURY

F. R. H. Du Boulay

6

THE FIFTEENTH CENTURY

In April 1378 an Italian was elected in Rome as Pope Urban VI. An English monk who happened to be there was asked by a French cardinal what the king and the leading men in England would think of this news, and he answered that they would be very glad, since all the temporal lords in England considered the French popes and cardinals (who had dominated the fourteenth-century papacy) as greater enemies to the kingdom than the king of France himself. Perhaps Adam of Easton spoke with some exaggeration, but he made a point of importance not only for his contemporaries but for those who wish today to understand the relationship between the Roman See and England during the century and a half before the final breach between them. By 1378 England and France had been enemies for as long as anyone could remember. The enmity was not total, as in a modern war. Truces were made, diplomats, scholars and others crossed the Channel without hopeless difficulty. But feelings were bitter and fear was often acute. Public opinion in England was to a large extent a local matter, influenced by local anxieties. A whole stretch of England, from South Wales round to Lincolnshire, faced France in the expectation of destructive raids, and in this fertile, well-settled area many monasteries and bishoprics had interests. Mottisfont Priory in Hampshire, to take but one instance, complained in 1410 that its property, situated mostly on the sea-coast, was frequently invaded by Frenchmen, Normans, Flemings and other enemies of the realm, and that the armed men who had to be billeted at the priory as a defensive garrison themselves did damage. The prior of Canterbury Cathedral also had to ask from time to time that men should not be taken into the armies from East Kent in such numbers that the countryside was left undefended. Prelates of eastern England, like the bishops of Norwich or Lincoln, had similar preoccupations. When the more articulate Englishmen, like monastic chroniclers, expressed themselves on the subject of foreigners it was usually in emotionally insular terms. Marriage ties between royal and noble houses might exist across borders, merchants might venture, and learned clerks of all nations might speak in the same tongue of theology and the moral law, but to the monks of St. Albans the Picards were 'the falsest kind of men', and the Scots, allies of France, 'enemies of the human race'. Foreigners also referred to the English in uncomprehending terms. The internationalism of the Middle Ages as a whole has been much overemphasized, and the growing nationalism of the later Middle Ages is an elemental fact. It is hardly surprising therefore, if the events which overtook the papacy had a strongly nationalistic colouring.

These well-known events may be summarized quickly. The behaviour of Urban VI so displeased his cardinals that five months after his election a strong body of them, mainly French, withdrew from his obedience and elected one of their number, who called himself Clement VII, claiming that Urban's election had been performed in mortal fear of the Roman mob and was therefore invalid. From this moment in September 1378 the allegiance of Latin Christendom was divided between what may be called the Roman and the French popes, and the loyalty of kingdoms and principalities was determined by motives which were mainly political. It should be said at once that men did not freely admit they were guided by political motives alone, and it would be unreasonably doctrinaire to suppose that nothing else counted. The schism in the papacy was scandalous, the more so because it sprang from a schism in the Church's own organization and not from the power politics of some secular ruler. Educated people everywhere knew the Church could have but a single head, however they might come to disagree about that head's exact function. Preaching in 1378 the archbishop of Canterbury took as his text *'Unus erit pastor noster'*, and an English letter to the Clementist cardinals spoke of their detestable ambition which tore the seamless robe of Christ and divided what could not bear division. The sense of scandal was immediately shocking, and continued to distress men in universities and even in governments. But politics held the field for a long time. An English boy of 15, just starting his university career in 1378, would not have seen the French ready to sacrifice their pope for the sake of unity until he was nearly 30. At 46 he would have seen the Council of Pisa issue in the election of a third pope, since the other two refused to resign, and not until he was 54 would he have been able to watch the combined efforts of English and Germans put an end to the confusion, and force through the universally-recognized election of a single pope. In this long period of schism, England and France adhered to their respective obediences for as long as they could, that is until 1408, and thereafter supported with declining enthusiasm the Pisan popes, while the supporters of the other two, mainly Italian and Spanish, grew fewer and fewer. Finally, Germany and England took the lead in the Council of Constance in persuading the Roman pope to abdicate and the council itself to renounce obedience to the other popes and vote unanimously for the Italian, Martin V.

In the years after 1378, wherever the English government possessed effective power, obedience to the Roman pope, '*Urbanus noster*', followed in due course. Conversely, political hostility to England brought with it a determination to adhere to the Clementists. In Ireland, the higher clergy and public opinion in the Dublin Pale were Urbanist, but the rest of the country was good soil for Clement VII, whom the population supported more out of a desire to make themselves unpleasant to the English than out of conviction. Scotland turned to Clement almost at once, and the monk of Westminster wrote that the English expedition of 1385 against the Scots was one against schismatics. Wales used the schism in a more constructive way to serve nationalistic ends. When Owen Glendower rebelled against Henry IV of England he transferred his allegiance to the opposition pope of the day (Benedict XIII, 1394–1409), but his mind was chiefly on an independent Welsh Church as the counterpart of the independent principality for which he hoped, restoring St. David's to its ancient place as a metropolitan see, served by Welsh-speaking clergy and guarding its revenues from export to England as jealously as ever England strove to keep revenue from France or Rome. In France itself, land of political schism, the division of allegiance was more painful still. Calais belonged to the diocese of Thérouanne where there was a feeling for Clement VII, but the whole region was in 1379 placed by a grateful Roman pope under the jurisdiction of Canterbury, where it remained with brief intermission until the reign of Mary I. There were divisions in Brittany, the Channel Isles and Gascony, but confiscations, deprivals and imprisonments in the end produced obedience to Urban. A Norman chronicler's assertion that Clementist clerks were burned in England was a fable, but a useful one for measuring the political temperature. More important to the European scene was the support for the Roman popes given by the German princes, Bohemia, Hungary and Poland, and the alliance formed between parts of this bloc and England. In broad outline, the Roman popes enjoyed the support of Italy and of the Anglo-German world, the French pope of France itself (save for the English dominated parts), Scotland, and Spain without Portugal. A wide view like this is subject to many small qualifications, and loyalties themselves shifted in a complex way as the two obediences confronted each other and then became three. But it makes clear the main tendencies, of hostility between England and the Franco-Spanish part of Europe, and of agreement and like-mindedness between England and central Europe, which showed themselves at Constance.

The initial support of England for the Roman line of popes did not imply a deep understanding between them. There were issues between England and the papacy which had a long past history, were never fully resolved in the future, and are central to the problem of Anglo-papal relationships quite apart from purely national considerations. In brief, they concerned the right to tax the English clergy, and the right to appoint clergy to English benefices, especially the important, well-paid ones like bishoprics, deaneries, archdeaconries, cathedral canonries and the richer rectories. Fundamentally these issues were financial. People with a legal cast of mind may think it better to describe them as jurisdictional issues, and there is certainly no intention here of denying the great importance given by medieval minds to questions of jurisdiction in themselves: trouble and expense were always lavished on claims to jurisdiction which men of corporate bodies believed were rightful. But at the same time it is hard to avoid the conclusion that the conscious day-to-day purpose of papal jurisdiction in the later Middle Ages was to enlarge and protect vital sources of revenue. Since the thirteenth century, popes, like secular rulers, had experienced the difficulty of getting enough income to hold and administer their realms. For the popes the difficulties could hardly have been greater. Not only were the older forms of revenue inadequate in an inflationary world, but for a large part of the fourteenth century they themselves had been exiles in Avignon, contending at a distance with war in the papal states and the substantial loss of their territory. They had had to borrow heavily, and had suffered depreciation of credit. It was to finance the recovery of the papal states as well as the livelihood of the papal court and administration that old forms of taxation were elaborated and new ones invented; and since the papal territories themselves were so unproductive of revenue, the main source had to be from outside, which meant the clergy and people of countries which composed western Christendom.

The first in time of these large-scale schemes to augment the papal revenue was the direct taxation of the clergy. The popes were pioneers of the income tax, and had since the late twelfth century required from time to time that the clergy pay as a 'subsidy' some fraction of the annual income they derived from their benefices. Unfortunately for the popes, their plans to tax the clergy met the determined resistance of the kings in the countries concerned, not least in England, and by the fourteenth century the king had succeeded in getting for his own purposes the greater part of the subsidies voted by his clergy. To the end of the period covered by this essay popes are found begging or commanding the English clergy to contribute to subsidies, particularly for crusades, but with very little effect.

The second main way in which the papacy sought to make up its needed revenue was for the pope to claim the right to 'provide' men to ecclesiastical benefices, and to impose various taxes on the occasions when he did so and when a man thus newly beneficed would, of course, have received a fresh personal source of income out of which he could be prepared to pay the papal court. The great Lateran Council of 1215 proclaimed to the world that bishops, like abbots, ought to be elected by their cathedral or monastic chapters, but in the making of bishops the future lay with pope and king, not in the electoral principle. Likewise with cathedral canonries and other lucrative benefices, popes from the early thirteenth century onwards made ever-widening claims out of the 'fullness of their power' to provide their own nominees until by the end of the fourteenth century there was hardly a case in which they could not put forward a theoretical right in canon law to provide. For this purpose the papacy classified benefices as 'consistorial' and 'non-consistorial': the first were those worth over 100 florins (or about £20) a year, and were provided by the pope in consistory with the assent of his cardinals; the second were those worth between 24 and 100 florins and were filled by the pope alone. Clerics who received consistorial benefices paid taxes called 'services' to the pope, the cardinals and to various officials at the papal Curia, as well as other fees and gratuities for all the authorizing documents which were needed by the new beneficiary, whether he had been appointed by papal provision or not. Recipients of non-consistorial benefices paid similar dues on a smaller scale called 'annates'. Services and annates are often confused, and Henry VIII's famous Act in restraint of annates applied to all these payments. The sums involved, though not vast, were considerable and on the average greater than those deriving from other forms of revenue which passed from England to the pope's treasury.

The strong English objections to this papal system of disposing of English benefices have been described in the previous essay. They were certainly not new in 1378. They were sustained partly because the king and English men of property who possessed rights as patrons to present clerks to benefices were hostile to the existence of a law which claimed these rights for itself, partly because the actual promotion of their kinsfolk or candidates was sometimes blocked by papal provisions, and perhaps chiefly because provisions appeared to operate to the benefit of people who were regarded as foreigners and even enemies. The provision of aliens from Italy or the Mediterranean world to English benefices was not as frequent as was sometimes imagined, but it occurred, and it was made worse by the thought that money in the form of services and annates was being paid over as a consequence of provisions, and was passing through the hands of the hated Italian merchants and papal bankers to the treasuries of popes and cardinals who were unfriendly to England. To Henry IV's parliament annates were 'a horrible mischief and barbarous custom'. Dislike of foreigners was strong in later medieval England. Yet not everyone took equal exception to the system. The lords and knightly persons who made up the main lay element in parliament were more consistently antagonistic than were the better-educated English clergy, or the king himself. Many of the clergy could see the benefits of papal provision. Universities had long been sending lists of graduates to the pope with the petition that he would provide them to livings. Some great lay lords had done this too, but in the late fourteenth century the opposition to papal provisions gathered fresh strength and the petitions were no longer freely allowed after the 1390's. In spite of this, English clergy continued to feel that a papal provision was somehow essential to a valid title, and sometimes went to great lengths to get one, even preferring to follow it with a royal pardon rather than getting a royal licence to ask for one first. The king himself could sometimes take power to make special arrangements with the pope, so that his own nominees should be placed in the posts where he wanted them, and he could also allow his subjects to evade the statutes of provisors if he chose. Despite disappointments and quarrels, these statutes were for the king more like a valve than a barrier, excluding the main flow but letting through what he wished. The same thing came to be true in France as the age of monarchy succeeded the age of particularism. But up and down England ecclesiastics of importance stood to lose rights of presentation to churches which they regarded as theirs according to lawful inheritance, purchase or a canonical right. To be able to present clerks to livings was not merely a game of prestige. Even if he took no money from his favoured candidate (and thus committed simony), the income from the church in question would maintain a man who could be the patron's servant in countless ways. Hence, when the Roman popes whom England supported after 1378, and who needed all the support they could get, began to emphasize these claims ever more strongly in order to strengthen themselves, they were at the same time acting with astonishing lack of political sense.

All the popes of this era were doing the same thing in one way or another, but in England it was Urban VI and, even more, Boniface IX who thus seriously shook loyalties. The worsening of Anglo-papal relations cannot be blamed primarily upon Richard II, nor upon his baronial opponents, for both sides wanted papal support, but upon the papal Curia itself. In 1390 the pope demanded a subsidy from the clergy, who began to pay it—for papal censures were no laughing matter to them—until the king declared the tax illegal. Next, the pope began to insist that English abbots come to Rome for papal blessing and there pay the appropriate taxes to the uttermost farthing. Throughout this time he offered offices like papal chaplaincies and many kinds of spiritual privilege such as the right to have portable altars to those who would pay for them. But most aggravating of all was his increased activity in providing to benefices. The case of Edward Bromfield shows the sort of thing that might happen even in Urban VI's early days, and illustrates a common enough experience. This monk of Bury St. Edmund's was sent to Rome by his house as their proctor in 1378, and by making suitable requests and payments got himself appointed to succeed the lately dead abbot of the monastery he was meant to represent, even though he had expressly undertaken to do no such thing. Returning with a full set of papal documents confirming his provision he persuaded a party in the monastery to accept him but aroused trouble and antagonisms in the outraged monastic family. It was the royal government which took action. Arrested by knights and squires and haled off to Westminster, he was asked by the Chancellor why he had presumed to act as abbot without royal licence. He answered that he came to bring health to the diseased sheep. 'I reckon', retorted the Chancellor, 'that you will have neither sick sheep nor healthy ones there. You have entered against the royal right and the approved customs of the realm, not as a shepherd nor even as a hireling, but as a wolf. And you and others like you ought to realize that people who hurt the royal majesty must be shut up in prison. . . . You will go to the Tower.' Bromfield came to a happy end, if the bishopric of Llandaff can be called such, for ten years later and after various vicissitudes he was provided to that see without opposition, and the bull of provision alluded to the injuries he had borne *in causa papae*.

The harsh feelings which papal actions aroused are unmistakable. When Urban VI's death was known in England in November 1389 the remarkable suggestion was made that all relations with the Roman court should be stopped and the election which the cardinals would make should be ignored until the English lords and commons had reviewed the whole situation. This was not yet a subtraction of obedience from the Roman line of popes, let alone from the papacy as such. The time had not yet come for either of these courses, but it was a sign that the first English enthusiasm for the 'true pope' had evaporated, and that papal demands now occupied the forefront of men's minds. The commons were determined to get rid of the burdens. They rehearsed the anti-papal statutes of the previous century and demanded the complete prohibition of provisions, expectatives and the translation of bishops from one see to another on the pope's initiative. They wanted papal collectors expelled, and draconian penalties inflicted on the disobedient. A memorandum of these days paints a picture of the golden age of the past, when free elections were the rule and benefices were filled with virtuous and educated men, before papal taxation drained the realm and provisions peopled the churches with the ambitious and the ignorant. Like most *laudatores temporis acti* the commons did not understand very well why things had changed, and placed on Roman shoulders some of the blame which ought to have been reserved for social and economic changes which were occurring in England. But still, nobody denied papal authority, and requests to Rome to alter its ways were made in terms of deferential obedience. The answer made by the new pope, Boniface IX, was abrupt. By an authoritative bull he simply annulled all the offensive acts of the English parliament. They were to be erased from the records and the faithful forbidden under censure to obey them. It was not possible for this order to be published in England, so the text was fastened to the door of St. Peter's in Rome. Naturally enough there were reprisals. More surprisingly, the effects of these reprisals were mostly fairly brief. It was forbidden to send lists of university graduates to Rome with petitions for their promotion, and this ceased to be done freely, though the occasional roll was allowed through by the king. There were some temporary restrictions on Italian merchants. English clerks were ordered back from Rome, and a statute was enacted which made little impact at the time, though it lived on in the statute books until a revolutionary use was found for it much later. This was the so-called 'Great statute of *Praemunire*'. Its intention in 1393 was quite narrow: to protect English clerks in England from papal censures when they used the English courts to claim benefices, and to protect English bishops from being moved from one diocese to another without consent of themselves or of the king. It became an offence to admit papal documents ordering such matters. The subject-matter was precise and limited, and the statute seems soon to have been forgotten. But the text was capable of wide interpretation and was sanctioned with extremely severe penalties, and it was to be revived in the future, most notably by Henry VIII when he wished to crush the canonical independence of his whole clergy. But for the moment the point of interest is not the dislike of the king and the whole realm for papal actions, but the difference in attitude between the king's government and the larger mass of English political opinion. The classes represented in parliament offered to papal policy a strong, clear and unending hostility, so that when the Lancastrian kings in the earlier fifteenth century evaded papal demands for the abolition of anti-papal statutes by referring to parliament's importance and parliament's upholding of these statutes, they spoke nothing but the truth. But kings themselves were not so unswervingly anti-papal, for they had no need to be. Richard II and Boniface IX continued to need each other despite the outrageous conduct with which the Curia and the kingdom reproached each other, and they were moving towards a concordat in Richard's last years of political tyranny. Even today it seems strange how each ruler in his way could be so out of touch with realities: how the pope could continue in irritated optimism to send nuncios demanding subsidies and the annulment of the English statutes where their predecessors had all totally failed, and how Richard could press for the canonization of his deposed and murdered predecessor, Edward II, as a significant way of strengthening his own position. Drawn together in this business understanding they were prepared to share between them the administration of the Church in England.

This desire for mutual political support based unfruitfully on self-interest is visible on the Continent also. When Clement VII died he gave place to Benedict XIII, a Spaniard who bled the French clergy white and gave not an inch in negotiation. It was this inability of popes to understand that politics, even spiritual politics, is the art of the possible that began to bring nations together and led to the councils which restored unity. There were three possible ways of ending the schism: to persuade both popes to resign (*via cessionis*), to arrange for one side at least to withdraw obedience to its pope (*subtractio obedientiae*), or to bring about the summons of a General Council which should make an effective adjudication (*via concilii*). During the first generation of the schism the French favoured the first, and the University of Paris, which commanded enormous prestige in Europe, tried in 1395 to persuade the University of Oxford to agree. But the English held that only a General Council duly summoned by the Roman pope could end the schism. In 1398 the French were disillusioned enough to withdraw obedience from Benedict XIII, and again made efforts to get England to abandon Boniface IX. Oxford and Cambridge were asked to advise the king, and Cambridge came up first with a calm and concise reply, followed in principle by Oxford. The university opinion was that Urban VI was a true pope and that his cardinals well knew it; that Boniface IX, his successor, had done nothing to provoke schism; that Benedict XIII on the contrary had sworn to end the schism even if it meant his own resignation. The best course, therefore, was for Benedict himself, and France, to return to Boniface's obedience. To withdraw obedience from Boniface would not only be rebellion, but would encourage rebellion everywhere. Cambridge also suggested that under certain circumstances Boniface might be able to resign freely, and that he might well summon a General Council to deal not only with the Western schism but also with the Eastern one, and with the reform of the Church. Given at this moment when Boniface IX had done little to endear himself to the English, this English university view is remarkable. It fastened clearly upon the legal issue; it tried to win political initiative for Boniface IX by inviting his opponents to recognize him by coming to his Council or else to forfeit their chance of public pleading; and it showed beneath all this a care for the reform of the Church itself. This was an outlook shared by many of the best minds in England. The English reforming spirit was alive and sharp until it was dulled after Constance by a failure of leadership. The English delegation was to play a leading part in the restoration of unity, but they did not achieve what many of them had at heart, a new order in papal government.

Between the 1390's, when the French were feeling for a way out of the deadlock, and the Council of Constance the situation became increasingly complex as the nations wavered and manoeuvred and the popes manoeuvred without wavering. It is necessary to simplify and to pay special attention to England, the subject of the present essay.

The French revulsion from Benedict XIII had led them to withdraw temporarily from his obedience in 1398 and permanently in 1408. Germany was divided by civil war and neither abandoned nor fully supported the Roman pope. England kept allegiance to the Roman pope until she too found it hopeless to do so any longer. Her case for withdrawal was a strong one. When Boniface IX died in 1404, his successors Innocent VII (who only lived a few months) and Gregory XII both bound themselves in the consistories they attended as cardinals and which elected them popes to resign if this course appeared necessary to attain unity. Yet when it came to the test Gregory was quite unable to shake himself free of family pressure to hold on to the papacy. Like so many others he was a prisoner of the family structure of politics, and had not the strength to prefer the Church at large to his kinsmen. Neither Gregory XII nor Benedict XIII would resign or even meet. In the event they were deserted by almost all their cardinals, who summoned princes, bishops and university professors to Council at Pisa. Henry IV of England pleaded with Gregory as others were doing. His letter in the summer of 1408 claimed that the schism had already cost 200,000 lives in the wars it had excited, and 30,000 of these in Liège alone where each pope had provided a different bishop. A copy of this letter was sent to the king of the Romans in Germany with the observation that he had the special obligation to watch over the unity of the Church. England was continually concerned about German opinion, and looked to Germany as a like-minded ally. At last, on Christmas Eve 1408, Henry IV withdrew England's long obedience to the Roman pope and ordered all money owing to the pope to be kept aside until reunion.

The Council of Pisa was a splendid failure. It included a great number of prelates and some 300 masters from the universities, which was a sign of the times. The English delegation was led by Robert Hallum, bishop of Salisbury, then a man of about 40, a devout and poetic scholar from Lancashire who disapproved of the death penalty for heresy and cared greatly for ecclesiastical reform. With refreshing unanimity the Council deposed both popes as schismatics, heretics and perjurers, and elected the archbishop of Milan as Pope Alexander V, arranging to hold another council in three years. The action was revolutionary, though not by intention. It was a move of conservative desperation, and unfortunately it did not work. Remarks about the future Alexander V's willingness to bear the terrible weight of the papacy had already raised sardonic laughter in Council, and his promotion was followed by the usual shower of privileges. Within a year he was dead, and replaced by someone far worse, the Neapolitan 'John XXIII'. The prestige of the Pisan popes vanished like smoke, and before long John XXIII gave in to the insistence of the new king of Germany, Sigismund, his only protector from political destruction, that he summon another great council. Its location was to be Constance.

The Council of Constance (1414–18) was the end of an era in more ways than one. It healed a schism nearly a lifetime long by receiving the free abdication of the Roman pope and deposing the other two. It inaugurated a papal monarchy of new strength when it elected the able young Italian subdeacon, Oddo Colonna, as Martin V. More to the present purpose, it marked the moment when serious concern by England and the papacy in each others' affairs began to grow fainter. These events were not altogether disconnected, and the key to them lies in the development of national identities. Nationalism was symbolized well enough in the Councils themselves. What had been informal practice at Pisa grew at Constance into the council's basic organization: a group of five nations, French, German, Spanish, Italian and English, each made up of prelates and university men, each lodged in different quarters of the town, meeting apart for sectional debate, negotiating in private and voting in public sessions as nations, with one vote for each nation. It is interesting that the scheme was proposed by the English, the smallest of the nations, and was found useful by the others in holding the balance against the cardinals and the Italians. It shows also that national Churches were acquiring a new significance within the Universal Church itself. Within this scheme there were natural sympathies and antipathies. Just as at an earlier time the English and the Germans had found each other on the same side in support of the Roman line and had shared other policies, so now at Constance English and Germans saw eye to eye in wanting Church reform, and especially reform in the papal government. The facts that England and Central Europe had produced the arch-heretics of the day, Wyclif and Hus, and that English and German authorities wished passionately to condemn and be rid of these heresies, should not obscure the reforming impulse vigorously at work within the two nations. Heretics and reformers shared many of the same expectations. Wyclif looked forward to a new age for the papacy and the Church, and was only severed from many colleagues by his later extremism. Among the orthodox too there was variety of temper within the wider movement, from the radical German publicist Dietrich of Niem to Bishop Hallum who again was leading the English delegation, and who, standing in fear of no man, as a contemporary remarked, told John XXIII to his face he was unworthy to be pope. Whether the reformers would have delayed reunion and whether they could have brought their plans to effective fulfilment are open questions. Hallum died and almost at once Bishop Beaufort of Winchester arrived at the Council, and under the new leadership of this brother-in-law of the English king the nations were manoeuvred *Uncle* into the decision to elect before reforming. The schism was ended. But whatever the priorities of task, the very nationalism which was ordering and informing the Council's procedures gave England at that moment a national prominence. It was an advantage of the day, expressed no doubt by able men, but deriving from England's military and political victories in France rather than from her weight or experience in ecclesiastical politics. There were no English cardinals, but Henry V had just launched his attack in Normandy, and Agincourt had been won as the Council opened. The French were still the great enemies of England, but were weak and divided amongst themselves. The situation produced for England an artificial strength at the Council, where the cardinals were complaining that the English nation had only twenty representatives and very few prelates but a vote equal to that of any other nation. Only the hostility of the other nations to the cardinals' group allowed the English to be made equal to the others, as a counter-weight. When before long the balance changed, the French could attack the English position, arguing that they were too small a people to appear as a fifth of Christendom. To this the English answer had about it a stubborn arrogance, doubly interesting in the light of future events:

> . . . whether nation be understood as a people marked off from others by blood-relationship and habit of unity or by peculiarities of language (the most sure and positive sign and essence of a nation in divine and human law), . . . or whether nation be understood, as it should be, as a territory equal to that of the French nation, England is a real nation.

This was all very well, and no worse than the obstinate national pride of the Spanish, or of the French, who could not stop talking about their university. But if Catholic affairs were ruled according to such partisan comparisons there was small chance that when English arms failed on the continent and English civil wars were discussed contemptuously in European cities England would be much honoured in the Roman Curia. And that is what happened.

The two preoccupations at Constance had been unity and reform. The English and Germans had wanted reform first, but in the end had led the way to unity. When this had been achieved there seemed no reason why the rest should not follow, especially as other nations felt the same way. Reform of course meant somewhat different things to different people, but to the English and Germans the differences were minimal, and some of the points they desired were embodied in two similar agreements, or concordats, between Pope Martin V and their respective nations. In the English concordat of 1418 the pope agreed to appoint only a moderate number of cardinals and to draw them from the various provinces of Christendom. He gave diocesan bishops the right to examine indulgences and letters authorizing absolution of those who made visits to particular places, and to suspend those which appeared scandalous. He promised to make no appropriations of parish churches on his own initiative alone, by which their revenues would be added to those of religious houses or churches he wished to favour, to the detriment of the parishes thus treated. Appropriations completed during the schism were allowed to stand provided the local bishop did not think them scandalous, and in future bishops were to have greater powers of decision on this question. This was the concordat's most important concession. The privilege bought during the schism by numbers of prelates below the rank of bishop to use pontifical insignia like the mitre was abolished. More important, clergy were not to be dispensed in future to hold a plurality of benefices 'except noble persons and men of very good birth'; as part of this move to protect the cure of souls, the dispensations to men who had obtained benefices exempting them from proceeding to holy orders were annulled, monks were not in future to receive dispensations to obtain benefices, and archdeacons who had the duty of visiting churches were not to be allowed to do it by proxy. Finally, some of the offices in the papal administration were to be open to suitable men of the English nation as well as others. In most of these matters, the

English diocesan bishops were to have a much greater say in what was and what was not permissible, and the points which were granted were sound ones reflecting the clerical and university mind at its best: the care for learning, for souls, for a decent competence, the preservation of a certain social discrimination in an unstable world, and for some acknowledgement of English abilities at the centre of the Church's administration.

But the English Church was not to be ruled by an Oxford-Rome axis, and the text of the concordat, copied and distributed freely and as a 'perpetual reminder', fell quickly into oblivion. Within England, the failure to carry on the reform must probably be blamed on the bishops, who had gained in power but with few exceptions never measured up to their responsibilities. As to the mutual failure of England and Rome to pursue reform in a spirit of encouragement and respect, the explanation must be seen again in political terms. Constance had taken place at the height of England's success in France and her influential friendship with the Germans. Within a generation the situation was reversed. Henry V died in 1422 and was succeeded by a baby who grew up to be an incompetent king. The English were defeated by a resurgent France, deserted by their Burgundian ally in 1435 and thrown out of the country, save for Calais, by 1453. Within England want of central authority permitted a series of civil wars which lasted off and on until the reign of Henry VII, and gave the worst possible impression to outsiders. The land appeared to withdraw into her own disorderly affairs and to become uninteresting to Europeans. In point of fact, England was neither poor nor weak but in the grip of remarkable social and political changes transforming her into an insular, bourgeois power of pronounced self-sufficiency. But at the time this was not apparent, and Anglo-papal relations became governed by a mutual incomprehension sweetened only by mutual hostility to France.

After Constance the pope was expected to summon General Councils regularly, but always disliked doing so and by mid-century had won his way clear of them. His first victory was in 1423, when Martin V sent legates to the Council of Pavia-Siena but avoided going himself. His success was largely due to the English delegates who used wrecking tactics, not out of a forward-looking devotion to papal absolutism but in the hope of getting papal approval for English ecclesiastical jurisdiction over the conquered parts of France. An infinitely harder fight awaited the pope in the years 1431 to 1449, when he was threatened theologically and militarily by the Council of Basle. Yet in the end he won here too, took over the Council himself, and at its continuation in Florence and Rome brought about a momentary union with Eastern Christendom. Here also England played a small part for the pope, but again it was less a result of spiritual principle than of political disillusionment. True, attention to principle was not wholly lacking: both pope and council had asked for English support in 1432 and a small delegation went to Basle, supported at home by a Convocation and a king who took a high view of the papal office. Convocation held that a council could not function against the pope's wish, and Henry VI objected to attacks 'by the sheep on the shepherd'. But politics were paramount. What effectively turned the English against the Council of Basle was the snub and the defeat they received there. No longer were they allowed to vote as a nation, equal to the other major nations. On the contrary, procedure was now to be by deputations of mixed nationality in which heads were counted, and the influence of the small English party was reduced almost to nothing. It made no difference to argue, like the brilliant canonist William Lyndwood, that since each nation sought a special kind of reform so procedure ought to be by nations, and that in any case Henry VI was king of France as well as of England. Far from convincing the Council, England had to watch Burgundy make up her quarrel with France and the German emperor show his feeling that the English were no longer masters in France and that he had better come to terms with the French king. England's diplomatic defeat was severe, and her support for the pope which had been useful though mainly negative was a policy without sequel.

In this way England supported the Roman and papal monarchy under Martin V and Eugenius IV (1417–47) as she had done at the start of the schism, mainly out of policy, marginally out of doctrinal recognition, wholly without warmth. The more particular

Anglo-papal relationships of these post-council years were not happy. This was mainly because the popes still could not abandon their full claims to provide bishops and clerks to English benefices. Probably they were nourished with hope that Henry VI's conspicuous piety and Bishop Beaufort's evident detachment from insular patriotism could be turned to upset the old order so stubbornly defended by the king's predecessors. Beaufort was to be the chief instrument in recovering 'the pristine liberty of the Church in that most Christian nation', and it was imagined in Rome that other men favourable to this cause could be promoted to English bishoprics and persuasive propagandists sent to England as papal collectors and diplomats. The dearest papal wish was the abolition of the statutes of Provisors. To Martin V these complex enactments were simply 'that execrable statute', and he wrote letter after letter to those he thought might help to bring about repeal, pouring out his mind in reproach:

> Christ said to Peter and his successors 'feed my sheep', but the kingdom's statute does not allow them to do this but wishes that the king feed them.

To some he sent thanks, to others threats. To Beaufort he promised the same support in his campaign that Alexander III had once given St. Thomas of Canterbury, though the limited nature of that help was not mentioned. To the Duke of Bedford in 1426 he likewise sent compliments and urged him to see the statute was really lifted, 'since it produces, now that the schism is over, a kind of separation between England and the rest of the Church', and in the next paragraph he alluded to a marriage dispensation the Earl of Huntingdon had asked for, remarking that if her due rights were restored to the Roman Church they would find him reasonably inclined in this and similar matters. If Beaufort was the pope's best hope, Chichele was his whipping boy. Beaufort was an aristocrat, like Martin himself. Chichele was the son of a Midland businessman, and had begun his archiepiscopate in the popeless interval before Martin V's election, when he instead of the pope had been able to confirm the appointment of new diocesan bishops in England. Chichele was no Cranmer but he was a reformer, and loyal to the kingdom's welfare. He had waited for Henry V's permission before establishing relations with Martin V in 1418. He had been angered and humiliated when the same year Beaufort was made a cardinal, allowed to hold his see *in commendam*, and appointed a legate *a latere* for life throughout Henry V's dominions. He had sent a list of complaints to the pope in 1421, mostly to show how the pope was ignoring his position as metropolitan. In 1426 he had to accept Prosper Colonna, the pope's nephew and then 16 years of age, as archdeacon of Canterbury: the royal council had agreed to this promotion as a special favour, but it is obvious none of these activities was in the spirit of the concordat of 1418. On his side, the pope was annoyed when Chichele organized a Jubilee indulgence at Canterbury for 1420, especially as a jubilee arranged by Rome clashed with it; and in any case the pope listened to gossip against Chichele in Rome which charged him with anti-papalism. In 1427, at the height of his drive to get the statutes of Provisors abolished, Martin V suspended Chichele from the legatine powers he possessed as archbishop until he had gone personally to the king and council to beg them to do away with the statute. This Chichele did with tears, as it was reported, in the refectory of Westminster Abbey. Parliament was immovable, but Chichele had proved his earnestness, and his legateship was restored. It is ironic that the archbishop really believed in the value of the papal provision of good university graduates.

Eugenius IV continued Martin's policy 'a little less cleverly, a little less quietly'. He too aimed a blow at Chichele, when Archbishop Kemp of York was created cardinal and in 1440 given precedence for that reason. It has been shown by Dr. Ullmann that this incident marks a stage in the rise of the cardinals to their supreme position of jurisdiction above all other ecclesiastical dignitaries under the pope, and yet that at the same time the pope was with great skill denying them a share in his own plenitude of power, and stating more precisely than ever his own position as Vicar of Christ. This reassertion of papal monarchy is indeed visible in both the doctrinal and the temporal spheres, and it bears upon our theme. At Florence in 1439 Eugenius declared that the holy apostolic see and the Roman pontiff hold the primacy over the whole world, and this Roman pontiff is the successor of blessed Peter, prince of the apostles and true vicar of Christ, and to him in blessed Peter was passed by our Lord Jesus Christ full power to feed, rule and govern the universal Church.

Concurrently, during the decades after Constance, the papacy appeared no longer as the mainly French organization it had been in the fourteenth century, but ever more clearly as an Italian princedom ruled by a small number of rich Latin families. From 1417 to 1503 there were nine popes, all of whom were Italians except the two Spanish Borgias, all elected in fairly small consistories heavily weighted with Italians of noble family, preoccupied with Italian politics and divided by temporal ambitions. Though the competition of the moment was rancorous, dynastic ties and traditions could stretch without final interruption across the years of schism and uncertainty: the Venetian family which produced Gregory XII (1406–15) produced also his nephew Eugenius IV (1431–47), and Eugenius's nephew Paul II (1464–71). Men of their preoccupations had little thought for a remote kingdom enjoying its own form of isolation. A glance through the indexes to the great histories of the papacy by Mandell Creighton or Pastor will reveal few references to England amidst the affairs of the Roman Church in the later fifteenth century.

Estrangement was something implicit in the structure of these kingdoms rather than any result of positive offence given and taken. There was, it is true, a constant traffic between England and Rome, and this will be considered later, but mutual concern on the grand level of temporal or spiritual politics was small. From time to time a nuncio appeared, to suggest peace in English conflicts or to appeal for a subsidy, but the visits were not made by men of mark and bore little fruit. Nicholas of Cusa never reached England. Francesco Coppini, sent by Pius II in 1459 on crusading business, was a talkative little man who enjoyed being entertained by the great, but he burnt his fingers in English politics and withdrew from the scene in disgrace. Rome's most constant interest in England was now as a possible source of special taxation. This theme runs as a continuous thread through the years, and dreary though the subject-matter may at first appear, it illuminates two facts of outstanding importance: the residual but abiding sense of papal authority among the English clergy, and the growing sense of royal authority among all Englishmen.

Popes asked for taxes on clerical incomes in England at least fifteen times during the fifteenth century, but their requests were mostly unsuccessful. In 1389 the king forbade the bishops to levy money for the pope. Martin V demanded a subsidy for the Bohemian crusade, but his request was shelved in committee on account of 'the small attendance and the approach of the harvest'. When Martin imposed a Tenth on the whole clergy they said it was 'difficult and unusual'; the archbishop tried to persuade them to give some answer that would please the pope and in the end a grant was at least agreed to on condition no offence was done to the king. Reasoned, lengthy and conciliatory excuses became the common response in the second half of the century. The urgency of the pope's case is perfectly clear to us and was apparent enough to contemporaries. It sprang from the need to repel the Ottoman Turks who were thrusting through the Balkans and through the Mediterranean to Italy itself, and no one could know that this impulse would have spent itself for the time when Mohammed II died in 1481, not twelve months after the massacre at Otranto where the archbishop had been sawn in two. To the senior English clergy sitting in St. Paul's chapter house in London events even in 1464 were sufficiently dramatic to merit some response, and Edward IV himself thought 'some notable sum of money as may honourably, reasonably and thankfully content our holy father' ought to be levied, seeing that 'our holy father had determined to put his person into the blessed viage [crusade] against the tyranny and cruelty of the Turk'. But there were difficulties. In a letter to the archbishop of Canterbury the king described the direct papal levy on the English clergy, sympathetic though he was with its object, as a dangerous precedent, and he therefore proposed that the clergy should be summoned in their separate dioceses to vote money, and that this money should be granted to himself, not to the pope. He would forward it to Rome. Archbishop Bourgchier accepted the idea and wrote a revealing letter to the diocesan bishops summarizing in the English language the points which ought to be brought to the attention of the local clergy: the pope was giving a courageous lead to Christendom and deserved thanks and consideration; he had even spared England some of the demands he had made in other realms 'where they are not and may not be disobeyed'; here too in England such a demand for the sake of the faith might not conveniently, lawfully or reasonably be disobeyed; yet, he went on, such a precedent was perilous, and the best solution was to 'devolve the excuse' upon the king; the clergy might then offer a lesser sum than they had been asked for, grant it to the king, and the king would offer it to the pope on behalf of the Church in England; in this way the clergy might be saved both from severe expenses and the imputation of disobedience, and the pope himself, it was hoped, would be satisfied, the more so if the king sent some honourable ambassador to explain the situation in person. This memorandum to Pius II is an articulate and moderately honest summing-up of the English clerical attitude. In 1481 another papal demand at a critical moment received less courteous treatment, for it was remitted to a committee of Canterbury Convocation in April and discussed with decreasing interest until November, when the chairman reported that sickness and death had so reduced the committee's ranks that they could not fulfil their duties. The matter was referred back to the next Convocation and dropped. But it is in these financial negotiations of the fifteenth century that Anglo-papal relations appear in a clear light: the passive recognition of the pope's leadership of Christendom, the faint acknowledgement of his right to obedience, the dislike of taxation, and the effective dominance of the king who was close at hand. The sting was in the tail: by a sufficiently impressive diplomatic mission the clergy were confident the pope would be induced to accept the arrangements the king would devise.

At the end of the fifteenth century England returned to the international scene in a more important role and was brought again into a more ostentatious political relationship with the papacy. As had happened a hundred years earlier, the king was glad to avail himself of the political and moral support the pope could lend to his throne, and the pope for his part valued the friendship of a king who counted for something in diplomacy and might help to keep the French out of Italy. The old differences of opinion about provisions were not utterly forgotten. When Robert Sherborne went to Rome in 1506 to defend himself against charges of forging bulls of provision to the bishopric of St. David's, he was asked probing questions by the papal prosecutor about a statute called Praemunire and laws forbidding causes to be taken to Rome. But they were no longer important issues, for the tacit agreement between pope and king was working well. More will be said of this shortly. Public relations were courteous and on several occasions elaborately friendly. After the battle of Bosworth Henry VII rapidly declared his obedience to the pope. Though he was not closely interested in the war against the Turks, and though Ferdinand and Isabella, parents of his daughter-in-law, hinted that Alexander VI was capable of using money for the crusade for other purposes, he allowed the pope's jubilee indulgence to be preached in 1501 (in unexceptionable terms), and contributed £4,000 himself to a crusading levy. The papal chancery did rather more for Henry than he for it. Very soon after Bosworth Innocent VIII provided a dispensation for the marriage of Henry and Eliza-beth, 'eldest daughter and undoubted heiress of Edward IV . . . in order to end the dissensions which have prevailed between their ancestors and their respective houses or families of Lancaster and York', and a sheaf of documents declared that Henry's children by Elizabeth or any other lawful wife would be legitimate. Rebels against him, even in Ireland, were declared excommunicate *ipso facto*. Henry's attempt to use canonization as an instrument of political propaganda was no more successful than Richard II's had been, but it is interesting that it was made, and allowed gently to drop rather than brusquely rebuffed. The pope agreed that en-quiries should be made about the saintly life of Henry VI, and a book of his works and miracles was compiled. Henry's mortal re-mains were removed by papal authority from Windsor to West-minster. A fresh attempt was made to obtain the canonization of St. Anselm—his cultus four hundred years before had been eclipsed by the glory of St. Thomas—and an Order of Canonization was inscribed hopefully into the register of Archbishop Morton. Henry VI was never declared a saint, but it is clear that an accord was established between the pope, the king and the king's close counsellor, Archbishop Morton. Morton pursued a policy of using Rome to support his metropolitan jurisdiction. He obtained bulls confirming his right to hear appeals from the suffragan bishops of England and Wales and supporting the ancient claim of the archbishops to prove the wills of well-to-do people all over the province. The power of the archbishop to visit and correct religious houses in his province though outside his diocese was supported by both king and pope. A scandal in the great and hitherto exempt abbey of St. Albans was treated by a royal order to Morton to reform it. Certain small houses were suppressed. Opposition by St. Swithun's Priory, Winchester, to undergoing visitation from Canterbury was crushed by the papal judges delegate and the prior excommunicated. The archbishop won a bitter little battle against the bishop of London over visitatorial rights in the priory of Holy Trinity, Aldgate. Morton and Henry saw eye to eye about the centralized maintenance of law and order, even amongst clerical persons. The privileges of sanctuaries in harbouring criminals and debtors were limited, and the legal privileges of clerks accused of crimes further diminished. Archbishop Morton was made a cardinal, and papal privileges were granted to the royal chapels of Windsor and Westminster. By the end of his reign Henry VII had received the Cap and Sword and the Golden Rose from Pope Julius II as tokens of honour. During his reign too, the king had no difficulty in getting the men whom he wanted as bishops provided by the pope in due canonical order, and matters of convenience to the realm of England, like the transfer of jurisdiction over the Channel Isles from Coutances to Winchester, were arranged without trouble.

These policies were negotiated through diplomatic interchanges which were now often much more splendid than they had been in the past. Henry VII took over the English Hospice in Rome, and for a time the formerly self-supporting lodgement for pilgrims became part of the royal administration, housing men of rank.

Political figures from England were seen in Rome in greater numbers and finer style than before.

A counterpart to the carefully dignified royal representation in Rome was the presence of Italian bishops in English sees. Once regarded as a kind of papal aggression against a monarchy in need, this is now seen to be a matter of royal policy. Henry VII virtually set apart the bishopric of Worcester to maintain a diplomatic agent at the Roman court. What more natural than that this should be an Italian to whom protocol and tactics were familiar? Similarly, there were Italian bishops at Hereford in 1502 and at Salisbury in 1524, under Henry VIII. Possibly these western or west midland sees were thought especially suitable now that the Marches were quiet, a half-Welsh king on the throne, and a Council of Wales established at Ludlow. Yet it would be wrong to imagine the bishops as foreigners without qualification. Giovanni de' Gigli, provided to Worcester in 1497, was as anglicized as it is possible for a professional cosmopolitan to be. Born in Lucca, qualified in Italy in the canon and civil laws, well read in classical literature, he had held preferments in England since he was about 40. He was often in England, but in court circles, not in his diocese. In 1481 he appeared before a stony-hearted Convocation to speak eloquently on the pope's need for money to fight the Turk, and described how Sixtus IV had sold his jewels for this purpose. But he was no unbending ultramontane. His little treatise on 'The Observance of Lent' was passed round his English friends, and he wrote an 'Epithalamium' to celebrate Henry VII's marriage. 'Why should not an ecclesiastic', he said disarmingly, 'in a time of general rejoicing utter his congratulations about an event on which depends the prosperity of the people and the lasting peace of a great nation?' His self-justification hits off the official temper of the time.

Only in writing about very modern times could the historian of Anglo-papal relations think of beginning his work with unpolitical people. In the late Middle Ages popes and kings thought in political terms even when it was a question of ecclesiastical order and defence, and the Church's liberty and exaltation were assumed to be defensible by diplomacy, crusade and censure. Hence, the earlier sections of this essay were of necessity about politics. But even in the fifteenth century politics were not the sum of everything, and neither politics nor pastoral care functioned without an unceasing communication between England and the papal Curia. Not only highly-placed people were involved, but multitudes of individuals and corporate bodies, both clerical and lay. It will be best to deal first with the English clergy, and then with the laity. But first a word is needed about the mechanism itself.

By the fifteenth century papal government had become very highly organized, and whatever charges of venality can be brought, its dependence upon professional expertise meant that skilled men are sometimes found serving different obediences during the schism and carrying on the same work afterwards under the unified papacy. The same sort of continuity in the professional administration is to be observed in England during the political upheavals of the later Middle Ages, and it has been compared not unjustly with the continuity of a modern civil service.

Leaving altogether aside the government of the papal states, the Curia was broadly divided into three departments. The chancery was the secretarial department and issued thousands of letters in the course of the year. The financial department, the Apostolic Camera, employed agents all over Christendom as well as its central staff: most important, there was a system of papal collectors who were ecclesiastics of fairly high rank and were sometimes scholars and diplomats as well, and there were also merchant companies based in Italian cities who acted as papal bankers, transferring and lending funds in ways not much less advanced than those practised by modern finance houses. Thirdly, there was the judicial department, where the principal court was the Sacred Roman Rota. Much of its business was concerned with disputes about benefices. Questions of conscience and dispensations were dealt with by the Apostolic Penitentiary, which may be regarded as part of the papacy's judicial department for the convenience of a thumb-nail analysis. To the chancery came streams of petitions from every country of Latin Christendom, asking for benefices and privileges of all sorts. To the judiciary likewise was directed a torrent of appeals in cases concerning canon law, requests for absolution from serious offences, and dispensation from impediments and irregularities of all kinds, whether the subject were a royal person wishing to contract marriage or a clerk uneasy at having cut off someone's finger. Anything could be directly settled by the pope, but most matters were delegated by him, and most often to suitable dignitaries who would represent him in the land where the cases originated. Between the Curia and England, then, the flow of business was two-way: from England petitions, appeals, information, money; from the Curia documents embodying decisions, demands, exhortations and sometimes blessings. The living traffic was no less varied. From England came the ambassadors of kings and the great, usually called 'orators', with their attendants, and a far larger number of representatives or 'proctors' to put forward cases for the people and institutions who employed them. There were pilgrims, penitents, witnesses and plain fortune-hunters. In the other direction were sent the pope's representatives, from the legates *a latere* down to his collectors and special nuncios. The journey between England and Rome took something like eight weeks, more or less, and could rarely be accomplished without discomfort or loss. To the medieval mind the traveller was an afflicted person and the hostel had something of an orphanage's charitable character.

The greater number of communications between England and Rome concerned the English clergy. This is only to be expected since, although the pope was the common father and superior of all, the clergy were by their order and profession subject to his jurisdiction in greater detail. At the higher level the pope never ceased to make canonical provision to English bishoprics when they became vacant. In spite of English objections to papal provisions and the severe statutes designed to protect the king's subjects against papal censure when they disobeyed him about benefices, the pope did not lose his formal part in the making of English bishops until the breach under Henry VIII. What in fact took place was a habitual understanding between him and the king by which the men the king wanted were promoted according to the forms of ecclesiastical law. The same practice can be seen in other countries. Monarchies were in the ascendant. No king wanted a radical breach with the pope, and popes saw the convenience of dealing with kings. So the forms were preserved and the losers were the local interests like the cathedral chapters. This understanding can best be illustrated by a couple of letters written in 1436 by the papal collector in England to Pope Eugenius IV in Rome. Piero da Monte was then a young diplomat in his early thirties, trained in law at Padua, a careerist and a stylist with a fund of self-satisfaction. Part of his work was to inform Rome about vacancies which occurred in important churches. Although he was prone to exaggerate his own effectiveness he was also capable of seeing and describing a situation clearly, and the viewpoint of the English government could hardly have been put better than it was by this servant of the pope.

> Your Holiness may hold it as most certain that none will be admitted as bishop in these vacant English churches unless he is one of the number on whose behalf the royal highness has supplicated.

Da Monte begged the pope to let the king have his way, since the king has stood by him in his vicissitudes, and

> especially since he desires to have bishops who are much to be recommended in their holiness of life, maturity of age and good education. . . . For we find it often done in our times by Roman pontiffs to prefer to churches those whom princes postulate. . . . For since by the gift and munificence of princes churches are built, endowed and adorned, who will not judge it equitable if, when they need pastors, the will of the princes should sometimes be heard?

This is precisely the argument of the first Statute of Provisors, and Da Monte went on to observe that the Church would never have gained such temporal abundance if princes had thought they were going to be deprived of all honour and prerogatives in them. Consequently, they should be allowed their way provided that they remain faithful to the Church. Another letter written at about the same time shows in detail how the accord was worked in practice:

Although I have often written to Your Holiness about the provision to be made in vacant churches in this kingdom, the letters are often stolen because of the danger of the roads; but not neglecting the matter I am repeating the information. Of the higher benefices, four cathedral churches are vacant, namely Ely, Bangor, London and Lincoln, and there has been much questioning here for a long time about the provision to be made to them by Your Holiness; not that there is any doubt amongst the important people here about the right of provision, but rather about the persons to be elected. They have, however, arrived at unanimity at last, and so I think it best to inform Your Holiness of this opinion.

For Ely the king desires the appointment of the bishop of St. David's, a suitable man in age and character and possessing many virtues. To Bangor he wishes the Duke of Gloucester's confessor to be preferred, and this man is a religious from the Order of Preachers. It is requested that the bishop of Norwich should go to to Lincoln, and they say that the bishop of Rochester, a man devoted to Your Holiness and the Apostolic See, ought to be set over Norwich. For Rochester they name the abbot of [St. Mary's] York, and this is the man who worked so hard at Basle for the dignity of the Apostolic See. The man to be preferred to St. David's is Keeper of the king's Privy Seal. The elect of London is canonically Dean of York, a very old man and of good family. This is the king's plan for these churches, and I think he should have his way provided the dignity and authority of the Apostolic See suffer no harm, since he always shows himself worthy, and his assurances have been accepted by Your Holiness.

Every move in this reshuffle of the English hierarchy was authorized by the pope.

The king did not invariably get his way, and there were some misunderstandings and hard feelings on both sides, but these became very rare after the middle of the fifteenth century. The king's mastery of the situation was confident. He had complete control of the temporal possessions of the bishoprics which supplied their holders with income, and sometimes he granted these to his candidates before the canonical formalities had been completed. But the English bishop did not receive his temporalities until he had renounced before the king all words in the papal letters prejudicial to the king and his crown. The king neither could nor wished to take the place of the pope in matters of spiritual jurisdiction, but he insisted that the bishoprics as material estates were held of him. By the end of the fifteenth century the practical dominance of the king in the selection of bishops was more than strong, it was habitual, and accepted without question by all officials who administered the dioceses.

The pope's practical jurisdiction over the mass of the clergy, however, was more positive and necessary to them than the system of disposing of bishoprics would suggest. The best evidence for this is the great series of papal registers which recorded some of the copious correspondence from the papal court. The letters which were directed to the British Isles have so far been printed in English summaries up to 1492, and those which fall within the span of the present chapter fill ten large volumes. In the early fifteenth century the registers were arranged under subject headings, and many of these sections were relevant to the clergy, regular or secular, alone. Their headings describe their contents: 'concerning the regulars'; 'provisions'; 'vacant dignities'; 'vacant prebends'; 'benefices about to become vacant', and—concealing the greatest variety—'concerning different forms' (*de diversis formis*). Later in the century the registers were simply divided chronologically into 'books' of bulls. The amount of business was vast and pages of similar-looking entries conceal a great variety. It will be best to offer a general view followed by a few examples. The largest class of papal letters to the English clergy dealt in one way or another with benefices, granting them, reserving them for future papal grant, permitting others to grant them, confirming holders in possession, resolving disputes about them. This activity continued unceasingly throughout the period, but the schism involved it in many ambiguities and inconveniences, for a pope might annul the acts of his predecessors, or make grants notwithstanding future annulments. Gregory XII, for instance, reserved the see of Exeter in 1407 for his own provision for as long as he lived, *even if he resigned the papacy*. Another type of letter granted personal privi-

leges and exemptions to the clergy: making them papal chaplains, for example (the equivalent of modern *monsignori*), or allowing them to say Mass at times and places not usually permitted,
or permitting old or disabled monks and friars to live outside
their monasteries. This group is much more numerous at the beginning of the period than later on. Privileges were saleable com-
modities and the hard-pressed popes of the schism sold as many as
they could. This too promoted disorders (apart from the scandal
of commercialism itself), such as excessive papal interference in the
affairs of religious houses by exempting religious from the authority of their own superiors. An example of this comes from the
Benedictine priory of Luffield in Northamptonshire, where in
1399 Boniface IX allowed a monk who had ruptured himself
lifting heavy weights to absent himself from choir and visit friends
and relatives as he pleased without asking leave of the prior. After
the schism this kind of licence dwindled away. A most important
category consisted of dispensations to the clergy from impediments or irregularities or the normal obligations of their office. A
priest might be dispensed from residing in his parish to study for a
time in a university. Not infrequently a cleric was aware he had
been involved in the shedding of blood and had thus incurred an
irregularity which needed dispensation before he could properly
resume his functions. These cases throw a colourful light on contemporary life but are sometimes difficult to interpret correctly.
The petitioner might be a ruffian trying to safeguard the lawful
enjoyment of his living; he might be the prey of scruples or self-
deception; or he might be a perfectly normal man caught up in
the circumstances of everyday life. At one extreme was the papal
declaration in 1398 that a vicar in York cathedral had not incurred
any irregularity by having at the age of seven accidentally chopped
off a joint of his baby sister's finger with an axe. At the other was
the absolution granted the same year to a priest from Exeter
diocese from various grave sins and irregularities he feared he had
committed and incurred over the years since he had received the
first tonsure. These were: 'distributing offensive weapons to
people; assisting in the arrest of supposed robbers who were subsequently executed; going as a student at Oxford with the Chan-

cellor of the university, with drawn sword, to some lodgings where the ringleaders of a riot had gathered, and there being present when a rioter shot one of his companions to death; receiving gifts from clergy and people, against the canons, when taking part in an ecclesiastical visitation, and advising others to do the same; helping friends who had lawsuits about a benefice pending in the Roman court by getting their opponents arrested and imprisoned in England under pretext of the statute of Praemunire until they gave security to the king that they would not pursue their causes; as a priest, hindering the passage of ecclesiastics going on business from England to the Roman court; speaking certain words tending to reveal (*sonancia in revelacionem*) the confession of a priest which he had heard; violently attacking ecclesiastics and drawing blood in consecrated places, though not seriously injuring them; in spite of having incurred the penalties for all this, holding the church of Westbere in Kent, and then receiving deacon's orders simoniacally, and priest's orders from a bishop simoniacally promoted; saying mass for about five months in places unconsecrated, and in places consecrated but under interdict'. Probably the commonest kind of dispensation obtained from Rome was by men who were illegitimate and wanted to be ordained and beneficed. These petitions were classified according to whether they concerned the children of unmarried parents ('simple bastards'), of adulterous parents, or of clergy. In the earlier fifteenth century there were about 7 to 10 dispensations a year for simple bastards and slightly fewer for sons of the clergy, and in the second half of the century the first class remained stable while the number of dispensations for children of clergy roughly doubled. Dispensations for adulterine children were rarely more than one a year throughout the whole period. These figures include Ireland from which a considerable proportion came. They are too few to have any statistical value but they illustrate the proportion of different sorts of dispensation to each other and their general nature.

Letters were written and journeys made between England and Rome by or on behalf of layfolk just as constantly as in the case of the clergy, though the total volume was rather less. The jurisdiction of the Church, and therefore of the pope, touched laymen in three principal ways: over marriage, the last will and testament, and moral conduct. To these should be added all those matters which concerned the organization of spiritual life, such as indulgences and private vows. Certain sections of the papal registers therefore had special bearing on lay people. Those headed 'concerning plenary remission' recorded hundreds of indulgences granted to individuals or to all who performed certain exercises, under the usual general conditions of being penitent and confessed. The sections 'concerning matters of confession' show privileges being granted to people to choose their own confessors and receive from them indulgences as well as sacramental absolution. Privileges like these were also intended to attract money to the papal treasury, and to have them noted in the official register cost more still, so it is generally true that the people involved in special privileges were at least moderately well-to-do. But although the papal clerks were fond of describing such Englishmen as 'of noble race', this by no means signified that they were all aristocrats. Knights, citizens and men and women of modest status from every diocese are to be found in the papal registers as the recipients of papal letters: a much wider spread of the population had money to spare in the fifteenth century than a hundred years earlier. The point may be illustrated by a papal letter of 1405 confirming that William de Burton, citizen of York, is freed with all his children 'from the yoke of servitude and the burden of bondage and villeinage'. He had already been thus manumitted by the archbishop of York who was lord of Burton, near Beverley, but it was evidently William himself who went to the trouble and expense of getting ratification both from the king and the pope, to make trebly sure, and he would have been able to pay for all these measures. The year 1405 may suitably be used to supply other examples of papal letters to the laity. A Lincolnshire man whose father had committed suicide while of unsound mind got permission to have the body exhumed from the chapel of St. John's Hospital near Boston and buried in the parish church of Whaplode. The faithful were exhorted to contribute to the upkeep of the Severn Bridge at Bridgnorth and granted indulgences if they did so, but this privilege was not to be handled by pardoners and would be void if it was. A confraternity of the Blessed Sacrament in the London parish of St. Mildred in the Poultry was allowed to have daily Mass in St. Mary's chapel, Conynghope Lane. The German-speaking merchants in London were permitted to have Mass and confession from German-speaking priests in the Guildhall and elsewhere. A Londoner seeking a nullity decree had been refused by the local ecclesiastical court and had appealed to Rome. Since he had not prosecuted this appeal with due rapidity, the bishop of Worcester was delegated to cause him to give a pledge to do so within a certain time or else obey the judgement already given. Of these cases and others like them a great number were decided by papal judges-delegate in England, and their decisions were regarded as the decisions of the pope himself. But even if the suitors did not go to Rome they needed representatives to state their case at the Roman court, advise on the best procedure and pay the expenses in the most economical way possible. These professional services were just as necessary in the Church courts as at the Common Law, and they were supplied by proctors who might well be appointed specially by a client for an individual case, or who might be full-time resident proctors in Rome acting for any client who hired them. A vivid impression of one of these, William Swan, is obtainable from a letter-book he kept, which has survived. Swan was a married man in minor orders who came from Southfleet near Rochester in Kent, and went to Rome about 1404. At first he worked in the court of Gregory XII, wandering about Italy and hoping that his master would some time meet Benedict XIII and come to terms. The election of a third pope at Pisa in 1409 disillusioned him but he continued in the papal Curia during Constance and worked there till about 1430. The letters show a man of intelligence and skill, the owner of a working collection of books, and a constant traveller to whom travel was dangerous, for the loss of his case-notes and official documents would destroy his credit and his livelihood and be more fatal than mere loss of cash. Illness too was a danger. He got dysentery at Viterbo and stayed for a time in the hospital of the Holy Ghost, attended by doctors and incurring 'an impossible pile of expenses'. He was nursed to health by a woman called Alice Tudor who had a suit going at the Curia, and Swan wrote gratefully about her and the other devoted women amongst whom his health returned: *'sed vita mea valet inter omnes feminas'*. He wrote too to his family, with longing that his wife should come out and join him, and learn German which, he said, was the *lingua franca* of the Roman Curia. This must have been at the time of Constance.

The Arundel-Talbot marriage is an example of Swan's work. John de Arundel and Elizabeth Talbot discovered after their wedding that they were related in the third and fourth degrees and wanted to get a dispensation to *continue* in the married state. This was granted, but there were delays in getting the documents. At one stage a papal merchant, Simon de Albertini, had the bull and wanted to be paid for it, and Arundel and Swan appealed to Innocent XII. But the pope insisted that the litigants should find a large sum, 'for he said that John and Elizabeth would be persons of noble stock, and had more than 100,000 marks' worth of property, and that a third of these goods should belong to the Apostolic Camera'. Swan pleaded with determination that they were young and under their parents' control, and had practically no money of their own. The successful handling of cases like this would greatly advance a proctor. The promoter of the suit in question was Lord Furnival, kinsman of Elizabeth and Treasurer of England, and Swan hoped Lord Furnival would persuade the king to grant a licence for him to accept from the pope a prebend belonging to the cathedral of Chichester or London. Just before the Council of Pisa, when he saw trouble coming for the Roman pope in England, Swan advised his clients not to apply for papal provisions even if they had secured licences from the king to do so, because if the Church were to be reunited under a single pope many of the papal graces might have to be revoked. He also realized and advised that litigation about benefices would at this time be much better done in the King's Bench than at the papal Curia.

Men like Swan had a foot in both worlds. If the situations he described have power to move us to anger it must be remembered that he himself wrote coolly, without anger. Venality and delay were not confined to Italy even if they appear there at their most outrageous. The jurisdiction of Rome was sought as assiduously as that of Westminster. They complemented each other and possessed behind their disfigurements potentialities for good.

How did the papacy view England, and what feelings had people in England towards the papacy during the late middle Ages? These last questions are most difficult to answer. The papal court kept registers to show how much the various bishoprics of Christendom should pay as 'services' when a new bishop was provided. To look at these assessments is one way, if only a partial one, of comparing the wealth of the Church in different countries. Western Christendom in 1418 comprised 717 sees, and of these only 40 owed services in excess of 3,000 florins. It is therefore remarkable that of these 40 richest sees no fewer than 12 were in England. At the very top came Winchester, bracketed together with Rouen, and not far below came Canterbury and York, in the same class as the great German-speaking prince-bishoprics like Cologne, Mainz, Trier and Salzburg. Others in the top class might be found scattered over the vast extent of France and Spain, but concentrated also in this island: Durham, Ely, Exeter, Lincoln, Norwich, Salisbury, Bath and Wells, Coventry and Lichfield, and London. The fact is of added interest as one recalls the constant reluctance of the English clergy to contribute money to the rulers of Church and secular governments, their continual assertions of poverty, and the claims of some of them that Rome was the avaricious devourer of English revenues. The various strands of truth and misapprehension which went to make up this uneasy relationship can easily be dissected. The financial need of the popes was great and sometimes desperate, but their methods were better calculated to repel than to attract help. At the same time, the English clergy were often justified in claiming to be hard pressed. For one thing, a rich bishopric was not the same as a rich clergy; there were many rectors and also priests working for stipends or wages whom taxation hit harder than their better-endowed fellows. Nor was taxation in the Middle Ages so regular, accepted and foreseeable a system that men budgeted for it as a matter of course. Further, the English clergy were contributing as a whole at the end of the Middle Ages, according to Dr. Scarisbrick, at least two and a half times as much to the English crown as to Rome. Of course, the clergy disliked these taxes. They grumbled in Convocation, and they were particularly afraid of having to account to royal tax collectors rather than clerical ones appointed by themselves. But the king was at hand, and powerful, and could not be refused, while the pope was far away. It is this contrast in effective power which explains clerical reluctance to contribute to papal funds rather than any theories of royalism or papalism. Yet this situation was not likely to have been keenly appreciated in Rome. The view taken of England by the papal Curia must therefore have been coloured by the financial question: England was a hard place to get money from, and papal agents were treated with coolness if not opprobrium. For the rest, it is doubtful how much the popes and their curial officers thought about England at all, except in the way of routine business. In the later fifteenth century urgent matters nearer home were enough to displace reflections on a remote and intractable island, the more so as a reasonable *modus vivendi* about appointments had been formed. But even in the days when England was at the forefront of continental affairs it is astonishing what ignorance there could be about her amongst otherwise well-informed people. At Constance, for instance, there were able men of all nationalities lodging for years within a few streets of each other, and Ulrich Richental, an intelligent if rather complacent townsman, describes the scene for us. Though sharp on detail under his nose his notions became less accurate the farther afield his gaze roamed. To the French he alluded with respect if not liking, and knew that their claims to renown were their king and their University of Paris. But the English nation, he had heard, included not only Ireland but Arabia, the kingdom of the Medes and Persians, Greater and Lesser India, Ethiopia,

Egypt and Nineveh, with some nine kingdoms beyond Turkey. He admitted to vagueness here, but not to the promptings of prophecy.

By all accounts the impact of the English at the time of Constance was out of proportion to England's size, which to the English themselves seemed greater than it was. They were disliked for this. Later on the reactions of the papal mind to England seem to have been more irritation and sarcasm than anything else, and it is difficult to believe the English were ever liked at the Curia during the whole period. 'The pope has ordered', noted William Swan, 'that no one shall have more than one expectative grace and one collation, least of all an Englishman. . . .' To Cardinal Beaufort Martin V wrote in 1427 protesting strongly about the arrest of his collector and official, John Obizzi, in England. The deed, he said, was contrary to the common law of the country itself, and he could not quell the bitter observation that this had happened in England, a kingdom 'which considers itself better than all other Christian nations in devotion, faith and divine worship'. Up to the time of the schism there had been numbers of able Englishmen working in the papal court, but by Martin's time this situation had ended. In 1438 Eugenius IV complained of the lack of Englishmen at the papal court, and besought the king's councillors and Cardinal Beaufort to do something about this; but closer attention to the letter shows his sentiment to have been disingenuous, and indeed a threat that the pope would not promote Englishmen if his own provisions in England were not to be accepted. Another dry view of England was taken by that natural autobiographer Aeneas Sylvius Piccolomini who visited Scotland on a political mission in 1435, and this has direct value for the present purpose since he became Pope Pius II in 1458. Arriving at Calais he found himself already an object of suspicion to the English authorities, and was detained until Cardinal Beaufort ordered his release. In London he was refused a safe-conduct to Scotland in the justified fear that he would encourage the Scots to move against England; he was also in bad odour as the secretary of Cardinal Albergata who had helped to break up the alliance between England and Burgundy. But he saw London before departing back to Calais, and thought it remarkable, adding some ironical references to the village of Strood near Rochester where men were said to be born with tails as a punishment for having cut off the tail of Becket's horse. Passing on to speak of St. Thomas's shrine at Canterbury he found that 'it is considered sacrilegious to offer any mineral less precious than silver there'. Back on the continent he took ship for Scotland, where he arrived after a terrible storm, and walked ten miles in thanksgiving to the church of Our Lady at Whitekirk. Though reticent about his mission itself he noted that 'there is nothing the Scots like better to hear than abuse of the English'. Dreading a long sea trip on the return he now entered England disguised as a merchant, and near the Tweed was startled to be asked if he were a Christian. Newcastle seemed to him the first sign of a 'familiar world and habitable country'. York he found admirable, especially 'a most brilliant chapel of which the glass walls are held together by very slender columns'. Before long he discovered that a foreigner could only leave the country if he had a passport from the king, and as he thought it unsafe to ask for one he bribed the keepers of the port of Dover—'a thing which is easy to do as this class of men loves nothing more than gold'— and so sailed back to Calais.

In the later years relationships between England and Rome appear to have lapsed into greater formality, unlit by direct observations. Travellers from England brought reports of the occasional scandal or heresy, like the furore created by the London Carmelites in the 1460's, and routine business. But English affairs seemed neither dangerous nor consequential to Rome. The realm was satisfactorily faithful but unproductive, and affection was not looked for.

One of the historian's hardest tasks is to portray public opinion, and the ordinary difficulties of this are enormously increased when the period of time under consideration is not only remote but long, and when the subject of public opinion is something as large as the papacy. Whatever conclusions are reached, therefore, must be regarded as provisional, especially as so few fifteenth-century people committed their views to writing and hence made them available to posterity.

There is no doubt that relations with Rome were accepted as normal. Whatever disputes there might be about papal provisions or political matters, it was taken for granted that the pope was the supreme judge on earth in spiritual matters and that the law applied by the courts under his jurisdiction was the canon law of Rome. That most English of canon lawyers, William Lyndwood, who spoke as Keeper of the Privy Seal in 1433 on behalf of Henry VI's lordship over France and the rights of the English nation in the councils of the Church, referred in the same breath to the pope's lawful presidency over a General Council, and in his law-book drew attention constantly to decisions made by the lords of the Roman Rota. At the same time, the earlier part of our century witnessed a far-reaching moral critique of the Church and the papacy. This criticism of papal 'politicality', acceptable enough today, was made in extreme and general form by Wyclif and his followers, who pushed their views well over the brink of heresy and beyond the agreement of most of their fellow-countrymen. When they said that 'the disciples of Christ have no power forcibly to demand temporal things by means of censures' they touched what seems to us the papacy's weakest spot, and showed in an articulate and violent form the same mind as many other men of that age, lay and ecclesiastical. Before the very Consistory which had elected Gregory XII, the Secretary of the Roman court had uttered a similar warning: 'beware, fathers, that while you guard the City you do not lose the world, and that universal spiritual obedience does not perish for the sake of a little temporal lordship'. Some campaigned actively for reform, this side or that of orthodox frontiers, like Robert Hallum in England or Dietrich of Niem in Germany. Others contented themselves with harsh words of criticism, like Thomas Gascoigne, a vitriolic Oxford don and one of the first to use a dictionary of definitions as a polemical weapon. His *Book of Truths*, written in mid-century, was ostensibly a theological dictionary, but explanation was coloured everywhere by opinion, and his opinion was not favourable to prelates or pope. 'There are three things today that make a bishop in England', he wrote of Provisions, 'the will of the king, the will of the pope or of the court of Rome, and the money paid in large quantities to that court; for thousands of pounds of English money are paid here in England to Lombards for exchange, to the impoverishment of the realm.' Gascoigne often exaggerated, and not everyone agreed with him about this. The part played by the pope in the promotion of university graduates had, as we have seen, its supporters amongst intelligent men who were otherwise critical of papal actions. The pope's part in the promotion of bishops, too, aroused much more dissatisfaction in the earlier part of the fifteenth century than later; and at the very highest level, dislike of having cardinals and papal legates in England was more acute at the early period. Archbishop Courtenay refused the Red Hat in deference to the opinions of his beloved Londoners. Beaufort met strong opposition when he was made cardinal, and had to refuse the legateship. Kemp's cardinalate outraged Archbishop Chichele. But as the fifteenth century drew on this attitude was modified, and the promotion of Englishmen by the pope was viewed with equanimity or pleasure. Archbishop Bourgchier became cardinal in 1467 and nobody objected. Archbishop Morton was made cardinal in 1493, and Henry VII was gratified. Objections to papal promotions only became violent again in the days of Henry VIII's marriage problem. In the late medieval period, the more secure the king became, the greater appeared the distance from Rome and the more benign their relationships. On the political level, this detachment encouraged benevolence. Henry VII was emphasizing his distance when he said his sailors were not equipped to travel beyond Pisa and could not well take part in attacks on the Eastern Mediterranean. Henry VIII, even before the rupture of relations, observed that England lay in a remote corner of the world, cut off by nature from all other kingdoms, with whose business he had no mind to meddle. The Italian observer who picked up current opinions in late fifteenth-century England wrote, 'the kingdom of England is not quite independent, I do not mean of the Empire but of the Apostolic See'. He recalled William the Conqueror's homage to Pope

Alexander II, but noted that 'the English histories make no mention of this, and it is a forgotten thing'.

Popular feelings are harder to interpret even than governmental ones, since their expression is less considered. The hysterical London crowd that lynched Archbishop Sudbury in 1381 cried out that they feared neither pope nor interdict, but this sentiment was common enough at moments of enraged self-interest. 'This year', wrote a London chronicler in 1468, 'the pope sent a bull to the Cordwainers, and cursed those that made long peaks [toes] more than two inches in length, and said no Cordwainer should sell shoes on a Sunday, nor put a shoe upon a man's foot, nor go to fairs upon the Sunday, on pain of cursing. And the king granted in a council and in the parliament that this should be put in execution, and this was proclaimed at Paul's Cross. And some men said they would wear long peaks whether the pope liked or not, for they said the pope's curse would not kill a fly.' 'God amend this,' he added piously. There was undoubtedly an undercurrent of doctrinal anti-papalism, but this was in no sense equivalent to what may be called the high-church anti-papalism of post-Reformation times. It was an aspect of Lollardy, which objected to the whole apparatus of hierarchy and institutional, sacramental religion, and it was not very common for Lollards to become peculiarly eloquent on the subject of the pope. A partial exception to this was Stephen Swallow who said in 1489 that 'the pope is an old whore, sitting on many waters, having a cup of poison in his hand', and that he was Antichrist, and that his pardon availed nothing. But he was saying equivalent things of all cardinals, bishops, priests and religious. Most instances of anti-papal statement in fifteenth-century England can be linked more or less directly with the feeling that the papacy was a threat to men's livings or their pockets, either because of the demand for money or some curb on economic activity. Yet it was possible to feel like this and still think of the papacy as an indispensable institution. To men of affairs like the Paston correspondents the Curia was simply 'the court'. An expression of these ideas appears in a letter of 1473 in which Sir John Paston commented on a petition he was making at the Curia:

... I have answer again from Rome that there is a well of grace and salve sufficient for such a sore, and that I may be dispensed; nevertheless, my proctor there asks 1,000 ducats. . . . But Master Lacy, another Rome runner here, who knows my proctor there, as he says, as well as Bernard knew his shield, says that he means only 100 ducats, or 200 at the most; wherefore after this comes more. He wrote to me also that the pope is always doing this nowadays. . . .

The views of the royal judges were almost as ambivalent as the popular ones. When in 1486 a cargo of alum, from which the papacy derived important revenues, was captured by English seamen, and the pope threatened censure against those who had taken it, the English judges in an authoritative discussion decided that the king had the right to safeguard merchants in his realm, and Justice Hussey recalled that under Edward IV a legate had only been allowed to enter England after swearing he brought with him nothing in derogation of the king or his crown. Other judges added instances, and one remembered the burning of papal letters concerning Beaufort's legateship by Humphrey Duke of Gloucester in the reign of Henry VI. On the other hand, the judges had no less authoritatively agreed in 1467 that the pope could write to the archbishop of Canterbury and compel him to summon his clergy to grant an aid to defend the faith, just as the king, they said, could enforce contributions to defend the realm, and neither could exempt anyone from paying something to the other.

Anglo-papal relationships had thus reached the pass where compromise was the rule, but it was a rule based upon the convenience of parties who attended to each other only intermittently, and it was unsupported by any comprehensive agreement, let alone theory. The king's subjects accepted the papacy as the 'well of grace sufficient for their sores', but mingled with this attitude was a purchaser's contempt for the overcharging salesman, a relationship more unpromising than any nationalist estrangement. Can we speak of affection? It is hard to say without more research. Pilgrimages to Rome, especially to the *Scala Coeli*, were as common a pious exercise as any; but pilgrims were not always devotees of the papacy. Piero da Monte in Henry VI's time told the pope of the reverence for the Holy See he found in England; but he usually said what he thought would please. Books and bequests have been cited to show the religious devotion of late medieval England, and this is true without doubt. But it was not a devotion in which the papacy figured strongly, however implicitly the papacy was accepted as an institution, though the historian is right to ask how often in the past the papacy has in fact been reverenced by the mass of Catholic Christians. But when all is said, it is hard to see how the articulate and determined papalist position of Thomas More, John Fisher and the Carthusians in the 1530's could have been adopted merely on the inspiration of the moment, and it seems likely that further historical investigation will discover certain centres of an active moral loyalty to the papacy in the last decades of Roman Catholic England. It has been suggested that such existed in Rochester and other parts of the south-east, to go no further. Archbishop Warham is not one of history's strongest characters, and he spent much of his pontificate overshadowed by Wolsey. Death saved him too from a final issue with the king. But at one time he was accused of violating the statute of Praemunire because he had consecrated the bishop of St. Asaph before the papal bulls of provision had been shown to the king and the temporalities granted, and during these days he dictated his answer and showed his mind, harking back in thought not to the homage he had done the king on his own appointment, but to the traditions of Becket which he represented and his cathedral perpetuated:

> I intended nothing against the king's highness, but I intend to do only that I am bound to do by the laws of God and Holy Church and by mine order and by mine oath that I made at the time of my profession. . . . If the Archbishop of Canterbury should not give the spiritualities to him by the pope provided as bishop until the king's own grace had granted and delivered unto him his temporalities, then the spiritual power of the archbishops should hang and depend on the temporal power of the prince, and thus be of little or none effect. . . . It were indeed as good to have no spirituality as to have it at the prince's pleasure. . . . And if in my

case, my lords, you think to draw your swords and hew me in small pieces . . . I think it more better for me to suffer the same than against my conscience to confess this article to be a *praemunire,* for which St.Thomas died.

SELECT BIBLIOGRAPHY

J. Bossy, *Christianity in the West 1400–1700* (1985)

B. Tierney, *The Foundations of Conciliar Theory* (1966)

E.F. Jacob, *Essays in the Conciliar Epoch* 3rd edn (1963)

——, *Henry Chichele and the ecclesiastical politics of his age* (Creighton Lecture, London 1952)

——, 'Petitions for benefices from English universities during the Great Schism': *Trans. of the Royal Hist Soc.,* 4th ser. 37 (1945), pp. 41–59

R.N. Swanson, *The Church and Society in later medieval England* (1989)

A. Hamilton Thompson, *The English Clergy and their Organisation in the later Middle Ages* (1947)

Margaret Harvey, *England, Rome and the Papacy, 1417–64* (1993)

——, 'Perceptions of the papacy in the later middle ages': *Unity and Diversity in the Church* (*Proc. of the Eccles. Hist. Soc.* 1995, 1996), pp. 145–69

W.E. Lunt, *Financial Relations of the Papacy with England 1327–1534* (Cambridge, Mass. 1962)

J. Scarisbrick, 'Clerical taxation in England, 1485–1547': *Journal of Eccles. Hist.* 11 (1960), pp. 41–54

P. Heath, 'Between Reform and Reformation: the English Church in the fourteenth and fifteenth centuries': *Journal of Eccles. Hist.* 41 (1990), pp. 647–78

M. Aston, *Lollards and Reformers* (1984)

C.M. Barron & C. Harper-Bill, eds., *The Church in Pre-reformation Society* (Essays pres. to F.R.H. DuBoulay, 1984)

F.R.H. DuBoulay, *The England of Piers Plowman* (1991)

E. Duffy, *The Stripping of the Altars: Traditional Religion in England 1400–1580* (1992)

INDEX